The author has gone to great lengths to avoid referencing specific financial product brands or product providers. This text is meant to be informative in nature and it is intended to provide general information on the concepts of insurance, investments, wealth accumulation, and financial planning. This book is not intended as advice. The author encourages you to seek qualified counsel regarding your specific financial and legal issues.

For wills, trusts, and estates, you should seek the services of a licensed attorney in your state of domicile. You should also seek legal counsel when considering entity planning and appropriate structure for your small business.

For tax planning issues, seek the services of an advisor specializing in tax consulting. The highest credentials in this field are the Certified Public Accountant (CPA) and the Enrolled Agent (EA). Many CERTIFIED FINANCIAL PLANNER™ Practitioners also have a specialty in taxation. There are also many capable tax professionals that do not have a professional designation.

Tax rates, tax regulations, and certain retirement plan contribution limits are subject to change.

The opinions in this text do not reflect the policy of any particular firm, investment company, or other financial institution. Contributing financial advisors may have expressed opinions not shared by the author.

Every effort has been made to provide the most accurate information possible, but no guarantees or warranties are made or implied.

This book is dedicated to Laurie, Garrett, and Lindsey. *The Wealth Management Manual* took over eighteen months to complete, often at the expense of being a participating spouse and father. They have exhibited the patience of Job and I am indebted.

Very Special Thanks

To my parents, Norman and Eleanor Diehl. Thanks for raising me to believe in myself and the abilities of those around me.

I am told that a book can fail or succeed, live or die, based on the quality of the editing. Lisa Gregory took a rough manuscript and helped create a tool that I hope is helpful in your personal wealth management. Thanks, Lisa. I would also like to thank Lila Day and Jeanie Holbrook for their proofreading assistance

To Greg Floyd, JD, and member of The Texas Bar Association, I greatly appreciate your contribution and review of the section on Wealth Transfer and Estate Planning. It is always recommended to seek wise counsel. Thanks for yours.

I am grateful to Beau Ballinger with the Financial Planning Association. Beau, thank you for your help in narrowing the list of advisor contributors for this book.

And finally, to the advisor contributors to *The Wealth Management Manual*, I am humbled to be able to share these pages with each of you. I have learned much from your contributions and am honored by your participation. In a candid and unscripted way, you mirrored many of the themes I had intended for *The Wealth Management Manual*. I am grateful.

It was my original intention to have advisor interviews as a separate and final bonus section but as I dove into your responses, I soon realized that your contributions needed to be an integral part of the manuscript. Your thoughts were too important to be buried in the back of the book.

Your responses allow each of us insight into the way you think and, in many instances, the way you feel. Thanks for your contribution, not only to this book but to the advisory profession that your participation elevates. The Financial Planning Association tells us that advisors like you are the heart of financial planning. I think they're right.

The
Wealth Management Manual

(for the average investor)

Published by Aventine Press
1023 4th Ave #204
San Diego CA, 92101
www.aventinepress.com

ISBN: 1-59330-436-6

Printed in the United States of America

WEALTH MANAGEMENT MANUAL

Table Of Contents

WEALTH MANAGEMENT MANUAL

Table Of Contents

PREFACE

This book is a message about choice. As we speak, American society is moving into the initial stages of what will prove to be the largest wave of people turning age 60 and older in the history of known civilization, the graying of the Baby Boomer generation. A recent study by the United States Department of Labor tells us that by the year 2010, only three years away, there will be 5 million more jobs than people to fill them.[1] As the years pass, this labor pool shortage will only worsen as more and more American workers retire with fewer and fewer people to fill their shoes. I grew up in a family of four children. I have two children. A diminished generation of taxpayers will be unable to support a Social Security system burdened by the largest demographic of senior citizens in the history of the world.[2]

But there is good news and great opportunity for people who plan, those who take stock of their current situation and plan for the future. Over the next 50 years, this Baby Boomer generation will transfer 41 trillion dollars in wealth.[3] Money transferred to their children or grandchildren, assets transferred to an alma mater or a foundation for cancer research. Money donated to carry on the work of their spiritual faith. Money, in itself, is neither good nor evil, but a powerful leveraging tool that magnifies all that we believe and all that we can accomplish.

In this book we'll discuss money, how to acquire it, how to keep it, and you will consider what money means to you. We only get one shot at this life and it is inevitable that some rain will fall. In this book you'll be reminded that what's important is not the dollars you accumulate but rather what those dollars can accomplish. We'll look at proven strategies for wealth accumulation and wealth protection. We'll discuss things I know you'd rather put off. Things like a will, estate planning, and a living will so that in your final years, your loved ones are not saddled with having to make your life and death decisions.

If you want to learn the latest option trading strategies or how to time the market, this is the wrong text for you. But if you're a parent or a grandparent wanting to provide the best for the children in your life, if you want to guarantee that an unfortunate traffic accident and liability doesn't wipe out your life's savings, if you want to make sure that you don't outlive your money, then let's spend some time together. Let's talk about what your money is doing and what it can do. Let's find out together what is important to you and how you and your family can use your available resources to create and protect the quality of life that is so important. Over the next several chapters, we'll look at tools to assist you in protecting and accumulating wealth. This book is about designing the architecture of your life and then implementing the tools to build and protect your life's work.

INTRODUCTION

The afternoon sky is warm on your back as you and your son walk in the deep sand, the Pacific surf pounding the shore and water rushing up to your bare feet. The air is dry and the mountains of Cabo San Lucas reach to the sky and as he runs in and out of the salty foam, you pause for a moment, looking back up at the hills and villas of Pedregal. It's a perfect day spent with the people you love. Your wife and four year old daughter are back up the hill at the villa, probably still in the swimming pool as they have been most of the day. It's one of those moments in time, one of those snapshots that you and your children will cherish for the rest of your lives.

This is what money can do for us, allowing more time with the people in our lives who really matter. One of the things I cherish most is the time I have with my family. Anyone who has children realizes how incredibly fast they grow up and before we know it they are coming home from college for the holidays to have Thanksgiving dinner with Mom and Dad. As I mentioned earlier, you'll need to decide why you want to accumulate wealth. Is it to buy more things or is it to buy more time? For me, I can say with confidence that I want more time. More time to savor a great cup of coffee, more time to read my favorite book, more time to walk along the beaches of Cabo San Lucas with my family. But there are challenges to accumulating wealth and even greater challenges to keeping it.

In many ways the world is a much different place than it was a decade ago. Just a few years ago America was faced with unprecedented terrorism as radical extremists attacked the World Trade Center and the Pentagon using commercial aircraft, and our government tells us another attack of similar proportion is almost certainly inevitable. We have evacuated New Orleans, a major U.S. city, and now there is debate about the viability of its reconstruction. A subsequent hurricane just a few weeks later resulted in the evacuation of an estimated 3 million people from the Texas Gulf Coast and incredibly, gas (albeit briefly) reached $6.00 a gallon in one area of the United States. The go-go stock market of the 90's seems a distant memory and investors are still gun shy from a market that lost almost fifty percent of its value between the 2000 and 2003.[4] Even as we speak, Congress and the current administration are debating the future of Social Security.

But America has survived several wars, a depression, and more than a couple of recessions. And with your willingness to do the right things, to make the right choices, you should survive also. But I don't want you to just survive. I want your financial life to be a success. We've mentioned some of the challenges facing our nation but there is so much opportunity. The barriers to investing in the stock market have never been lower due to low-cost brokers like TD Ameritrade and Scottrade. You can now benefit from professional investment management by investing as little as $50 a month and premiums for certain types of life insurance have never been lower. The pharmaceutical industry is developing new drugs each year and new companies, non-existent five years ago, are redefining their respective industries.

Together, we're going to discuss strategies to help you earn and keep your wealth. A fundamental truth we should establish immediately is that there are only two ways to make money...

1. People at work

2. Money at work

You will never be able to quit working until you have money that you can put to work in your place. As you consider your motivation for wealth accumulation, I want you to know that I consider it a very worthy goal to seek strategies that enable us to spend time doing the things that really matter. Not so that we can quit work just for the sake of being lazy, but being in a position to be able to afford the things that really matter. For instance, you may have always wanted to donate time to Habitat for Humanity or contribute time to your church or synagogue, but if you're working extra hours at a high stress job, you may not have the time or the energy to contribute to these meaningful endeavors. This book is about your freedom to choose, and that freedom starts in the very first chapter of this book. This book will provide a roadmap that will show you ways to grow and protect your wealth, but the ultimate decision to take action is in your hands.

Over the course of your lifetime you'll need to be concerned with four main financial areas.

- **Protecting your hard earned assets.**

- **Increasing your assets through prudent investment strategies.**

- **Determining the distribution of assets during your retirement.**

- **Transferring your assets to the ones you love, avoiding probate and minimizing estate and income taxes.**

We will take a look at each of these four areas of your wealth management program. But maybe you don't think of yourself as wealthy. This book is written for the average American, the average investor. For a homeowner in New Orleans who lost her uninsured $95,000 home to a hurricane; that was her largest asset, that was her wealth. For the person who became permanently disabled, losing his ability to earn an income; that was his greatest asset. But the person who saved $500 each month in his 401(k) and ended up with $675,000 in his retirement account created wealth!

For average Americans living in the land of opportunity, *The Wealth Management Manual* is written for you. As we spend time together, I hope you will gain a new appreciation for the things you have. You'll learn how to protect your home, autos, and property from loss and you'll also discover how to protect yourself from the thousands of lawsuits filed each and every day.

In the wealth accumulation section, you will be reminded of things that you have probably known for years. Pay yourself first. Don't put all your eggs in one basket. Try to minimize taxes and beat inflation.

Americans are living longer and as you approach your retirement years, your investment nest egg may need to last 30 years or more. If you invest too conservatively, you will not be able to keep up with inflation and your investment account could run out of gas. If you invest too aggressively, you risk losing money to stock market fluctuations.

And finally, after a long and rewarding life, you'll want your estate to go to the ones you love or the organizations you care about. You will probably be interested in taking care of a surviving spouse, avoiding probate, and minimizing taxes.

We'll cover a lot of ground during our time together. We'll address wealth protection, wealth accumulation, wealth distribution and wealth transfer. But this book is not really about these four key topics. This book is about choice; it is about you designing the architecture of your life. Protection, accumulation, distribution and transfer are the four main corners, the main supports of your life planning structure.

As Steven Covey says in *The Seven Habits of Highly Successful People*, "Begin with the end in mind."

Where do you want to be in five years, in ten years, and in twenty years? Is there anything that you have always been passionate about but never pursued? Do you want to learn to paint? Do you dream of raising horses? Maybe you considered writing a book. For years I dreamed of writing a book and now I have! I always wanted to try my hand at winemaking and in January of 2006 I produced my first two cases of Cabernet Sauvignon. I can't find anyone willing to drink it, but that's another story.

Thanks for joining me on this wealth management journey. I hope you don't mind, but I've invited a few friends to join us. Some of the nation's top CERTIFIED FINANCIAL PLANNER™ Professionals will be answering your questions about investing, retirement, long term care and financial planning. They will also offer suggestions on how to select a financial advisor, what questions to ask, and what documents to request.

The contributing advisors have been featured or quoted in almost every major media venue including *USA Today*, *The Wall Street Journal*, *Worth Magazine*, *Kiplinger's Personal Finance*, *Forbes*, *Bloomberg*, *The New York Times*, *Money Magazine*, *Investors Business Daily*, *ABC Nightly News*, *CNNfn*, *MSNBC*, and the list goes on and on. As an author, I am very privileged to have these top shelf advisors contribute to *The Wealth Management Manual*. And, more importantly, I think you will benefit from hearing fifteen different opinions on key financial topics. Take your time and feel free to write in the margins and highlight areas of interest. Use this book as a tool to help you map out where you would like to go and help you determine the most efficient way to get there.

At first glance, this is just another book about money. In truth, I think it would be more accurate to say this is a book about life, with a strong emphasis on money. In any case, we're on a journey together. Sometimes the train will speed along and there will be other times when we will go at a snail's pace. The minutia of investment options will need to be digested in small bites. If you stay on board until our final stop I think you'll agree your ticket was a good investment.

Before we get started, let me take a few moments and introduce you to our traveling companions.

The Wealth Management Manual

Our Advisor Panel

As a CERTIFIED FINANCIAL PLANNER™ Professional and a Chartered Financial Consultant, I felt that readers would benefit from my years of experience in the field of financial services.

I like to take complex concepts and boil them down to something that is understandable, something that can be easily digested. I wanted to take something as complex as financial planning and refine it into a strategy so simple it could be written on an index card or a beverage napkin.

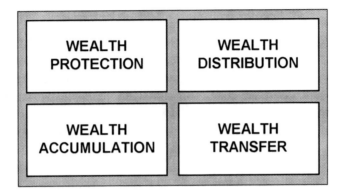

I think I have accomplished what I intended, but let me explain that this book is not really about money. Instead, this book is about the time and freedom money can buy.

There are so many things more important than money. Time with your kids is more important. For me, fishing for rainbow trout along a river in Colorado would be more important. A lazy Saturday morning with my family and a full pot of coffee would be more important. For you, time at your church or synagogue or simply spending time with friends might be more important, and financial planning can allow you to focus on those more important things in life.

This is not a do it yourself book. It is my desire that reading these pages will enable you to wisely seek professional financial counsel, and then empower you to ask the right questions and take the right steps leading to financial independence. I am certain that you and your family need an

Unbiased Advocate in Your Corner

You need someone in your corner that has your best interest at heart. Later in *The Wealth Management Manual* you will learn how to select a financial advisor and what questions to ask. If someone is applying for a coaching position, you need to know if they have ever fielded a winning team.

But I do not just want you to hear my opinions. I want you to hear the opinions of some of the nation's top financial advisors. All of the contributors to the Wealth Management Manual are CERTIFIED FINANCIAL PLANNER™ Professionals.

In January 28, 2006, Jeff Opdyke from *The Wall Street Journal* wrote "The CERTIFIED FINANCIAL PLANNER™, or CFP designation is considered the gold standard in this crowd. CFPs are required to be knowledgeable about financial planning topics including insurance, employee benefits, investments, taxes, and retirement and estate planning. They must also have at least three years of experience, pass a 10 hour exam, and starting in 2007, hold a bachelors' degree. The ChFC designation, given by the American College is also well regarded."[5]

According to Terry Savage of the *Chicago Sun Times* "A CFP is a CERTIFIED FINANCIAL PLANNER™ - and it is *the* designation of choice for professionals in this area. I'd highly recommend using only a CFP as an advisor."[6]

Walter Updegrave of *CNN/Money* says "The first credential to which I would attach the most credence is the CFP or CERTIFIED FINANCIAL PLANNER™, which is awarded by the CFP Board of Standards. Planners with a CFP must agree to abide by a strict code of ethics that, essentially demands that all planning decisions be made in the client's best interest. The second credential I think is credible for overall financial planning is the ChFC or Chartered Financial Consultant designation awarded by The American College."[7]

Six of the contributors hold a Masters in Business Administration, three are Certified Public Accountants, three are Chartered Financial Consultants and one contributor is a Chartered Financial Analyst. One contributor is an attorney.

Two of the contributors have been voted by *Worth Magazine* to be among the top financial advisors in the nation. Wayne Starr, CFP®, ChFC, MBA has earned this accolade six years in a row!

As a group, they have been quoted or interviewed by *CNN*, *The Wall Street Journal*, *The New York Times*, *Forbes*, *Worth Magazine*, *USA Today*, *Fox News*, *Money Magazine*, *Kiplinger's*, *Bloomberg*, *Investors Business Daily*, and *ABC Nightly News*, just to mention a few.

Several of the contributors have served as financial expert witnesses before courts in their local jurisdictions and also before the Securities and Exchange Commission. At least two of our contributors teach financial planning at the university level.

I promise your time will be well-spent within the pages of *The Wealth Management Manual*. I do not want you to read fifteen versions of the same opinion. Some of the financial planners love annuities, while some do not. One advisor believes in an investment management style that is diametrically opposed to that of his colleagues. At least three of the advisors are very passionate about 529 college savings programs, while other advisors might never recommend their use.

If the average fee for advisors of this caliber is $200 an hour, it might cost over $2800 to have a 60 minute consultation with fourteen of the nation's top financial planners. After reading *The Wealth Management Manual*, I think you'll agree it was time and money well spent. So let's get started.

OUR ADVISOR PANEL

- Matthew Tuttle, CFP, MBA
- Kristi Sweeney, CFP
- Wayne Starr, CFP, ChFC, MBA
- Dana Sippel, CPA/PFS, CFP
- Cary Carbonaro, CFP, MBA
- Jim Reardon, JD, CFP
- Diana Grossman Simpson, MBA, CFP
- John Scherer, CFP, CLU, ChFC
- Randy Smith, CFP, MBA
- Kathy Stepp, CPA/PFS, CFP
- June Schroeder, CFP, RN
- Tom Wargin, CFA, CFP
- Chad Starliper, CFP, ChFC, CLU, EA
- Mike Busch, CPA, CFP, CEBS

Matthew Tuttle, CFP®, MBA

He is a CERTIFIED FINANCIAL PLANNER™, author and educator. He helps his clients make smart choices about their money so that they can achieve their goals for the reasons that are important to them. Matthew is a frequent guest on *CNNfn* appearing on the *Your Money* show and *Dolans Unscripted* with Ken and Daria Dolan. He is also a frequent guest expert on *Channel 12 News* in Stamford, Connecticut.

Matthew is frequently quoted in the *Wall Street Journal, Forbes,* the *Journal of Financial Planning,* and a number of other publications. He has been profiled in the *New York Times, The Stamford, CT Advocate,* and *The Greenwich Times.* He writes articles for the *Fairfield & Westchester County Business Journal* and the *Stamford Senior Flyer.* He has written articles in over 25 publications nationwide. He has also been interviewed for ESBN Radio. Matthew was the host of the *Money Show with Matthew Tuttle,* heard every Sunday from 10:06am to 10:30am on WSTC/WNLK AM 1350 & 1400.

In addition to his media experience, Matthew also teaches personal finance to consumers as an adjunct professor at Westport Continuing Education, Norwalk Community Technical College, Stamford Continuing Education, Darien Continuing Education, Greenwich Continuing Education, Katonah Continuing Education and the 92nd Street Y. He has also taught continuing education to

CPAs at Baruch College, the CPA/LAW Forum and through the CPA Report. In addition, Matthew has spoken at accounting and trade association meetings across the country.

Matthew has written two chapters for the *Life Insurance Answer Book*, the desk reference guide for Life Insurance Agents, and is sought after for his testimony as an expert witness in financial planning court cases. Matthew earned his MBA in Finance from Boston University.

Kristi Sweeney, CFP®

Kristi Sweeney, a CERTIFIED FINANCIAL PLANNER™ certificant, is a fee based financial advisor and benefits consultant. She is the principal of Sweeney & Associates, LLC, in Greenwood Village, Colorado. Kristi has focused her financial planning practice on assisting families with special needs.

A graduate of the University of Wisconsin, Kristi has a major in social work. She is convinced that financial preparation is preventive social work. The impact of disability on her family when her husband had a stroke as a young man helps her understand and advocate appropriate planning for businesses, individuals and families.

She is a member of the Estate Planning Council of Southeast Denver, LLC. She served on the board of directors for the Metro Denver Association of Health Underwriters. In her current capacity as Public Relations Chair on the board of directors for the Financial Planning Association of Colorado, she helps the community understand the importance of a financial plan.

Kristi is an active proponent of the Rocky Mountain Stroke Association, after completing a five year tenure as one of the original directors on the Executive Board. In 2001, she served on a national task force for The National Stroke Association. In the past few years, she has participated in national educational conferences concerned with financial planning for families who have special needs.

Kristi earned her Life Underwriters Training Council Fellow designation in 1993. She became a CERTIFIED FINANCIAL PLANNER™ Practitioner in 1999. Kristi conducts special needs workshops for parent organizations and is a presenter for professional and business groups.

Kristi has lived in the Denver community with her family for thirty-five years. She has been a caregiver for her husband for over twenty of those years.

Wayne Starr, CFP®, ChFC, MBA

Wayne has more than 25 years of financial services experience, specializing in all phases of financial planning, as well as investment management. He joined BKD Investment Advisors in October 1999 through the merger of Neill & Associates, of which he was president. His experience also includes 13 years at Midwest Mutual Insurance Company in positions including underwriting vice president, administrative vice president and marketing vice president.
Wayne's professional affiliations have included various officer positions in the local chapters of the Institute of Certified Financial Planners and the International Association for Financial Planning. He has served on the board of directors of the Financial Planning Association. Professional designations include Chartered Financial Consultant since 1984 and CERTIFIED FINANCIAL PLANNER™ Practitioner since 1987.

Worth Magazine has named Wayne to its list of top planners in the U.S. six years in a row. He has been published in *Forbes*, as well as being a regular contributor in the *Kansas City Star*.

He received a B.A. degree in business administration and social science from the University of Northern Colorado, Greeley, Colorado, in 1965 and earned an MBA degree in 1973 from Drake University, Des Moines, Iowa.

Dana Sippel, CPA/PFS, CFP®

Dana consults with clients on a wide variety of financial planning topics, tax strategies and investment advisory issues, with a special emphasis in the area of personal and trust tax planning.

Dana earned his accounting degree from the University of Maryland in 1986 and became a Certified Public Accountant in 1987. In 1990, Dana earned his designation as a CERTIFIED FINANCIAL PLANNER™ Practitioner. He recently added the AICPA's Personal Financial Specialist designation to his credentials.

Dana is a past President and board member for the Maryland Chapter of the Institute for Certified Financial Planners (now part of the National Capital Chapter of the Financial Planning Association). He is currently a board member of the Northern Virginia Chapter of the Virginia Society for CPAs, the Financial Planning Association, the American Institute for CPAs, the Maryland Association of CPAs, and the Virginia Society for CPAs. He is also a member of the national Honorary Accounting Fraternity – Beta Alpha Psi.

Dana has been featured in *USA-Today, FOX News, Medical Economics*, and speaks on a number of tax and financial planning topics.

Cary Carbonaro, CFP®, MBA

Cary has an MBA from Long Island University and is a Registered Investment Advisor. Her tenure in Private Banking and the Institutional Investment Services Industry spans over fifteen years, including eight years at JP Morgan Chase, three years at Citibank (Vice President) and two years as a Director at Lord Abbett Investment Management.

Cary received her certificate in financial planning (CFP®) from the College of Financial Planning and is a NAPFA Registered Financial Advisor. NAPFA (National Association of Personal Financial Advisors) is an organization committed to fee-only financial advising.

Cary has taught at the University of Phoenix, and has a NY State teacher's certificate. She taught the CFP® program at Kaiser College and is currently a national instructor for the Kaplan Professional/Dearborn division for the accelerated CFP®.

She has been quoted in various publications, including *Mutual Funds Newsletter, Financial Net News, Bloomberg, Money Magazine, Kiplinger's, Investors Business Daily* and the *Orlando Sentinel*. She serves as an *Orlando Sentinel* "Money Matters Hotline" expert and was a major contributor to a nationally published book titled *TIPS from the TOP: Targeted Advice from America's Top Money Minds* published in January of 2003.

Cary participates in the *Kiplinger's Magazine* annual Jump Start your Retirement Hotline and is a Five Star Advisor with the Paladin Registry. She has served as a Judge for the 2006 Financial Frontier Awards sponsored, by the Financial Planning Association and Janus.

She is a member and serves on the board of the Central Florida FPA (Financial Planning Association) and is the 2006 President of the Financial Planning

Association. She, along with 80 of America's other top financial advisors, founded National Advisors Trust Company, FSB to provide Corporate Trustee and Custodial Services at a substantial discount for clients. They collectively manage more than $20 billion in total client assets.

Jim Reardon, JD, CFP®

Jim is President and CEO of People's Wealth Management, LLC, a fee based investment advisory firm in Topeka, Kansas. Jim holds licenses in law, real estate, securities and insurance. He is a graduate of Kansas State University and Washburn University Law School.

Jim has been a CERTIFIED FINANCIAL PLANNER™ Practitioner since 1987. He has served on the board of directors of the Financial Planning Association of Greater Kansas City for the past four years. He has served on an advisory board on *International Professional Standards* and a national task force on *Self-Regulatory Issues* for The National Financial Planning Association(FPA). He is currently serving on a FPA committee to review proposed changes to the *Code of Ethics* for CERTIFIED FINANCIAL PLANNERS™.

Jim hosted *Financial Strategies,* a weekly radio talk show, for over five years. He has presented over two dozen educational programs for trade and professional organizations such as the Kansas Medical Society, Mid-America Beverage Wholesalers and the Kansas Contractor's Association. He has presented retirement programs for employee groups including Hallmark Cards, AT&T, Burlington Northern and the State of Kansas. Jim and two of his clients are featured in the Spring 2006 *Mutual Funds Special Issue* of *Kiplinger's Magazine.*

Jim has served as an expert witness to three Topeka area law firms. He has presented papers and lectures for the Kansas Bar Association and the Kansas Society of CPAs. He has addressed student groups at the Kansas State University School of Business and Kansas University Law School. He currently serves in the mentorship program at Washburn University Law School. In May of 2006 he addressed a combined meeting of the Missouri Society of CPAs and the Greater Kansas City Financial Planner's Association.

People's Wealth Management, LLC specializes in providing active portfolio management and advisory services to law and accounting firms, charitable foundations, non-profit organizations, pension plans and moderate to high net-worth individuals and their families.

Diana Grossman Simpson, MBA, CFP®

Diana is the Managing Partner of Fee-Only Planning Professionals, LLC in Birmingham, Alabama.

As a "fee-only" financial advisor, Diana specializes in retirement planning, tax reduction strategies, estate preservation, insurance and investment strategies, pre-divorce settlement analysis and small business consulting.

After receiving her Masters of Business Administration (MBA) from the University of Alabama at Birmingham (UAB) in 1992, Diana began her new career with American Express Financial Advisors. In 1998, she received the CERTIFIED FINANCIAL PLANNER™ (CFP®) designation after completing the required coursework through the College of Financial Planning. She was recruited in 1999 to become the Managing Director of her current firm, which was a new, start-up company focusing on hourly consulting services.

Diana is a current member of the National CFP® Board of Professional Review, a current board member and lifetime member of the UAB National Alumni Society, current President of the board of directors for the Epilepsy Foundation of North and Central Alabama, the Past President of the Financial Planning Association, Alabama Chapter, and Past President of the UAB MBA Alumni Chapter. Diana has also previously served as a business consultant to the Junior Achievement of North Alabama Applied Economics program.

She is quoted often in local media and has been quoted in such national publications as the *New York Times, Kiplinger's Personal Finance, Money Magazine*, and others.

John Scherer, CFP®, CLU, ChFC

John Scherer helps small business owners, retirees and other 'regular' people lead more comfortable and rewarding lives by integrating their money with their values through commission-free financial coaching.

As Principal and founder of Trinity Financial Planning, John guides clients through the financial maze of taxes, insurance, college education, estate planning and investments to their personal finish line without the underlying conflict of interest and buying pressure inherent in a sales-based agenda.

John earned his CERTIFIED FINANCIAL PLANNER™ (CFP®) designation in 2000 as well as the Chartered Life Underwriter (CLU) and Chartered Financial Consultant (ChFC) designations in 1997 and 1998, respectively. He is a member of the Financial Planning Association (FPA) and of the Alliance of Cambridge Advisors, LLC, a nationwide alliance of leading financial planners bringing fee-only advice to middle America, where he currently serves on the Board of Directors as Treasurer.

Randy Smith, CFP®, MBA

Randy Smith, a CERTIFIED FINANCIAL PLANNER™ Professional and Southwest Airlines Captain, has been a practicing financial planner for 13 years. His professional development as a pilot and financial planner has led him to unite the two disciplines and specialize in retirement goals for Southwest Airlines employees. With most of his clients flowing from Southwest, he understands their needs and is well versed in their benefits.

Randy has lived in Texas most of his life. He graduated from Plano High School in 1974 and North Texas State University in 1977 and 1979 with degrees in Business, Marketing and a Masters in Business.

Randy has been a pilot for Southwest Airlines for 23 years. At Southwest, Randy met and married a wonderful and creative wife. He also has two intelligent and sports minded boys.

Randy joined the Southwest Airlines Pilot Association (SWAPA) Retirement Insurance Committee and was Chairman for three years. He completed a retirement benefits comparison booklet for Southwest Airlines pilots. He has published monthly articles in the SWAPA newspaper on personal finance and related subjects to better educate Southwest employees. He was also an instructor pilot in the Southwest Training Department for ten years. Education for the betterment of investors is his passion.

Randy has been interviewed by:

- *Money Magazine*
- *WBAP Radio* in Dallas

- *ABC Nightly News*
- *Retirement Dreams Roundtable*

His love of education inspired him to become a CERTIFIED FINANCIAL PLANNER™ Practitioner, a recognition that relatively few financial planners have achieved. Randy's knowledge in financial planning has allowed him to inform and guide his clients to achieve their financial goals.

Kathy Stepp, CPA/PFS, CFP®

Kathy Stepp is a Principal and Founder of Stepp & Rothwell, a fee-only financial planning and investment advisory firm in Overland Park, Kansas.
A graduate of Ohio State University, Kathy holds a Bachelor of Science degree in Business Administration with a concentration in Accounting. She also holds the designations of Certified Public Accountant (CPA), CERTIFIED FINANCIAL PLANNER™(CFP®), and Personal Financial Specialist (PFS). Kathy has served as a national spokesperson for the Citibank, MasterCard, and Visa consumer financial education program, "Keeping Your Financial Balance" and has appeared on CNBC and many television stations nationwide.

Kathy is a former national board member of the National Association of Personal Financial Advisors (NAPFA), the largest professional organization of fee-only financial planners, having served as a NAPFA national conference chair. She also is a former board member of the Financial Planning Association (FPA), Kansas City Chapter. She has been named among *Worth* magazine's and *Mutual Funds* magazine's "Best Financial Advisors" in the country, and she is frequently quoted in *The Kansas City Star*, *Worth*, *Medical Economics*, *Mutual Funds* magazine, and *Bloomberg*.

June Schroeder, CFP®, RN

June Schroeder, CFP®, RN, along with Tom Wargin, founded Liberty Financial Group, Inc, of Elm Grove, Wisconsin, a fee-only financial planning firm, in 1981. Her credentials, coupled with seven years as the Director of Economic Security for the Wisconsin Nurse's Association, make her uniquely qualified for her role as a "public wealth nurse."

She has written extensively for local publications, such as *Nursing Matters*, as well as *CNBC.COM*. She has taught courses on financial planning for

universities and technical colleges. June has been a regularly scheduled guest on a local TV news show since 1992. She hosted her own radio show for five years, *"Today's Woman: Your Money and Your Life"* focusing on making wise choices in all aspects of life to achieve financial security. Her writing, teaching and media appearances multiply her efforts to promote financial literacy.
June is an active member of the Financial Planning Association (FPA), as well as a number of business and professional women's groups. She remembers when she was one of only a handful of women at FPA meetings 25 years ago and feels that being a woman, especially now at 60 years of age, has been a great asset in reaching out to other women--one of her main focuses.
She lives with her husband, Michael McCormick, an army pilot turned computer nerd, and her four dogs in West Bend, Wisconsin.

Thomas M. Wargin, CFP®, CFA

Thomas M. Wargin, CFP®,CFA, is a founder of Liberty Financial Group, Inc., Elm Grove, Wisconsin. The firm, started in 1981 with June Schroeder, provides fee-only financial planning and investment management for individuals and their businesses.

Tom currently manages funds for approximately 145 clients. He uses a strategic asset allocation approach coordinated with the client's financial profile designed in a simple, common-sense style.

Tom has conducted numerous seminars and workshops on financial planning and investments for management of Fortune 500 companies, as well as for management organizations and small business owners. As a small business owner himself, Tom provides special insight into their particular problems.

Tom has designed numerous tools to assist in the evaluation of retirement plans, retirement planning, insurance planning, education funding, tax planning and portfolio management. He has written articles on financial planning and portfolio management, and has been quoted in *The Business Journal , The Milwaukee Journal-Sentinel, U.S. News and World Report,* and *Netfolio.com* .

Tom is married to Judy and they have four boys. In his spare time he enjoys woodworking, home improvements, and playing with his grandson. He also bakes a mean lemon meringue pie!

Chad Starliper, CFP®, ChFC, CLU, EA

A native of Knoxville, Tennessee, Chad received his Bachelor of Science degree in Marketing from Clemson University in 1998, where he was a scholarship player on their nationally ranked golf team. He is a CERTIFIED FINANCIAL PLANNER™ (CFP®) practitioner and was conferred the designation of Chartered Financial Consultant (ChFC) by The American College. Chad is a NASD Series 7 and 66 registered representative (licensed with Securities Services Network, Member, NASD, SIPC) and holds Life, Health, and Variable contract licenses. He has specialized in sophisticated comprehensive financial planning since 2000. Chad is frequently quoted in such noted publications as *Investment News* and *Financial Planning*, and has been a professional reviewer for a national publisher. He serves as a moderator on Financial Planning Interactive, the leading online forum for financial planners worldwide. Chad has been a speaker on matters ranging from debt management, retirement planning, investments, taxation, to estate planning. He is currently a member of the Financial Planning Association, the Knoxville Estate Planning Council, and serves on the board of directors for the Society of Financial Services Professionals.

Mike Busch, CPA, CFP®, CEBS

Mike Busch, President of Vogel Financial Advisors, has been affiliated with Vogel Financial Advisors and Philip Vogel & Company since 1988.

After graduating from Texas A & M University with a degree in accounting, Mike continued his education by earning marks as a Certified Public Accountant, CERTIFIED FINANCIAL PLANNER™, and Certified Employee Benefit Specialist. Mike's areas of expertise include portfolio design and investment management, tax planning, insurance analysis, retirement planning, employee benefits, and estate planning. Mike is past President and Chairman of the Dallas/Fort Worth Financial Planning Association and was elected to the Board of Governors of the Estate Planning Council of North Texas. In 2005, the Plano City Council appointed Mike to serve as Chairman of Plano's Retirement Security Plan Committee. Mike is proud to have been named by his peers and recognized by *D Magazine* as one of "The Best Financial Planners in Dallas".

Mike is frequently interviewed and has appeared in numerous magazines, newspapers, and journals including *The Washington Post, The Journal of Financial Planning, The Miami Herald, Investment News, The Seattle Times, Financial Advisor, American Way Magazine, The Dallas Morning News, The Bureau of National Affairs,* and *Consumer Reports.*

Wealth Management
Defined

Wealth management today is more than planning your money; it's also planning your life.

June Schroeder, CFP®, RN

What is Wealth Management?

Wealth Management is a relatively new buzzword in the field of financial services, and I am convinced that the average consumer does not know what it means. More importantly, the average consumer is not the benefactor of wealth management services.

The term is all encompassing and describes everything that is usually addressed in a comprehensive financial planning relationship, and then some. The CERTIFIED FINANCIAL PLANNER™ Board of Standards carefully details the process at www.cfpboard.org and the following has been reprinted with their permission.

FINANCIAL PLANNING PROCESS

1. Establishing and defining the client-planner relationship.
The financial planner should clearly explain or document the services to be provided to you and define both his and your responsibilities. The planner should explain fully how he will be paid and by whom. You and the planner should agree on how long the professional relationship should last and on how decisions will be made.

2. Gathering client data, including goals.
The financial planner should ask for information about your financial situation. You and the planner should mutually define your personal and financial goals, understand your time frame for results and discuss, if relevant, how you feel about risk. The financial planner should gather all the necessary documents before giving you the advice you need.

3. Analyzing and evaluating your financial status.
The financial planner should analyze your information to assess your current situation and determine what you must do to meet your goals. Depending on what services you have asked for, this could include analyzing your assets, liabilities and cash flow, current insurance coverage, investments or tax strategies.

4.Developing and presenting financial planning recommendations and/or alternatives.
The financial planner should offer financial planning recommendations that address your goals, based on the information you provide. The planner should

go over the recommendations with you to help you understand them so that you can make informed decisions. The planner should also listen to your concerns and revise the recommendations as appropriate.

5. Implementing the financial planning recommendations.
You and the planner should agree on how the recommendations will be carried out. The planner may carry out the recommendations or serve as your "coach," coordinating the whole process with you and other professionals such as attorneys or stockbrokers.

6. Monitoring the financial planning recommendations.
You and the planner should agree on who will monitor your progress towards your goals. If the planner is in charge of the process, she should report to you periodically to review your situation and adjust the recommendations, if needed, as your life changes.

Copyright © 2006, Certified Financial Planner Board of Standards, Inc. All rights reserved. Used with permission.

A financial advisor using the above six step process would be able to address your concerns, your goals, analyze your current resources, and determine future steps needed to realize your goals.

The financial planning relationship endorsed by the CFP® Board of Standards is an ongoing one between the client and advisor. Many advisors practicing the wealth management business model serve as Chief Financial Officer to their clients, providing a greater depth of services to a usually much smaller client base. I know one advisor who has a very successful practice with only eighteen clients.

Wealth management advisory firms frequently advise their clients on anything and everything financial. This might include consulting on home mortgage options, automobile financing, real estate cash flow investing, and buy-sell agreements for a closely held business. A wealth management team will include or have a referral relationship with a CPA and an attorney.

The team approach is effective for a wealth management practice because it takes into consideration the fact that specialists are needed to perform the various required functions. For example, estate planning has to be done by an attorney.

It is the age of specialization, yet high net worth clients are desiring a broader range of services from their financial professionals. The team approach is the answer to that dilemma.

I asked our advisor panel to share their personal definition of wealth management. Let's read what they had to say.

WEALTH MANAGEMENT DEFINED
ADVISOR ROUNDTABLE

MARK DIEHL:
What does Wealth Management mean to you? I think it is a term many people are familiar with, but they may not understand what it encompasses.

Kathy Stepp, CPA/PFS, CFP®: We believe the most important aspect of wealth management is the concept of 'balance'. We help clients balance their long-term goals with their present lifestyle. The idea is to determine the appropriate living expense level that can be maintained while saving enough to amass the investment capital needed to continue that lifestyle beyond the desired age of retirement. We recognize that the living expense level and the desired retirement age differs from client to client, making the specific financial plans different for everyone. However, the concept of balancing spending and savings responsibly during the working years in order to maintain a balanced lifestyle is valid for all clients.

Wayne Starr, CFP®, ChFC: It's not just about growing assets for you and your family. It's about protecting those assets as well, so they will last as long as you need them. Then it's also about having your wealth work for you to meet the goals for a life that is ultimately well-lived.

At BKD Wealth Advisors, wealth management has three components: grow, preserve, and protect.

To me, wealth management means bringing to bear all aspects of financial planning. In addition, it encompasses the management of a client's assets. Even when money management is the focus of the relationship, wealth management means taking a global view of the client's situation in order to customize the approach to growth, preservation, and protection.

Wealth management is not product driven; it is solution driven. It should be objectively delivered. Wealth management has become the title for the financial planning/investment management business. The consumer needs to be clear about where the advisor places his or her emphasis.

Diana Grossman Simpson, MBA, CFP®: Wealth management, at its very core, involves making rational decisions about money. If people weren't prone to making emotional decisions about their finances, I would be out of business. It's not just about knowing how to invest. The fundamentals are simple – buy low, sell high, be tax-savvy, and invest for the long-term. It is simple, but not easy. Most people struggle with even these basic rules, because they are emotional about their money. Professional money managers know when the market is down, it's time to buy – stocks are "on sale". But this is precisely the time the individual investor is ready to sell; he is afraid that the market will go down forever. And believe me, I feel their pain! This most recent bear market was terribly painful. I spent almost three years telling people, "The market will turn around." That's a long time to stick to your story! But that is what the market does; it goes up and down. And given the fact that the market had gone up so much and so fast in the late 1990's, in retrospect, it should have come as no surprise that the market had an extended downturn. I am very interested in the field of Behavioral Finance, which studies the reasons people make financial decisions. Although it is a complex area, it is clear that the majority make decisions based on emotion – either fear or greed. The emotion must be removed from the decision-making process in order for an investment strategy to work.

And it's not just about investments – people make emotional decisions about everything from purchasing a home to buying life insurance. The most value that a professional advisor can bring to the table is being able to remove the emotion from the equation.

Dana Sippel, CPA/PFS, CFP®: Wealth management is a concept that evolves throughout an individual's life. The basic premise of building a sound financial foundation is that it allows the accumulation and preservation of wealth. As the individual or family accumulates wealth the next step becomes making sure their wealth is prudently managed and protected from avoidable risks.

Initially, a young person needs to focus their efforts on securing intellectual intelligence that will allow them to progress in their career or business. Once this part of the foundation is built, the individual moves into the accumulation phase when saving, building equity in businesses, investment property and investment portfolios become important. Once the foundation of the financial plan is in place, the individual then works towards accumulating wealth that has the ability to generate enough income to achieve financial independence. Work has now become optional, allowing them to devote more of their efforts to pursue passions that may not have been a focal point during their earlier years.

Cary Carbonaro, CFP®, MBA: This is becoming a buzzword, but it is really what I do. I believe anyone who practices comprehensive financial planning and/or life planning is managing wealth. I advise my clients in creating solutions to manage their life, wealth, dreams, goals and so on. I help them in areas of their lives that go beyond wealth, like emotional and health issues. My previous experience in banking enables me to advise my clients in areas often overlooked by other advisors; debt management, mortgages, lines of credit, and all types of banking products. I notice that many small community banks are advertising wealth management services, but it could be just a way to market products. That being said, private bankers have been offering wealth management since the beginning of time. If they say it is free, I would not call that wealth management. You usually get what you pay for.

John Scherer, CFP®, CLU, ChFC: Wealth management to me is not much different than holistic planning: addressing all areas that affect a client's financial situation to maximize resources, minimize risk, and achieve goals with as few bumps in the road as possible. Perhaps what differentiates wealth management from regular holistic financial planning is that wealth management connotes having already achieved some amount of wealth, whereas regular planning is for people of all means.

Kathy Stepp, CPA/PFS, CFP®: Wealth management is a comprehensive term, with issues ranging from the macro to the micro. On a macro scale, wealth management is planning for the accumulation, use, and distribution of wealth over time. On a micro scale, wealth management is dealing with the details of tax planning, investment management, insurance planning, cash flow management, employee benefits, education funding, special needs planning, and any other aspects of one's financial life.

Tom Wargin, CFP®, CFA: In years past, wealth management was considered necessary only for the truly wealthy to manage the issues that came with sufficient assets to create tax, inheritance and legal problems. Wealth is not just dollars to us. It involves more than that. Wealth management encompasses how you make money--your career choice. How you spend and save, how you invest and how you use it to foster your beliefs and values. It also means dotting the i's and crossing the t's when it comes to issues like beneficiary designations, durable powers of attorney and wills.

June Schroeder, CFP®, RN: Well put, Tom. Wealth management today is more than planning your money; it's also planning your life. In fact, that is a tag line on our flyer. That can be as basic as recognizing the abilities you were born with and what you like to do, facing the financial challenges of a disability, illness or change in status, or deciding which way to go on a career path. For example, recently we spent time with a client who dreads going to work. She has a high income but no time to enjoy it. We explored what she really wants out of life and it turns out to be very different from what she now has and does. Our goal: to help her plan for and accomplish what really matters to her: more time, less earned income and a garden. On the other hand, we have clients who feel guilty about having money, so we are planning to help them give it away!

Mike Busch,CPA, CFP®, CEBS: True wealth management is much broader than most people think. For many, the term is simply synonymous with investment management. Compounding the problem is the fact that many financial service providers brand their investment service as wealth management. In reality, wealth management encompasses every aspect of administering a person's wealth. So, in addition to the obvious investment issues, other facets include strategies to protect wealth, ensuring that the use of the wealth is in harmony with the individual's goals and objectives, and planning for the transfer of that wealth during lifetime and at death.

By now, you realize that wealth management is much more than investment planning and is not just for the wealthy. If you are worth $50,000 or $5 million, you have dreams and goals you would like to see through to completion. You probably have worked hard for what you have and you see the value of protecting those assets from risk. Over the next 300 or so pages we'll look at ways to prudently grow your assets and stretch them through your retirement years. On the day you leave this earth, you'll want to make sure your remaining property goes to assist your survivors, or possibly an organization that shares your vision for contribution. We have a lot of ground to cover, so let's get started. After meeting our contributing advisors, I think you'll agree we are in good company.

The Wealth Management Manual

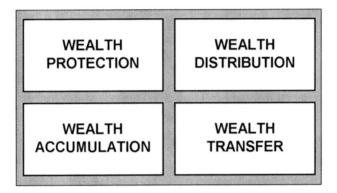

WEALTH PROTECTION	WEALTH DISTRIBUTION
WEALTH ACCUMULATION	WEALTH TRANSFER

The Big Picture

By the time you finish this book you'll see that you are much better off by taking a holistic view of your finances. You'll learn that your insurance program and your investments synergistically work together, similar to the offensive and defensive line of a football team. Knowing that the average worker now changes jobs at least seven times over the course of her career, we'll encourage you to take control of your own finances, minimizing your dependence on the ancillary insurance programs offered by your employer. In short, I want you to learn how to protect your assets, increase your wealth and, as you approach the end of your life, we'll show you methods that can streamline the transfer of your assets to your loved ones or to specific charities and non-profit organizations that promote the issues and beliefs you value most. You'll be in control of your financial life. This book will present four main sections, addressing critical areas of wealth management. So let's get started on the road to financial independence!

It's not just about growing assets for you and your family. It's about protecting those assets as well, so they will last as long as you need them. Then it's also about having your wealth work for you to meet the goals for a life that is ultimately well-lived.

Wayne Starr, CFP®, ChFC, MBA

Section 1

Wealth Protection

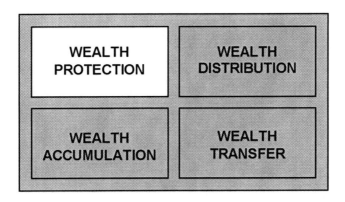

"Many, if not most, of the estimated 70,000 lawsuits filed every day in America target small business owners and mid-to-upper income Americans with less than $1 million in net worth."[8]

"The Lawsuit Lottery: the Hijacking of America" by Douglass S. Lodmell and Benjamin Lodmell,

Protecting Wealth from Liability & Lawsuits

As we delve deeper into strategies that will help you accumulate wealth, we'll discuss some of the more academic theories of investing and simplify these concepts, leaving you with a thorough understanding of the most effective strategies for asset growth. But before we move into growth strategies, we need to make you aware of your immediate risks and the solutions available to protect what you've already acquired.

There are several ways to lose your money and assets, but one of the greatest risks is the threat of being sued for a negligent act, an honest mistake that could happen to anyone. And honest mistakes happen to people every day. Take just a moment and grab your yellow pages. Look at the back cover and the odds are great that the advertisement you'll see is for a personal injury attorney. Do you have any idea how much that back cover ad might cost in your area? In some cities that advertisement can cost tens of thousands of dollars, yet personal injury attorneys are willing to pay those high prices because they know it is an investment guaranteed to pay off. How many television commercials do you see advertising the services of your local personal injury attorney? An injury or death due to an automobile accident or an accident in your swimming pool or at your lake house, and your life's savings could be gone literally overnight. Certain assets are protected from creditors and some of these protected asset types are state specific. For instance, in the state of Texas, annuities are protected from creditors. In addition, IRAs are now protected from creditors as are 401(k) plans and qualified pension accounts.

> # 20 million lawsuits are filed each year in the United States.

But the simple fact is that we live in a very litigious society. According to *The Lawsuit Lottery: the Hijacking of America*, by Douglass S. Lodmell and Benjamin Lodmell, over 20,000,000 civil lawsuits are filed annually in America.

150 lawsuits are filed every minute of every working day.

That's right, twenty million! To quote the authors:

"By the end of the 20th century, the litigating public was filing as many as 150 lawsuits every minute of every working day -- with a take-home pay for plaintiffs' lawyers totaling $45 billion in 2002! The harsh reality is that many, if not most, of the estimated 70,000 lawsuits filed every day in America target small business owners and mid- to-upper income Americans with less than $1 million in net worth."[9]

But maybe you're thinking this could never happen to you. You drive safely and you don't think you're at risk for a lawsuit. Consider these facts as reported by the National Highway Safety Traffic Administration (NHTSA): In 2004, 6.3 million traffic accidents were reported by the police, in which over 41,000 people were killed and an approximated 2.7 million people were injured. According to the NHTSA, in 2003, 42,643 people died in car accidents and another 2,889,000 were injured in the same year.[10]

- **Motor vehicle crashes are the leading cause of death for people under the age of 33.**[11]

- **A motor vehicle death occurs on average every 12 minutes and an injury every 11 seconds.**[12]

- **About 113 people died each day in motor vehicle accidents in 2003.**[13]

Remember, if you have teenage drivers in the household and they are insured on your family automobile insurance policy, they are an extension of your family's liability. Several years ago it was possible to place teen drivers on their own separate policy. It was previously accomplished by both the teen and parents signing a waiver that the teenage driver would never drive the other family vehicles. He/she would be assigned to drive one vehicle, but it was soon discovered this was easier to commit to than it was to accomplish. Junior would inevitably borrow Mom or Dad's car to run to the grocery store or take his sister somewhere, and the ensuing accident would require Mom and Dad's insurance policy to pay for Junior's high-risk behavior. The main point to consider is this: if there are four drivers in the home, your liability risk is multiplied by four.

I must admit that if one of my family members was injured or maimed in a car accident, I would utilize the legal system and sue for the funds needed for rehabilitation, medical bills, and loss of income. I don't want to vilify the personal injury attorney because it is all too easy to go down that path, but I will advise you on the steps you can take to minimize your risk and provide your family with peace of mind. In the state of Texas, a person can have injury liability limits as low as $20,000 per person and $40,000 cumulative for one incident or one accident. Very low liability limits do not offer much financial protection.

But there are other risks you face besides automobile accidents. Does your home have a swimming pool? Consider these facts...

- **Drowning is the second leading cause of injury-related death among children under 15.**[14]

- **Between 60 and 90 percent of drownings among children aged 0 to 4 occur in residential pools; more than half of these occur in the children's own home.**[15]

- **For boys between the ages of 1 and 3 who have drowned, most of the victims were being supervised by one or both parents at the time of the drowning.**[16]

These are some sobering statistics and I don't want to dwell on them, but if I was your personal financial advisor, one of the first things we would accomplish together is to make sure that your liability limits on your auto and home insurance were at their maximums, then I would probably recommend you also take out an umbrella policy.

People who have suffered the loss or serious injury of a loved one deserve to be able to utilize the legal system to seek restitution for costs associated with medical payments and disability. By increasing your liability coverage, you provide a source for that money rather than having to draw from your personal savings or being forced to liquidate assets.

33

Step one: Have the highest limits of liability available on your auto insurance and your homeowners insurance.

> # A million dollars of liability protection for less than a dollar a day.

Step two: Purchase an umbrella policy from your insurance agent. The umbrella policy will increase the liability limits on your underlying home and auto policy up to $1 million. Some umbrella policies offer even higher levels of liability protection. The good news is that the umbrella policy is usually not very expensive, but your actual cost will depend on your location, your state, and possibly your past insurance loss history. In my area, an umbrella liability policy can cost under $200. a year, but a point to remember is that you're usually required to have the highest limits of liability on the underlying auto and home policy. This is probably a good place to mention that if your home has a swimming pool, the umbrella policy is a must! The increased risk of a guest drowning or being injured getting in or out of the pool greatly increases your chances of litigation.

Another benefit of increased liability coverage is your insurance company, at no additional charge, will provide you with legal representation for any incident that is applicable to your liability coverage. This legal representation is not charged against the $1 million of liability coverage but is an additional benefit. Basically, the insurance company doesn't want to cough up the million dollars to pay a claim without putting up a fight and since it's your insurance policy, they're automatically in your corner. Remember our earlier discussion of lawyers? The only way to survive in that game is to get one of your own. With the umbrella policy, you receive two substantial benefits:

- The money to pay a claim should you ever need to do so.

- And someone in your corner--legal representation supplied by your insurance company.

A million dollars covers a lot of sins so, all in all, not a bad deal for usually less than a dollar a day.

Just think about it this way . . .

If you're willing to write the small checks each year, you can probably find an insurance company you can count on to write the big check should the need ever arise. Trust me on this one--protect *your* assets. The umbrella policy is well worth the money and the peace of mind you'll enjoy is priceless! Below is a sample of a letter that you, the insured, might receive if you caused an automobile accident and your coverage was not sufficient to pay all claims filed against you:

Sample letter

CONSEQUENCES OF INADEQUATE COVERAGE

Jun 1, 2000

John and Jane Doe
111 Blankcheck
Been sued, TX 7000

Dear Mr. and Mrs. Doe,

This letter will acknowledge receipt of the suit filed against you in connection with the December 13, 2005 automobile accident.

We have forwarded a copy to our staff attorney, and have requested him to provide a defense of the lawsuit brought against you.

This attorney will give the matter all necessary attention and when you hear from him, please comply with all his requests. As a duly authorized representative of your insurance carrier, this attorney, under the terms of your policy, is entitled to your complete cooporation throughout the handling of this litigation.

Because the amount claimed against you in this suit is in excess of the protection afforded by your automobile insurance policy, there may be personal liability on your part. In view of the possible personal liability, it will be agreeable with XYZ Insurance Company for you to acquire legal representation of your own choosing, at your expense, to represent you personally and appear in this matter, in addition to the attorney that we have selected.

Your policy liability limit is $100,000 and the plaintiff is asking for $500,000 due to inability to work, medical bills and possible paralysis. At this time, your potential personal liability exposure is the remaining $400,000 that exceeds your automobile policy liability limits.

Susan Walker
Claim and Litigation Specialist
XYZ Insurance Company.

Can you imagine getting that letter, knowing that you could be on the hook for $400,000? How would you feel if you were in a state where wages could be garnished to satisfy a legal claim? How many years would it take to pay $400,000 deducted out of your paycheck a little bit at a time, once or twice a month? Would that slow down your wealth accumulation program?

- Increase your liability limits on your automobile policy

- Increase your liability limits on your homeowner's policy

- Purchase an umbrella policy for the excess liability.

Entity Planning

There are certain liability risks to the small business owner. If you have a small business established as a proprietorship or a partnership, your family and personal assets are at risk as a result of your business activities.

There are other ways to shelter your assets if you are involved in a business. If you're a doctor, attorney, CPA, or a financial advisor, you will have some type of professional liability insurance. Business owners will carry liability insurance as well. Another possible way to protect your assets from a business liability is through entity planning. Entity planning is beyond the scope of this book, but I'll give you a brief example of how it works.

Example: You are a realtor and your business is established as a sole proprietorship. One day you are driving a prospective buyer to see a home they are interested in buying. On the way, you are on your cell phone as realtors often are, and you are not paying attention to the car in front of you that just came to a sudden stop. You rear-end the car in front of you, causing your passenger to crash through your windshield, landing on top of the vehicle now attached to your front bumper. Since you are a sole proprietor, your injured passenger will personally sue you for every nickel you have, and justly so. The person you rear-ended will probably have her lawyer call you as well. Those pesky back and neck injuries can be so hard to actually substantiate, not to mention the pain and suffering. In some states, this could result in garnishment of wages. In addition, your passenger will probably not be inclined to buy the house you were going to show him.

If your business was established as a "C" corporation and the corporation owned the vehicle you were driving, and you were an employee of the corporation, your airborne passenger could sue the corporation but probably not you personally. The "C" corporation puts a partition around the assets and any risks associated with the "C" corporation. In the above example, you could lose your business and any business assets, but not your home or any personal assets or accounts.

Let me give you another real life example. A few years ago a woman successfully sued a McDonalds restaurant for $2 million because she accidentally poured coffee in her lap that she had just purchased at the drive-through window. Evidently, she was very surprised to discover the coffee would create a hot, almost burning sensation when it touched her skin. The employee who made the extremely hot coffee that morning could not be sued. The employee was protected by the corporate partition. I understand she works at Starbucks these days. The McDonalds story can teach us four very important lessons . . .

1. Entity planning can protect individuals from liability. *Not always, but usually.*
2. A person interested in suing you can find a lawyer to take any case, no matter how ludicrous.
3. A liability case that you think is obviously frivolous might be viewed differently by a jury.
4. When getting coffee at a drive-through, always ask for a lid.

Entity planning is beyond the scope of this book, but I recommend that you read *Asset Protection* by Arnold Goldstein, PhD. There are many good books on the subject and Dr. Goldstein's book is in my personal library.

Protecting Your Wealth from Loss of Income

One of the greatest threats to your financial security is loss of income. When we think of the material things we want to protect, we often think of our homes, our vehicles and our personal possessions. Each of us has insurance that protects all three. But the greatest asset we have is our ability to get up every morning and create an income. Remember, earlier in the book I mentioned there are only two ways to make money.

Let's look at it another way. If you had a goose that laid golden eggs, would you insure the goose or the eggs? I think I would probably insure both, but I know that I would definitely insure the goose. If you had a money machine that cranked out money every day, would you insure it? I think you probably would. By the way, I think they call that counterfeitting so don't try it at home. It was just an analogy.

> # People at work
> ## or
> # money at work.

Let's try a different angle. Let's say that you have a home that would cost $250,000 to replace. You'll want to insure your home for at least $250,000 and you know it would be negligent not to have your home insured. In fact, the mortgage company will start to send you nasty letters if they even suspect that it is not insured.

Consider your annual income. If you make $65,000 a year, and we do not factor in inflation or pay increases, over the next 20 years you will earn $1,300,000! That's quite a sum of money. There are two major risks to your earning power: premature death and disability. Let's take a look at premature death first.

> # Insure the goose.
> *Unknown*, possibly the goose's husband.

Is It Life Insurance or Death Insurance?

Chad Starliper, CFP®, ChFC, CLU, EA: How important is life insurance? Well, I'd say it is non-negotiable. Most people are vastly underinsured; when they do have some insurance, many of them have been sold whole life when it is inappropriate for them.

Advisors may have various ways of calculating how much someone needs, but it is not that difficult to understand once it is laid out for them. I've gotten to where I almost start the process in front of clients on a legal pad—naming the issues that need to be funded one at a time and add them up.

Sometimes the very simple things need to be asked differently. For instance, we'll ask clients this question: "If you were driving home tonight and were killed in a car accident, how much money might your family need to continue on? Now answer this: if you could magically be brought back to life, how much insurance would you go back and buy to cover it?"

Excusing for a moment all of the time value of money and investment considerations, a breadwinner that dies tomorrow leaves behind certain financial obligations. For instance, a surviving spouse might need $50,000 per year in living expenses for the next fifteen years until the kids are gone. Well, at a 4% discount rate, that comes to about $556,000 needed in today's dollars—and that's pre-tax. Leaving out the cute math—just so none of the other advisors get mad at me—that single expense is pretty substantial. Where it is going to come from?

Randy Smith, CFP®, MBA: Yes, insurance is a must. You always insure against the loss of things and people. This, along with wills, is in my first discussions. Insurance analysis is always in a plan.

After years of research, the statistics are in. The average mortality for the normal healthy person is 100%. At some point, we all run out of gas.

Someone has probably tried to sell you life insurance and you probably own at least some life insurance today. Death is a tough issue for many people to address. Even life insurance agents frequently side-step the issue. Early in my career, life insurance was a part of my portfolio as a representative with a major financial services firm. I remember talking to potential clients about life insurance and saying, "If you die, the policy will pay your family $500,000." For some reason, I found it difficult to say the phrase "when you die." Over the years, I have realized that the question is not *if* you die but *when* you die. You might think you're immortal, but statistically the odds are not in your favor.

I know what many of you are thinking, so let's get this out on the table right now. The teachings of your faith may have taught you that, in a twinkling of an eye, you can be called up to heaven. That is my faith too and rest assured, I am right there with you on that one. But that may not happen for a long, long time after you're gone. In all of your planning, plan for the worst and hope for the best.

Everyone is somewhat familiar with life insurance. It is appropriately named for two reasons. The risk insured is a life. If the insured life ceases, an insurance company will write a check to the beneficiaries. The people who benefit from a life insurance policy are the living, the people who remain behind. One of the most selfless gifts that a person can give is the gift of life insurance. Imagine writing a check every month for $500 for a policy that will only benefit someone at your death.

There are always two questions that seem to arise when life insurance is being discussed.

1. How much life insurance do I need?
2. What kind of life insurance is best?

A rule of thumb frequently used by financial professionals is a total equal to seven to ten times your annual income. There are some interesting things going on in the life insurance industry these days. Across the board, almost everyone agrees that the average American is grossly underinsured. In addition, it seems there are fewer life insurance agents than there were just a few years ago.

Many employers offer low-cost term insurance to their employees. You may have $50,000 of term insurance through your employer. Some companies also offer a multiple of your salary, possibly two or three times your annual income. This optional life insurance is usually offered to you at a very competitive low monthly premium. Add up your total life insurance in force, being careful to include your employer provided life insurance and also any policies that you own outside of work.

Throughout the book I have attempted to provide you with information that will allow you to be in control of your life and your finances. With that in mind, do not be dependent on your employer provided life insurance. If you change jobs or your current employer makes benefit changes, you could lose important life insurance protection needed by your family. Employer provided life insurance is a very valuable employee benefit, but view it as icing on the cake. Develop your own life insurance program independent of your employer. Unless you're planning to die while working at your current job, you will want to have life insurance that can be portable. Remember, Americans today may change jobs as many as seven to ten times over their working careers.

Another consideration is that you must be insurable to purchase life insurance. If you put off purchasing life insurance until next year, you may find that you are uninsurable. As you postpone the decision to purchase life insurance, your potential monthly cost steadily increases. It costs more for a 55 year old to purchase life insurance than a 45 year old.

Bread winners must seriously consider insuring for seven to ten times their annual salary. You must determine what level of financial support you want to provide in the event of premature death. You'll probably want to make sure that your family is able to maintain the same standard of living, reside in the same home, the kids attending the same schools. In the calculation of your life insurance need, you might wish to consider providing funds for college education, home maintenance, or possibly a down payment on your child's first home. Make a list of things you would like to fund in the event of your premature death. There are also income considerations. Your family has grown accustomed to you bringing in an income each month. There a couple of strategies you might consider for income replacement when evaluating your insurance needs.

1. The capital preservation method assumes the death benefit will earn an income from dividends, capital gains, or interest. The family will live off of the earned income, thereby preserving the capital or principal investment.
2. Capital liquidation assumes the surviving beneficiaries will slowly withdraw money from the principal, gradually depleting the death benefit over a number of years.

3. Beneficiaries could also use a combination of capital preservation and capital liquidation, each month withdrawing a portion of income and also a portion of principal.

Remember that life insurance is the ultimate *love* gift. You will not be around to watch your grandkids enjoy their first home. You won't be there to watch your kids walk across the stage at graduation. Maybe some of the money from your life insurance policy will be used to pay for your daughter's wedding and, even though you won't be there to give her away, your gift will be cherished. When she was just a little girl, you cared enough to plan ahead and think about a possibility that, even then, was unpleasant to consider.

In 1992 my father purchased a life insurance policy from an insurance agent who was a close family friend. At the time, I was a newlywed with no children and my mother was fighting a losing battle with cancer. Years have passed. It is now 2006 and my mother is no longer with us. A few years ago the insurance agent who sold my father the life insurance policy passed away as well. My wife and I revel in the time that we spend with our two children, Garrett, age 10, and Lindsey, age 6. I am reminded that when my father purchased that life insurance policy, my kids weren't even born. My wife and I have earmarked some of that life insurance money for their college educations. I find it fascinating that my kids will be able to go to college thanks to an insurance agent who sold my father a policy before they were even born and thanks to a father able to see beyond his own mortality.

Term Life Insurance

I believe almost everyone is familiar with term life insurance. Term insurance is usually the most inexpensive form of life insurance and is preferred by many consumers and advisors, alike. Term life insurance is a commodity.

Here's the way it works. You pay a premium for a policy that guarantees a death benefit for a period of time, or a term. No cash value, no equity. The only way anyone receives any economic benefit is if the insured--you--dies. Actually, I stand corrected. There is someone who does receive an economic benefit, the insurance company. The life insurance industry tells us that only about 3% to 4% of term policies ever pay a death benefit to beneficiaries. Approximately 96% of term life insurance policies lapse due to non-payment of premium or expire worthless because the insured outlives the term period. If you buy a fixed premium thirty year term policy, you will own a policy for thirty years that will never increase in cost and provide a death benefit for your family. The point to remember is that you must die during the thirty year time

43

frame outlined in the policy. If you die the day after the policy expires . . .well, I think you get the idea.

The concept behind a term life policy is that it can provide much needed protection during those years when you are supporting a family or fulfilling a financial obligation, like a mortgage or a business loan. One of the weaknesses of term insurance is that policies are often designed to run out of gas at a time when you are at increased risk of death.

I think this may be a good time to discuss a viable need for life insurance in your retirement. As we will learn later in the book, defined benefit plans are quickly becoming a thing of the past. A defined benefit plan is the type of retirement program that pays you a retirement income for the rest of your life. Let's take a look at an example of a couple who invested fairly successfully over their working years.

John accumulated $450,000 in his 401(k) and his wonderful wife Jane accumulated $450,000 in her 401(k). In our example we will assume that John and Jane only have their 401(k) plans to count on in their retirement years. Together, they have a total of $900,000 which is not a small amount by any means. Both John and Jane come from families with strong gene pools. John's father still goes to Fort Lauderdale every year for Spring Break. Jane's mother is still dating, actively. The point is John and Jane could be retired for a very, very long time. They may need to make their $900,000 last twenty or thirty years.

The good news is that both John and Jane each have a permanent life insurance policy they bought years ago. They never looked forward to paying those insurance payments each month, but for some reason they kept paying their premiums year after year after year. Both of their policies have a $400,000 death benefit. John and Jane can leverage their retirement money using their existing life insurance. They decided that when one of them dies, they would like to leave the surviving spouse $600,000. Let's see how this works.

Jane Dies	To John from Janes's 401(k)	$200,000
	To John from life insurance	$400,000
John Dies	To Jane from John's 401(k)	$200,000
	To Jane from life insurance	$400,000

The life insurance allows John and Jane to spend the remaining $700,000 while they are both alive, together. One of retirees' major sources of retirement accumulation will be in their 401(k) plans. Life insurance allows you to leave money for pennies on the dollar. If John did not have any life insurance and he wanted Jane to have $600,000 at his death, it would cost him $600,000.

I want to be very clear about this. You *will* be buying a life insurance policy to protect your surviving spouse. You can pay $600,000 to leave your spouse $600,000, or you could pay $300,000 to leave your spouse $600,000. If you have a policy that is self-supporting at retirement, all the better. I advise you to be very cautious before canceling a life insurance policy.

You never know what your health may be a year or two from now and, if you cancel a policy, you may not qualify again. I know financial professionals have different opinions regarding the value and need of life insurance at different stages in life. I respect those differing opinions and many of their objections have validity. I just encourage advisors and consumers to look at all possible aspects of a situation before making any financial decision that could be irreparable.

I love term insurance but I must advise you about the weaknesses, as well as the strong points. If you buy a thirty year term policy at age 30, the policy will expire when you are 60 years old.

Advisors and salespeople in a discussion of term and permanent insurance can become very passionate. It's similar to discussing religion; there are strong opinions on both sides of the argument and you are never going to change anyone's mind. I can tell you that it is never going to be an inexpensive proposition to purchase life insurance as you enter retirement. If you think that life insurance may be a way to leverage your retirement savings for you and your spouse, then you might consider permanent life insurance. It is in your best interest to purchase permanent insurance when you are young.

Whole Life Insurance

Whole life insurance is a form of permanent insurance. As the name implies, it is designed to last your whole life. Whole life insurance usually requires a fixed monthly premium, either on a monthly, quarterly, or annual basis. There is no flexibility in the premium payment. In most cases, if you do not pay the premium the policy will lapse. Whole life insurance is usually a policy that provides certain guarantees: a guaranteed premium, a guaranteed death benefit, and also tax-deferred cash value accumulation. Permanent life insurance has higher premiums than term. A portion of your monthly payment helps build a cash value that grows very slowly over time. There has always been much debate about whether a consumer would be better off buying term insurance and investing the difference.

Universal Life Insurance

Universal life (UL) insurance is another form of insurance that has a cash accumulation component. The cash value component in universal life insurance increases in value based on current interest rates. During the 1980s when interest rates were in double digits, universal life policies enjoyed fantastic performance. Another characteristic is flexible premiums. The policy owner has a certain amount of flexibility when paying the premiums. A policy owner could skip one month's payment and send in two payments the following month. If someone wanted to accelerate the cash value accumulation, they could send in a little extra money each month, with the excess going directly to cash value. As with whole life insurance, cash accumulation in a universal life insurance policy grows on a tax-deferred basis. In the 1990s many universal life policies collapsed. This was due to three reasons.

1. Low interest rates had a negative effect on cash values.

2. Insurance agents sold many universal life policies improperly, under-funding the monthly premium and low-balling the actual cost of the policy to the applicant.

3. Many policy owners abused the premium flexibility and under-funded their policy premiums.

Universal life insurance is a good product if it is managed correctly. If you own a universal life insurance policy, you must over-fund the premiums. This is accomplished by sending in more than the minimum required payment. Contact your insurance agent and he/she can tell you the maximum allowable premium you can pay on your policy. If you have a period in your life where you need to miss a few payments, your policy cash value can help support the policy. View your cash value as a sort of escrow account .

1. You can borrow against your policy cash values. The insurance company can send you a check. By borrowing from your policy it allows the coverage to remain intact.

2. You can withdraw cash value.

3. You can use cash value to support the policy during a time when you may be unable to pay premiums.

Variable Universal Life Insurance

Variable Universal Life insurance is another type of policy that builds cash value. This product is unique because the policy owner has the ability to invest in market based investment options. A variable universal life insurance policy may have 30 to 40 investment options very similar to mutual funds. The policy has the potential to accumulate cash, but your cash value is based on two factors: the premium you pay and the performance of your investment choices. The policy owner bears all the risk of the investment and accumulation component in this type of policy. Like the universal life policy, it is important that you over-fund a variable life insurance policy. As with any market based investment, there is the potential for higher gains, and there is also the potential for greater losses.

Life Insurance and Taxes

Regarding the over-funding of premiums in permanent policies, there are premium guidelines that cannot be exceeded. The Tax Equity and Fiscal Responsibility Act of 1982 (TEFRA) carefully spells out guidelines that cannot be exceeded when over-funding flexible premium insurance policies. If these guidelines are exceeded, the policy becomes a modified endowment contract or M.E.C., losing many of its tax benefits.

The cash value in a permanent policy accumulates on a tax-deferred basis. When you withdraw money from your policy cash value, you will be taxed at your ordinary income rate on any amount that exceeds premiums paid. You can borrow from your policy with no immediate tax ramifications. Life insurance death benefits are free from income taxes; however, the death benefit can increase your estate to a point where estate taxes may become an issue.

You will want to have a qualified advisor review your policies to make sure your beneficiary designations and policy ownership are arranged in your best interest. You may have had some changes in your life that dictate changes in your policy ownership or beneficiary arrangements:

1. Were you recently married or divorced?
2. Have you adopted children? Do you now have step- children from a marriage?
3. Do you want money to go to a charity, church, or organization?
4. Would it be in your best interest to remove your life insurance from your estate? If you are the owner of your life insurance policy, it will be included in your estate at death.

Life insurance is the best way to replace critical income in the event of your premature death. Consider purchasing seven to ten times your annual income in personally owned life insurance. Also, if you are a stay-at-home husband or wife, you provide a significant economic value to your family. The cost of child care, house cleaning, daily personal errands, grocery shopping, and cooking would cost your surviving spouse thousands of dollars each and every month.

Disability

You may feel that you have disability insurance provided as a benefit from your place of employment, but you will probably find that your employer, like most companies, only has you covered for short-term disability. Many short-term disability policies only pay a benefit for six months, possibly a year, and then the benefits cease. You may want to consider an individual policy that you own personally. There are two benefits of owning your own policy:

1. As I stated earlier, I do not want you to have to depend on your employer for your financial security. The average American can change jobs or careers as many as six to eight times over the course of his lifetime. If you became uninsurable while working for one employer, you may change jobs and find yourself working for a new employer that does not even offer disability coverage. Buy your own policy and, in most cases, it is yours as long as you pay the premiums on time.

2. When you own an individually purchased disability policy and you are paying premiums with after-tax dollars, any monthly benefit that you might need to collect one day will be income tax free.

But maybe you do not think there is much risk of being disabled. Did you know that of all non-institutionalized persons age 15 and over in the United States, 17.5% have a functional limitation.[17] That is 34.2 million people! That does not include "institutionalized" people.

People have a physically severe functional limitation if they are unable to perform a physical function or if they need the help of another person to perform the function. An estimated 7.8% of those age 15 and older (15.2 million people) are severely limited in the functions of seeing, hearing, having speech understood, lifting or carrying, walking, or using stairs.[18]

> **Almost one in five people has a disability.**

A quarter of the population over 15 years old has some functional limitation, and nearly one-third of them has a severe limitation.[19]

An estimated 19.4% of non-institutionalized civilians in the United States, totaling 48.9 million people, have a disability. Almost half of these people (an estimated 24.1 million people) can be considered to have a severe disability. Almost one in five people has a disability.[20]

Knowing that one in five people has a disability, one could reach the conclusion that your chances of becoming disabled are greater than your chances of your house burning down. In my small neighborhood, there are one hundred homes and for the same ratio to hold true, every fifth home would have to burst into flames.

Disability does happen and it affects more than your ability to earn an income. It can happen to you or it could happen to a spouse. In addition to loss of income, there are emotional issues that most of us never consider. Kristi Sweeney, a CERTIFIED FINANCIAL PLANNER™ Practitioner, shares her personal story, a life-changing experience not only for her husband, but for the entire family.

Kristi Sweeney, CFP®: *I could not shake the feeling. I had a chilling fear that I would suffer a stroke, succumb to cancer or have a heart attack. Every so often, I could feel a tingle in my skull, a knot in the back of my neck and my heart skip a beat. A check-up proved there was nothing physically wrong with* *me. There was no wonder I was anxious. My doctor wasn't concerned but these symptoms worried me.*

These new sensations started soon after my husband had a major stroke when he was only 37 and at a time when he appeared to be in excellent health. I felt certain something unexpected and catastrophic would happen to me, too. Why wouldn't it happen to me if it happened to him? I had a disabled husband who could neither read, write nor talk and two suddenly bewildered children, ages 6 and 9, who had lots of years of growing up to do. Everyone in my family looked to me to hold their lives together and I was determined to do it. But would my health fail me? I wondered what would happen to my family if I was incapacitated or if I died?

Suffering from a condition that I now call "caregiver anxiety", my unease was caused by being too important in the lives of my loved ones. I knew no one could take my place.

I couldn't think of who would want to take my place! It was too much to handle. I paid household bills, managed financial accounts, drove my children's school carpools, made business phone calls, went to my husband's doctor's visits, completed claim forms, read to understand the residuals of stroke, made the meals, did household chores, tried to keep life as normal as possible for my children by having their friends to our house, going to the zoo, etc..

I also tried to find meaningful activities for my husband, whose life had taken such a drastic turn. I went with him when he attempted some volunteer work, I drove him to speech therapy, found an art teacher and drove him to classes. I researched enriched rehabilitation programs and medical therapies. I knew sometime soon I'd have to add in going to work. I'd lost my life partner and gained a pretty demanding dependent. I'd lost a fun life as a young wife and took on a heavy caregiver burden. My children needed me more because of the loss of their father who now had a major disability that was not going to change and who could not take care of them anymore. What would my family do if I wasn't around?

Realizing that I had to take charge of the one aspect of my life that I could control, I knew I had to add another self-assignment to the inventory of my chores. This new task had to move to the top of my list. So I started to organize my affairs so my family could make it without me. It seemed impossible and overwhelming at the beginning because I knew so little about planning.

Fortunately, the solutions were far simpler than I expected. Through careful and appropriate financial and estate planning, I eventually regained a normal sense of my own personal well-being.

With the help of my attorney, I set-up a testamentary trust, designated guardians for my young children, prepared power of attorney and living will documents, named a conservator and a guardian for my husband. Then, to protect my husband and children financially, I applied for insurance on myself. I purchased life and disability insurance (to protect the income I earn) and eventually long term care insurance (to protect assets if I were to become catastrophically disabled). This planning made me feel better. In fact, I thought this planning thing was such a great idea that by 1989, I went back to work and became insurance licensed, selling health insurance, disability insurance (especially) and life insurance.

Nine years later I went a little overboard with planning enthusiasm and started studying to learn all that I could about taxes, investing, wills and trusts. I loved all that I learned and was pretty convinced at the time that everyone should take this rigorous three year course with it's requisite arduous hours of study. I successfully passed the two day comprehensive exam and became a CERTIFIED FINANCIAL PLANNER about fifteen years after my husband's stroke.

Now I really had the knowledge it took to take command over my family's financial future. So, every few years I have updated our plan and I am in control –not of unexpected loss of health and disability, but assuring that my family will be well cared for. My knowledge has helped my clients as well and special- needs planning has become the focus of my financial planning practice.

In writing this book, it was my hope that you would glean some useful information, possibly making a substantial difference in your life. If you learned that you could buy an umbrella policy from your insurance agent for less than $275 a year and protect you family from financial loss associated with an unfortunate car accident, the price of this book would be money well spent. Writing *The Wealth Management Manual* has been an educational experience for me, as well. I thank Kristi Sweeney for sharing her story with us. This book is about quality of life, caring for the ones you love, and developing strategies that can help you deal with the unexpected.

The chances of you becoming disabled are relatively high compared to other risks you may face. When we used an earlier example of someone earning $65,000 a year, it is easy to see how a permanent disability can derail most of the family's financial plans. Many people do not consider that usually during a time of disability, health costs increase due to the treatment and maintenance of the disabled person. Can you imagine how you would be able to save for retirement or send your kids to college without an income? Do the math. Calculate your annual income and multiple by 20 years. Can your family afford to live without that income? Would your family even be able to live in the same home? When shopping for disability income insurance, consider two options that you may want to have quoted:

1. Waiver of premium. With most insurance companies, if you're disabled for a period of at least six months, you no longer have to pay the policy premiums as long as you are disabled.

2. Definition of disability. Read the "definition of disability" in the policy literature very carefully. If a policy defines disability as "your inability to perform any gainful employment" you could find yourself selling newspapers at the intersection. Ask your agent to carefully explain the "definition of disability" in the policy to your complete satisfaction before you purchase the policy.

Many people who are severely disabled need help to perform activities that most of us take for granted. Your chances of becoming disabled increase as you get older. As you might imagine, the insurance industry has created a solution for that dilemma and it is known as long-term care insurance.

Long-Term Care Insurance

The federal government's Medicare program does not pay for most nursing home or assisted living costs if retirees are no longer able to care for themselves. Retirees need to weigh the costs for long-term care insurance (LTC) and the risks that a lack of such coverage may pose to their finances should they have to accept a prolonged nursing home stay. Below are average nursing home costs from areas across the country. These numbers will give you a better idea of the risk to your bank account. Remember that as we get older our chances of needing some kind of long-term care greatly increase. One half of people over age 65 will spend some time in a nursing home. The average stay is usually less than three years.

Western states	**$46,000 to $62,000**
Southwest States	**$40,700 to $62,300**
Midwest States	**$41,000 to $71,300**
Southeast States	**$35,900 to $63,000**
Northeast States	**$59,100 to $105,500**

The above chart is based on findings from a study by GE Capital (as cited in Dolan, F. , & Harlow, V., 2004). Lifetime income planning. *Fidelity Investments,* 23.

Average Annual Nursing Home Costs[21]

Most policies also have the option of in-home care so long-term-care policies are not just for nursing homes. Various LTC policies are available through a handful of very solid insurance companies and most of the policy designs are very similar.

There are at least three ways to keep your premiums lower on a LTC policy or even a disability policy.

Three factors that impact the policy cost:

1. **Waiting period** – This is the time between when you first qualify to use the policy due to not being able to perform two or more ADLs, or Activities of Daily Living and when the policy actually begins to pay benefits. For instance, a policy with a 6 month waiting period would be less expensive than a policy with a 3 month waiting period.

2. **Benefit period** - A lower premium or policy cost will result from choosing a shorter benefit period or smaller benefit amount.

3. **Benefit Amount** - A smaller benefit amount will reduce your insurance cost, referred to as insurance premium. For instance, a policy that pays out a $200.00 daily benefit is more expensive than a policy that pays out a $150.00 daily benefit. Some long term care policies have a lifetime dollar maximum and once that amount has been reached the policy runs out of gas.

Just remember that regarding any type of insurance, the difference between what reimbursement or protection you need minus the level of coverage that you have, is the amount that you are self insuring for. Self-insurance is when you pay some of the claim out of your back pocket. If a long term care provider is billing $200.00 a day to take care of a loved one and the long-term-care policy pays $150.00, the $50.00 shortfall will come out of someone's back pocket.

When purchasing any type of insurance, remember that insurance is a promise to pay at some time in the future. Because an insurance contract is a promise to pay, it is very important that you deal with a financially strong organization. It is very possible, even probable, that you or your family may not need to access insurance policy benefits until many years in the future. I can't stress enough the importance of selecting a company that has withstood the test of time.

Wealth protection or asset protection is one of the four pillars of your wealth management program. Regardless of your station in life, you need to protect your property and your money. Over the last few pages you have learned that your greatest financial asset is your ability to earn an income. Our advisor panel shares their thoughts on wealth protection.

Wealth Protection
Advisor Roundtable

MARK DIEHL:
Do you feel asset protection is a key component of a well-rounded financial plan?

Chad Starliper, CFP®, ChFC, CLU, EA: Asset protection planning can get very complicated. For most people in non-litigious jobs—and who are not super wealthy—the first layers of defense are typically ownership structure and insurance. There are usually federal and state laws that protect certain assets from creditors, while other laws protect clients when property is owned a certain way. So structure is one way. Liability insurance is another, relatively cheap way to get additional protection.

If that is not enough, there are other ways of structuring entities, such as Family Limited Partnerships (FLP), Family Limited Liability Companies (FLLC), or through the use of various trusts. At some point there needs to be a structural shift away from owning assets outright in the name of the individual and more toward entity or split ownership or outright transfers.

Mike Busch, CPA, CFP®, CEBS: I am amazed how many people have an excellent offense but play lousy defense. In other words, they have been successful at accumulating wealth, but they do a poor job of protecting it. There are numerous risks to wealth. What is so dangerous is that you can have most of these risks covered, but it only takes one risk that you didn't plan for to really devastate you. Some of the steps that can be taken to shore up a client's defense include diversifying their portfolio and reducing the overall risk in the portfolio as the client ages. Umbrella liability coverage is an amazingly cheap way to protect against adverse legal judgments. Storing accumulated wealth in creditor protected assets and/or assets that are unattractive to potential creditors is also beneficial. Unfortunately, the biggest challenge to maintaining wealth is often our own actions. As strange as it sounds, we actually need to make sure we protect our wealth from ourselves. Our own psychology can be the greatest risk to our portfolios. The twin emotions of fear when the market is struggling and greed when it is advancing incite investors to make the worst possible decisions for their portfolios. Having the resources to deal with these emotions as they arise is critical in order to keep people from de-railing their financial futures.

Kristi Sweeney, CFP®: The importance of insurance cannot be underestimated. Adequate liability protection, auto and property insurance coverage is critical. More importantly, people need catastrophic medical, life, disability and long term care insurance. Being inadequately protected is an enormous risk to asset accumulation and preservation. For instance, during your working years, a disability lasting one year could wipe out $50,000 to $100,000 or more of savings without adequate long term disability insurance. If you could never work again, you will wipe out significant assets. In retirement, most people should have long term care insurance. A chronic condition requiring unskilled care is not covered by MediCare or MediCare supplemental policies. Round the clock care can cost $240 or more a day in the home.

John Scherer, CFP®, CLU, ChFC: Being properly insured is the cornerstone of holistic financial planning. It is important not to skimp on life insurance; especially when term insurance is so inexpensive. I always tell clients to make sure they get enough insurance. One million dollars is a lot of money if you win the lottery but it's not a lot if you have to raise three children for the next twenty years relying on that money.

Dana Sippel, CPA/PFS, CFP®: There are many major challenges to someone who is trying to maintain their wealth. The key is to determine what a person needs based on their accumulated assets, their profession and the risks associated with the different aspects of their life. There are several key components that need to be in place in order to preserve wealth. They are listed below:

1. Risk Management Program: It is essential to have a proper risk management program in place to shift any insurable risks to an insurance company. An example of a proper risk management program would be something as simple as having a life insurance policy to cover the income of the breadwinner in the family, so that in the event something were to happen to the breadwinner, the family would not be left in financial difficulty.

2. Property and Casualty Insurance: This type of insurance is necessary to protect property in the event of accident or liability issues. Property and casualty policies cover residences, rental properties, automobiles, recreational vehicles, boats, motorcycles and other similar items.

3. Umbrella Liability Policy: Umbrella policies are extremely important to expand the liability coverage beyond the amounts included under a typical property and casualty policy. Umbrella liability policies normally have limitations in the $1,000,000 - $5,000,000 range although some policy limitations can be up to $50,000,000. This policy is usually a relatively inexpensive but critical component of a comprehensive risk management program. In today's litigious society you must protect assets from lawsuits.

4. Officer/Director Insurance: This type of policy is necessary to protect those who serve on a board of directors from any liabilities incurred while carrying out their duties as a board member.

5. Professional Liability Insurance: Professional liability insurance is important for all professionals - doctors, lawyers, certified public accountants, architects or any profession where a lawsuit can be brought due to errors and omissions.

Matthew Tuttle, CFP®, MBA: We believe in always planning for the worst and hoping for the best. We can't control what will happen in the economy, the world, or the markets. The only things we can control are the ways we manage risk. We would recommend that the client consider all areas of risk—estate tax exposure, lawsuit exposure, spendthrift exposure, divorce exposure, etc. and plan for all of these. At a minimum we would make sure that clients title assets correctly, that trusts are used when necessary to protect inheritances, that there was proper life, disability, and long term care insurance and a well thought out philosophy regarding their use, that all ways to reduce taxes were explored, that any estate tax exposure was discussed and planned for, and that the client had an umbrella policy.

Wayne Starr, CFP®, ChFC: It is difficult to be a good investment advisor without delving in to asset protection issues. The issue of adequate insurance must also be addressed. Whether in a profession or not, adequate liability protection is critical. I have had a client very adversely affected by a medical malpractice judgment. The insurer was insolvent and the state fund did not come to his rescue.

Cary Carbonaro, CFP®, MBA: On the asset protection side, you should have an umbrella policy. You should also know state specific laws regarding what assets are exempt if you were sued. For example, your retirement plan including your IRA is exempt from creditors. In Florida, the homestead exemption for asset protection purposes provides the owner of property with a shield from virtually all non-lien creditors. This type of homestead exemption is only available if the property is your primary residence and a court makes a determination that the property is within a municipality or outside of a municipality. If your property is within a municipality, protection is provided for only one half acre of contiguous land. If your property is outside of a municipality, protection is provided for 160 acres of contiguous land.

Diana Grossman Simpson, MBA, CFP®: Insurance is critical to the success of a financial plan. Not just life insurance, but homeowner's, auto, liability, disability--it is so important to know that you are covered in case something goes wrong. Most people have life insurance, but when asked about it, they are not sure how much it is, how long it lasts or how much it costs. Usually, there is no real underlying strategy to their coverage – maybe they multiplied their current salary by some random number and settled on that amount as appropriate coverage. And I've found that often, spouses are unsure of the coverage on their partner, and don't know where the information is in the event of a premature death. I guess these are just not topics of discussion for most people – they'd rather not think about it – but I can help them sort through it.

John Scherer, CFP®, CLU, ChFC: Regarding asset protection, it is imperative to be properly insured against loss or damage of property, liability, death, disability and identity theft. Before getting into investment issues, adequate insurance protection must be in place.

In addition to insurance, a client can use limited liability companies (LLCs) and trusts to protect against frivolous lawsuits and unnecessary liability. I even have some clients who own their house and cars in separate LLCs in order to shelter their other assets; so that in case of a car accident which is their fault only the assets of the owner of the car, in this case the LLC and not they personally, are at risk. This is a very complicated issue and should be closely evaluated by all members of one's advisory team.

Wealth Protection Action Plan

1. Review and increase property coverage limits and liability limits on your auto and homeowner's insurance.
2. Consider the risk for flood in your area and insure appropriately.
3. Purchase an umbrella policy for increased liability protection. Inquire about discounts for multiple policies with your insurance carrier.
4. If you own a small business, speak to an attorney regarding entity planning.
5. Insure the goose. Secure a personal disability policy with the waiting period scheduled to end when your employer-provided short term policy stops paying benefits. When one policy ceases, the other will begin. Select a benefit period of at least 36 months, a lifetime benefit if you can afford it.
6. Have a life insurance analysis performed by your advisor. If you have dependents, consider purchasing seven to ten times your annual salary in life insurance.

Section 2
Wealth Accumulation

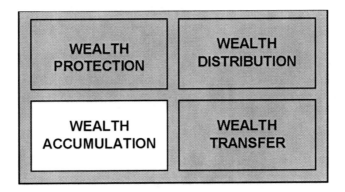

It's Not About Greed.
It's About Quality Of Life

The Wealth Management Manual is separated into four key areas: wealth protection, accumulation, distribution, and finally, wealth transfer. Everyone should be concerned about wealth protection, regardless of your stage in life. Wealth accumulation is about creating strategies to enable you to accomplish life's major milestone goals.

For me, this is the fun part of the book. No one wants to admit it, but a lot of people love money. They love to have it, hold it and they love to spend it. They would love to talk about their money if it wasn't just plain rude and frowned upon by society. For the record, I believe loving money is a bad thing. I love what money can help us do. I'd love to be able to help my children get a great education. In fact, I would love to be able to fund a small scholarship to help other kids acquire an education as well. Money is just a tool. Don't focus on the tools, but rather on the architecture of your life and the people you love. What good is having a garage full of hammers if you never build anything? One of the interesting things about money is that it really isn't a status symbol; it just allows you to buy status symbols. No one knows how much money I have in my bank account, but I love it when they admire my Mercedes 300 SL. Or actually, in my case, my Ford F150 Super Crew Cab. Hey, if a pickup was good enough for Sam Walton, it's good enough for me.

On the other side of the coin, money is serious business. Did you notice two separate puns in the same sentence? In the preface of this book I mentioned your underlying motives and feelings regarding wealth and money. Bill Bachrach, a leading coach to financial advisors teaches a system called Values Based Financial Planning. I think it is critical that you quantify what you want to accomplish and qualify the why. What are the underlying values behind what you want to do? For instance, let's say you wanted to retire at age 55 for these reasons:

- To donate time to your faith
- To volunteer in your community
- To spend more time with your kids and grandkids

These are great reasons to want to retire at age 55! I remember a colleague making the comment that he was not wrapped up in the desire for more money, that he aspired to make a difference in the world. I wonder how much time you can contribute to making a difference in the world if you're still focused on trying to make a mortgage payment or a car note? Is it possible that cash flow could affect your tithe? This book isn't about greed. It is about making wise choices so that you may have the financial freedom to impact your world, your community and your family in a very positive way.

As we get started, I feel it is important to explain some initial concepts that are simple to understand. Most people don't take the time to learn the nuances that can mean the difference between financial success and financial failure, at least as it relates to wealth accumulation and also wealth preservation. So, here we go.

There is a difference between stock trading and investing.

Stock trading is usually more speculative in nature and almost always less than a six month proposition. At its most radical extreme is the day trader who may enter or exit a stock position several times through the course of a day. During the 90s when everyone was a stock guru, day trading was very popular. As of the writing of this book, most of the day traders have literally traded themselves into oblivion. There are some common threads of logic that are carefully woven throughout this book and one concept I want you to glean from this is that I will show you how to wisely put your money to work and then go out and live your life and enjoy the things that life has to offer: your family, your health, a beautiful sunny day. Five years from now, if you find yourself glued to a computer screen sweating the four tick movement of an individual security you're holding, it will be safe to say that you did not heed any of the concepts in this book. There are so many things in life more important than money. Yes, I am a financial author and you did hear me right.

> There are so many things in life more important than money.

In fact, a few years ago I read a comment in a mutual fund sales brochure from the American Funds family of mutual funds.

"Your life should be more exciting than your investment portfolio."

I heard an investment professional make a statement many years ago and I still carry it with me today. "The markets can provide whatever a person is looking for, if that person knows what they are looking for." It probably took me at least a year to really understand that statement and then one day I had an epiphany. I finally "got it."

If you want excitement, the markets are an excellent place to get it. Growing in popularity is FOREX trading, or Foreign Exchange Currency Trading. FOREX trades 24 hours a day, five days a week. Most people who trade FOREX lose money and they lose it fast, due to the high leverage of 10,000 to 1. And the great thing about FOREX trading 24 hours a day is that you can lose money while you sleep. You don't even have to be awake. For excitement, you can trade stock options, but if you don't know what you're doing you can lose your shirt--and your shoes, your slacks--the list goes on.

Thrill Seeking and Wealth Building:
Two entirely different things.

I want to teach you how to slowly invest your way to a portfolio that can contribute to your financial peace of mind for years to come. The concepts we are about to delve into are boring, like watching paint dry.

Building your wealth is like any other journey. It will take some time to get there, but it will be worth it. In the first section of the book, we looked at some risk management techniques. We made sure that our seatbelts were securely fastened and our tray tables were in the full and upright position.

Now, I'm going to show you how to remove one of the two major sources of investment risk from your portfolio. I'm also going to show you how to take advantage of Nobel Prize winning investment strategies and implement these strategies in your own investment portfolio.

If you have had the great fortune to have accumulated substantial assets, through the next few chapters we'll discuss steps you can take to diversify your accounts and minimize your exposure to unnecessary risk. In the first section of this book we looked at risk management from an insurance standpoint, making sure that your wealth accumulation and preservation is not at risk due to a lawsuit or loss of income from disability. Now we're going to consider risk management in the selection of your investments and portfolio design.

Risk and Recovery

If your Account Lost	You Need This To Recover
10%	11.5%
20%	25.0%
30%	42.8%
40%	66.5%
50%	100.0%
60%	150.0%

Let's say that you are retired, and your total investment account lost 40%. All you have to do is read about what happened between 2000 and 2003 in the NASDAQ and S&P 500 and you'll realize that a 40% loss is very possible. If you lost 40% in your account and then averaged a 7.5% annual return in subsequent years, it would take you over eight years to recoup your losses. If you were in retirement and you had been withdrawing money to help fund your retirement, your account might never recover to its original balance.

As documented in an economic letter published by the Federal Reserve Board of San Francisco in March of 2003:

" . . . the environment surrounding the historic expansion of the U.S. economy from March 1992 though March 2001 mirrors in many ways the expansion of the 1960s. After a subdued start, productivity perked up to average 2.4% per year from 1995 onward. This improved productivity growth was accompanied by strong economic growth and a surging stock market, while inflation remained relatively low. A bottom for the stock market occurred in October 1990, followed by a "bull" market that accelerated rapidly after 1994, fueled by the high-tech boom. From December 1994 to its peak in August 2000, the stock market increased in value by $9.7 trillion, with the S&P 500 rising by an extraordinary 226%, or by 40% per year, for an average annual inflation-adjusted increase of 34%. From the fourth quarter of 1994 to the third quarter of 2000, the inflation-adjusted net worth per capita of households increased by over 8% per year. The market peaked in August of 2000, and over the next two years, the inflation value of the...

S&P 500 fell more than 43%."

Over roughly the same time period the NASDAQ dropped 77.8%

According to *CBS MarketWatch*, 94% of all stock mutual funds lost money in 2002. Lipper and Company calculates that the average equity mutual fund lost 21% in 2002.

Dana Sippel, CPA/PFS, CFP®: My suggestions for capital preservation first and foremost would be diversify, diversify, diversify. The safest way to protect your investment, if you'll excuse the cliché, is to not have all your eggs in one basket. We can all imagine a dozen eggs in a basket that gets dropped by accident. At that point all the eggs have the potential to break and there is nothing left to be done except watch and see if there are any whole eggs left. Most of us would rather not take that chance. It's just too risky. But if we put one or two eggs in different baskets the risk is greatly reduced. You may lose an egg here or there, but some of them, given enough time, may produce a chicken or two. The same can be said for investing. You need to make sure your portfolio is diversified and with the appropriate risk tolerance based on your life and your long-term goals for your portfolio.

I would also advise protecting yourself against a large investment in the company you work for through stock options, stock purchase plans, etc. due to the same logic mentioned above. We all remember the Enron scandal. Unfortunately, many employees of Enron had their life savings tied up in the company's stock. When the stock value quickly plummeted to zero, many employees lost their life savings. This situation could have been easily avoided by diversifying their investment portfolio. You do not want to be in that position if your company goes belly up. Not only is your paycheck gone, but your savings are lost as well.

Matthew Tuttle, CFP®, MBA: In investments there are four bad things that can happen: the stock market can go down, interest rates can go up, oil prices can go up, and inflation can go up. We would make sure that a client had at least one investment that was supposed to go up if one of those bad things happened. That way, whatever happens, you will still be okay.

It is so critical for all investors to make an honest assessment of the risk they are willing to assume. The "risk and recovery" chart that we looked at earlier should help you evaluate how much pain you can endure. Younger investors with longer time horizons have greater latitude in recovering from market volatility. When we talk about managing risk in the investment selection process, we'll need to consider the work of a gentleman named Harry Markowitz.

A Nobel Prize Winning Strategy

I believe this section is one of the most important sections of *The Wealth Management Manual.* What you learn in these pages will play an integral role in any success that you have as an investor. In 1952, Markowitz published a paper titled "Portfolio Selection" in the *Journal of Finance.*

Markowitz' theory was built on the concept that investors could develop diversified portfolios, seeking an optimum balance between risk and reward. In 1958, another gentleman, James Tobin, had been studying the possibility of adding a risk-free asset to the mix. I know all of this is very academic but I promise that we'll wrap up this section with information you can take to the bank. Did you notice that last money pun?

In 1964, William Sharp added his contribution to Modern Portfolio Theory with the concept of the Capital Asset Pricing Model (CAPM). All of this gets very complicated and I believe more information than most of us need or want to know, but 38 years after Markowitz' paper first appeared in the 1952 *Journal of Finance,* Markowitz, Sharp, and Merton Miller were awarded the Nobel Prize for what has become the broad theory for portfolio selection and asset allocation.

So what does all this mean to you and me? Gary Brinson, Brian Singer, and Gilbert Beebower performed a study of 82 large pension plans over the period of 1977 to 1987, a ten year snapshot. The study was titled "Determinants of Portfolio Performance II: An Update." Their goal was to assess the influence of passive and active asset allocations on the 82 pension plans. They discovered that 91.5% of the variation in portfolio returns was the result of passive, or benchmark, allocation. To put it another way, asset type selection was more critical to overall performance than individual security selection. Earlier, they had actually performed a predecessor study titled "Determinants of Portfolio Performance." In this analysis, 91 large pension plans were analyzed to determine the major contributing factors to portfolio performance and they looked at the period between 1974 and 1983. They determined that 93.6% of the total variation resulted from asset selection, not individual security selection.

These findings are important to the average investor because they tell us that our success in an investment portfolio is not determined by picking the hottest stock or the mutual funds on the cover of the latest edition of a particular magazine, but by being adequately diversified across different asset classes.

"93.6% of the total variation in portfolio returns is a result of asset allocation, not individual security selection."

Asset Allocation and How it Works

According to William F. Sharpe, as defined in his 1992 article *Management Style and Performance Measurement,* "Asset Allocation is generally defined as the allocation of an investor's portfolio among a number of major asset classes." In a few minutes we will take a look at each of the asset classes. Based on the investor's time horizon, risk tolerance, and investment objective, a portfolio is created, giving careful consideration to the investor's weighting of each asset component in the overall portfolio.

All of this is a very fancy way of saying, "Don't put all your eggs in one basket.'" As one asset may be increasing in value, another asset may be in decline, creating a "smoothing" of portfolio volatility. This sounds very complicated, but a lot has taken place since the initial work of Harry Markowitz back in 1952. The evolution of the personal computer and modern day asset allocation software has transformed the investment management profession.

The Asset Classes

T-Bills
Cash equivalents with less than three months to maturity

Intermediate – Term Government Bonds
Government bonds with less than ten years to maturity

Long –Term Government Bonds
Government bonds with more than ten years until maturity

Corporate Bonds
Corporate Bonds with ratings of at least Baa by Moody's
or BBB by Standard and Poor's

Mortgage – Related Securities
Mortgage backed and related securities

Large Capitalization Value Stocks
Stocks in Standard and Poor's 500 stock index with high
book-to-price ratios

Large Capitalization Growth Stocks
Stocks in Standard and Poor's 500 stock index with low price-to-book ratio

Medium Capitalization Stocks
Stocks in the top 80% of capitalization in the U.S. equity universe after the exclusion of stocks in the S&P 500 Index

Small Capitalization Stocks
Stocks in the bottom 20% of capitalization in the U.S. equity universe after the exclusion of stocks in the S&P 500 Index

Non – U.S. Bonds
Bonds outside the U.S. and Canada

European Stocks
European and non-Japanese Pacific Basin stocks

Japanese Stocks
Japanese Stocks

Many financial professionals are very strict followers of modern portfolio theory and one can't ignore the logic of diversifying across asset classes. With the modern asset allocation software available to advisors, it is simple enough to ask a series of questions concerning risk tolerance and a model asset allocation is generated. The allocation will usually be shown in the form of a pie chart and also accompanied in a spreadsheet format showing percentages of the component asset classes, totaling 100%.

One of the few weaknesses of asset allocation is that it doesn't take into consideration the personal preferences and values of the investor. Remember, this is your life and though your financial choices can help you along your journey, your investment choices should be consistent with your values. I could create an allocated portfolio based on your risk tolerance and the software program could determine that you should invest a portion of your assets in the Japanese economy. However, if your great-grandfather died in

> # Asset allocation, a place to start or a place to finish?

Pearl Harbor and you would never buy a Toyota or a SONY product because of your point of reference, you may not want to invest in any Japanese companies. If you are a devout conservative Christian you may be reluctant to invest in any company that derives their primary revenue from alcohol or tobacco. If an allocation analysis determines that the S&P 500 is an appropriate place for you to invest some assets, you might seek ways to exclude tobacco or liquor companies from the mix. Maybe your personal value system precludes you from supporting any company that harms the environment or manufactures firearms. Asset allocation is a great foundation on which to build a portfolio, but for many investors it is a starting place rather than the final word.

One phrase that you will hear frequently in the investing universe is the abbreviated word "cap." It is just a shorter version of the word 'capitalization." Some investment companies have redefined the list of asset classes down to just six or seven.

- Large Cap

- Mid Cap

- Small Cap

- International Stocks

- Bonds/Fixed Income

- Cash

Many of the mutual fund companies have general, but very similar, definitions of the various asset classes. For example:

Large Cap	Over $10 billion in capitalization
Mid Cap	$3 billion to $10 billion in capitalization
Small Cap	$1.5 billion to $3 billion in capitalization
International	Stocks listed on the MSCI Index

The MSCI EAFE Index is the Morgan Stanley Capital International Index which tracks Europe, Australasia, and the Far East.

I know all of this sounds very complicated but it is actually quite simple to create an effective asset allocation model based on a brief questionnaire. Modern

Portfolio Theory purists believe in something known at the Efficient Market Hypothesis. According to the Efficient Market Hypothesis, all information in a market, whether public or private, is accounted for in a stock price. Not even insider information could give an investor or trader an edge. People who rely solely on stock charts to select their stocks are using what is known as technical analysis. Investors who analyze a company's financial information, balance sheet, earnings growth, and debt ratio are performing what is referred to as fundamental analysis. According to the strongest form of the Efficient Market Hypothesis, neither technical nor fundamental analysis will give an investor any type of edge in security selection.

This concept is very important for you to know because most true believers of the Efficient Market Hypothesis only invest in index mutual funds. The passive school of investing does not believe anyone can outperform the indexes over the long haul. Fidelity cannot, Oppenheimer cannot, AIM Investments cannot. During the unprecedented bull market of the 90s, investors could do really well just by investing in a fund that tracked the NASDAQ 100 and the S&P 500 indexes. Remember that during the period between 1994 and the peak of the market in early 2000, the S&P 500 was averaging double digit returns each and every year. Give or take a few basis points, an investor in an S&P 500 Index mutual fund did extremely well during that period, his account increasing in value by almost 226%. Then 2000 came along, and the wheels came off. That very same S&P 500 Index mutual fund lost 43% over a three year period. In 2002 alone, the S&P 500 index dropped over 23%!

This may be a good place to point out that markets only do one of three things:

Markets go up.
Markets go down.
Markets go sideways.

When markets go up everyone is a hero. For the most part, all ships rise with the tide. Your plumber is managing his own account with TD Ameritrade and he tells you he is earning 24% on his portfolio. College grads are becoming stockbrokers because it is such an easy business and existing stockbrokers are starting their own hedge funds because everything they touch seems to turn to gold. There really isn't a bad mutual fund since all equity funds seem to be making money and, in a market where a major index is averaging 25% growth per year, index funds are the obvious place to be. Life is good and you feel confident that you will be retiring early. Maybe you'll start a new career and become a stockbroker.

When markets go down, which they inevitably will do, some unusual things happen. The first thing you may notice is that your broker does not call you as much as he or she used to. If the markets stay down for a prolonged period of time, you may notice that your broker has had a sudden career change and no longer works for the firm holding your account. Maybe he has gone into the witness protection program. The firm holding your account may not be calling you on the telephone, not because they don't want to, but because they are now understaffed. The index fund you are holding is dropping like the roller coaster on the big hill at Coney Island, and you are considering pulling the plug, but no one will return your call to give you any recommendations. It is never comforting when your are 65 years old and your 27 year-old investment representative is encouraging you to hold course on your rapidly dropping account which constitutes your entire life savings. You're wondering if your retirement is going to be your golden years or maybe working at the golden arches. And you can't help but wonder how the plumber who came to fix your sink last year is doing with his account?

When markets go sideways, so do index mutual funds. Because index mutual funds mimic a particular index, they will follow the market very closely. No better, no worse. This can be particularly disconcerting to people in retirement needing to count on some of their retirement savings for income. One day the market is up 100 points and the next day it is down 115 points. Your local evening news reports there are as many market losers as winners and the network financial reporter advises that analysts and market pundits do not see a end in sight. Retirement is achievable, but you may need to work a few extra years to further pad your retirement accounts.

You may be wondering which is the best way to invest. Is passive index investing the right way to manage you investments or is active management the most effective way to seek portfolio growth? And what about trading stocks or options? As I mentioned earlier I cannot ignore the statistical support for the efficient market and Modern Portfolio Theory. On the other hand, the successful long-term track records of many professional portfolio managers are hard to ignore. Peter Lynch of Fidelity Investments and Bill Gross of PIMCO have had great histories of successful money management. You may also remember that I said earlier that active traders do have the potential to earn large profits from the markets.

The real question is what strategy would work best for you and your family. Active traders make a large tradeoff between the required time commitment to trade successfully and the impact of that time commitment on their children and spouse. Another factor that cannot be ignored regarding active trading is the stress level. On several occasions I bought put options on stocks that I was anticipating to rapidly decrease in price. A put option is a type of option that allows you to benefit from a stock or security that drops in price. In fact, the faster the price drops the more money you make! Buying options is very speculative in nature and I still remember the feelings I had as I watched that stock move in the "wrong" direction. Eventually, the stock made the anticipated move downward and I picked up a 40% return in a matter of days. I was so excited and just knew that option trading was going to be the key to my early retirement. I immediately found another stock on which to do an option play and very shortly experienced a 34% loss. It sounds a lot like Las Vegas, doesn't it? You win a $100 at the blackjack table and, instead of walking away, you stick around to give all or most of it back to the house.

Options can also be utilized in a conservative fashion, often safer than simply owning stocks outright. Call options or covered calls can be written on stocks and exchange traded funds, providing a certain amount of downside protection and generating immediate portfolio income at the same time.

We talk a great deal about diversification across asset classes, but one can also diversify across investment styles. Many times I suggest that a client place assets in index funds, which are passively managed, and a portion of assets in actively managed mutual funds. For instance, an S&P 500 Index fund can populate the same portfolio as an equity income fund and a small capitalization fund. The index fund and the equity income fund would experience at least some level of stock overlap, but a small percentage of overlap is not always a bad thing.

Stock or security overlap occurs when you hold two or three mutual funds that have some of the same stocks in the portfolio. For instance, I know of one mutual fund company in particular that has a very short list of stocks their portfolio counselors are allowed to invest in. The list is short because it has been reduced to stocks of only the highest quality companies. The problem with shopping from such a short list of available companies is that, inevitably, some of the same stocks are in most of the mutual funds they manage.

To put the level of risk in perspective, you must know that a particular mutual fund may only hold 1% to 2% of a company's stock. Overlap may make the company in question comprise 3% to 4% of your portfolio. In the big picture, still not an undue amount at risk on any one company.

It is important to be aware of the risk associated with holding one security. This may be a good time to explain the differences between the two major types of risks investors face.

Risk Defined

Unsystematic Risk
Systematic Risk

Unsystematic Risk is the only type of risk that can be diversified away. Unsystematic risks are the risks associated with a single company or stock holding in your portfolio. For example, let's say the year is 2001 and that 100% of your investment portfolio is invested in Enron. If Enron drops from $80 a share to .80 a share, it will have a drastically negative effect on your portfolio. Unsystematic risks are:

- **Financial Risk**
- **Business Risk**
- **Default Risk**
- **Regulation Risk**

As we take a closer look and define each of these substantial risks, remember that these types of risks can be almost completely avoided with proper portfolio diversification.

Financial Risk is the risk related to the amount of debt that a company has outstanding. Financial risk is the liability side of the balance sheet.

Business Risk is the risk associated with a particular business. Remember Enron? This risk includes the speculative nature of the business, management style and business philosophy. Business risk is usually associated with the asset portion of the balance sheet and you can see how business risk and financial risk might go hand-in-hand.

Default Risk is the risk associated with the possibility that a corporation may not be able to adequately service its debt. This is a type of risk that is of concern to bond investors. Bonds that are issued by municipalities and corporations are subject to default risk. When you invest in a bond, you are lending money to an entity. Default is when that entity does not have the resources to repay the debt.

In contrast, let's say I was a stock investor of a company that went bankrupt. Bondholder investors of that company would be concerned about **default risk**, about the company not being able to repay the debt to bondholders. Investors who had purchased stock would be concerned about the **business risk.** This is the risk of the value of the common or preferred stock declining due to poor business management.

Regulation Risk is the risk that the current legal environment can have on the future of a particular business. Regulatory changes such as tax rate changes or zoning changes can have an adverse effect on a business.

Now let's take a close look at the risks that are unavoidable. As a matter of fact, you will be affected by many of these risks whether you invest in the stock market or not. These types of risks are referred to as **Systematic Risks**. You can keep all of your money in a fixed interest bank account, in a coffee can in your backyard or in the stock market, and you will still be at the mercy of many of these types of systematic risks. But before we define each of these risks, you should know that the markets tend to financially reward investors who are willing to accept at least a certain amount of risk.

Systematic Risks are:

- **Purchasing Power Risk**
- **Exchange Rate Risk**
- **Interest Rate Risk**
- **Reinvestment Risk**
- **Market Risk**

Purchasing Power Risk is the risk that a dollar today will be worth less than a dollar tomorrow. Can you remember how much a gallon of gas cost ten years ago? How much did a stamp cost ten years ago? It is possible that inflation can erode the real value of your invested assets. As the price of goods increases, the purchasing power of your assets decreases. Purchasing power risk in unavoidable.

Exchange Rate Risk is the risk associated with changes in the value of foreign currencies in relation to the value of the dollar. This risk can impact companies and also consumers that deal with oversea companies. Do you or any of your friends drive a foreign car? Do you drink coffee? Does the mutual fund in your 401(k) plan at work possibly invest in Toyota, SONY, or Samsung?

Interest Rate Risk is an easy type of risk to understand. Many of us talk about interest rates frequently because we are keenly aware of how rates personally affect us. You may be considering refinancing your home or financing a new car and interest rates are a concern. If you're like me, every other day I get an offer in the mail from a credit card company offering a lower interest rate. Interest rates influence businesses and also investors. Interest rate risk is the risk that interest rates will have a negative impact on the value of securities. Typically, an inverse relationship exits between interest rates and the value of stocks and bonds. When interest rates go up, it is not uncommon to see bond and stock prices go down. The Federal Reserve Board will influence rates and tighten the money supply when they want to slow the economy down a bit.

Reinvestment Risk is the risk that cash flows distributed from current investments will be reinvested at a rate of return less than the rate of return on the current investment.

Market Risk is the risk that stock prices will be influenced by the direction of the broader market. One phrase that I use with investment representatives and clients is that "all ships rise and sink with the tide." No matter how capable the captain is at the helm of your ship, he is unable to control the seas below.

Unsystematic risk can be diversified away, but many of the systematic risks are components of a financial environment we are unable to control.

Measuring Risk

The classic definition of risk is the uncertainty of future outcomes, or the probability of an adverse result. As mentioned previously, the total risk an investor faces can be separated into two categories: systematic and unsystematic risk. Total risk is the sum of systematic risk and unsystematic risk as measured by the standard deviation of returns.

Beta is a measurement of systematic risk. The broad market is defined as having a beta of 1.0. A security with a beta of 1.50 would be considered to be 50% more volatile than the market. A security with a beta of .50 would be considered to be 50% less volatile than the market. Pertaining to investments, volatility and risk are the same thing.

Most investors would like to enjoy the benefits of high returns and avoid the account draw-downs associated with market losses, but risk and return go together. You may have heard the term "risk premium." Investments that have a certain amount of risk also exhibit the potential for greater returns. Likewise, conservative fixed-income investments will always have a lower yield. This is the classic risk, return tradeoff. Prudent investors will create diversified portfolios with the highest expected return for a given level of risk.

High Risk – High Return	Consistent
Moderate Risk – Moderate Return	Consistent
Low Risk – Low Return	Consistent
High Risk – Low Return	Inconsistent
Moderate Risk – High Return	Inconsistent
Low Risk – High Return	Inconsistent

When reviewing the above example you should know that it is very possible to invest in a high-risk investment and experience a low return but it is highly improbable that you could invest in a low risk investment and earn a high return. Using Morningstar's Principia Software, I have discovered scores of mutual funds that have a high beta, a high degree of risk and consistently lower returns. While past returns are not a consistent indicator of future returns, remember that you do not want to assume a higher level of risk unless there is also substantial potential for higher returns.

Likewise, if your projections to meet your retirement accumulation goals 20 years from now are based on an assumption of an annualized return of 9%, you're never going to hit that target by investing all of your money in certificates of deposit.

In the development of your investment program you will need to consider two very important factors; your personal tolerance for risk and the time horizon of your particular investment or portfolio. For instance, your retirement account may have a target accumulation date 20 years from now, while the account for your grandchild's college fund will be needed in 10 years. Longer term time horizons can be invested a little more aggressively than financial goals with shorter term targets. When considering your tolerance for risk you might ask yourself what would keep you up at night. At what point would your investment program make you nervous or uneasy? Investors should try to accomplish at least four things when designing portfolios.

- Portfolio returns sufficient to meet their most important goals.
- Peace of mind.
- A well-organized and designed portfolio.
- Tax efficiency

In another area of *The Wealth Management Manual* we will discuss portfolio organization in greater detail but this is an appropriate time to address the assumption of risk and desired investment returns. The challenge is to find a balance between an acceptable level of risk and investment returns sufficient to meet your most important lifetime goals; a secure retirement, college funding for children or grandchildren, or possibly transferring assets to family members or charities at your demise.

To continue our discussion, realize that any stock can be a risky investment if only held for the short term but over the long-term the stock market has exhibited a definite bullish tendency. Stocks are only appropriate for the investor who can be committed to his/her investment for the long-term. You have heard me say long-term and short-term several times during this conversation and I've never really defined what they mean. It is subjective but I can tell you that I am very uncomfortable recommending equity investments for anyone that will be in the investment less than five years. If your time horizon is under five years, the odds are very good that your account value could be less than your initial investment. You might want to consider CDs, money market accounts, and short term bonds for investment time periods that are 5 years and shorter.

If an investor tells me they have a time frame of 5 to 10 years and they want to invest in equities, I might suggest a balanced mutual fund because it is one of the most conservative ways to participate in the market.

> # Any stock can be risky if held for the short term.

We have discussed Modern Portfolio Theory, asset allocation and the twelve major asset classes. You have learned that, for the sake of simplification, many investment firms reference a shorter refined list of only six asset classes. Now that you have a thorough understanding of the different types of risk you may face as investor, we'll look at the basic building blocks of the major asset classes: stocks, bonds and cash.

Stocks, Bonds, and Cash

There are alternative financial vehicles in addition to stocks, bonds and cash. Options fall into a category known as derivatives. In addition, one could speculate in the foreign currency exchange market (FOREX) or one could speculate in futures or commodities. Stock options can be used very conservatively by the prudent investor but, in my opinion, the FOREX, futures and commodities markets are very speculative and the only participants certain to profit are the brokers. That being said, commodities often have a negative correlation to equities and there are professionally managed commodities accounts available. I must admit that commodities are not my area of expertise. The purpose of this book is to show you how to invest wisely, putting your money to work profitably while maintaining a strong emphasis on capital preservation.

We are going to dissect the three major building blocks. We'll start with stocks and then we'll have a comprehensive review of bonds and mortgage-backed securities. After our analysis of the building blocks of a diversified portfolio, we'll discuss how managed money can reduce unsystematic risk, create immediate diversification and provide you with professional world-class portfolio management.

Stocks

In our discussion of stocks, I will start with what are generally perceived as the most conservative stocks and then work back to the more aggressive stocks. It should be mentioned that some of these stocks will overlap into different categories. For instance, blue chip stocks and income producing stocks have some of the same companies populating both lists.

Blue Chip Stocks are the highest quality or at least the highest regarded stocks available. Most people view blue chip stocks as holdings that are very safe. Blue chip stocks generally populate such indexes as the Dow 30 or even the S&P 500. Coca-Cola, General Electric, Wal-Mart, and Philip Morris are examples of blue chip stocks. As mentioned above, many blue chip stocks are also income producing stocks because profits are returned to the shareholders in the form of dividends. As companies reach a certain size, they may have no interest in getting bigger.

Income Stocks are companies that find themselves in a situation where growth of infrastructure is no longer attractive. Typically, these are large well-established companies that return excess profits to the investor in the form of dividends. Utilities pay dividends, as well as companies like AIG Insurance, Conoco, Pfizer, Bristol-Meyers and General Electric. Remember that General Electric was mentioned above in the discussion regarding blue chip stocks.

Defensive Stocks are companies that usually hold up pretty well in times of economic weakness. These companies sell a product or service that consumers can't do without. In economist terms, these products are considered inelastic, meaning that price has little effect on the amount of demand or consumption. Examples would be gasoline for your car, electricity for your home, milk and certain food staples. If the price of electricity goes up, I may try to cut back on my consumption, but since I live in Houston, Texas we will sacrifice other things before we would ever consider going without air conditioning in the summer. Cigarette prices continue to climb, yet career smokers somehow find room in their budgets to continue buying.

Growth and Income Stocks have the potential to do both, as the name implies. Their prospects for growth are usually lower than a true growth stock and their dividend income does not really stack up to a true income stock. Because the potential for both growth and income exist, they are often attractive stocks for the moderate investor. Total return tends to hold up pretty well in down markets and slightly under-perform in bull markets.

Growth Stocks are companies that take most or all of their profits and reinvest them back into the growth of the company. These types of corporations may experience above average growth in earnings and assets. In an earlier chapter, we talked about asset classes based on size: large cap, mid cap, and small cap. The word "cap" is an abbreviation for capitalization. Growth stocks can fall into any of the three asset sizes. There are small cap growth stocks, mid cap growth stocks and large cap growth stocks. Growth companies take earnings and reinvest those earning in expanding infrastructure: more equipment, more warehouses and bigger buildings. The main thing to realize is that these stocks do not pay any income and may be inappropriate for the investor seeking cash flow to supplement retirement income. An older investor may benefit from growth stocks in their portfolio but should consider allocating a smaller percentage of total assets. Many growth stocks can be overpriced because market exuberance and emotion can push prices higher and higher.

Emerging Growth Stocks are several steps deeper into the realm of potential higher returns and definitely higher risk. These are young companies that may have gone public only recently and have little or no track record. They often exhibit potential for growth but have a corresponding level of risk. You will see these types of stocks in aggressive growth funds and emerging growth funds.

Speculative Stocks are companies that are experiencing significant volatility due to extreme circumstances. Both younger companies and established companies can become speculative in nature. At one time, Lucent Technologies was a solid holding in most blue chip portfolios, yet today it is trading at $2.63 a share. Enron was a household name--and still is--but dropped from $83. per share to .60 a share in a matter of weeks, from a solid investment to a speculative risk in the blink of an eye. Investors in speculative holdings should be prepared for heightened volatility and unpredictable stock prices and returns.

Bonds

Fixed income investments are usually appropriate for the investor interested in income, capital preservation, and liquidity. Bonds are debt instruments. When you own bonds or a bond mutual fund, you are participating in a loan to an entity. There are bonds that help finance the federal government and bonds that help finance municipal governments. Municipal governments are at the state, city, county, and local level. Investors can enjoy tax free dividend income from municipal bonds and municipal bond funds. We'll discuss municipal funds in greater depth as we progress through the bond section of *The Wealth Management Manual.*

When we began the section on wealth accumulation and investing, we learned about certain types of risk Bonds and bond mutual funds are vulnerable to default risk, purchasing power risk, reinvestment rate risk and interest rate risk.

Default risk is the possibility that the entity may not be able to repay the dept in its entirety. Certain rating agencies specialize in the ratings of companies and entities to determine their credit worthiness. Bond issues from entities that display a higher degree of default risk usually pay a higher interest rate.

It really is no different that a credit card company wanting to charge you a higher interest rate because of a low credit score. Corporate bonds that exhibit a higher degree of default risk are known as high yield bonds. The term "high yield bonds" has a certain ring to it, but you may also be familiar with their other moniker, "junk bonds." Two of the largest and most well-known bond rating agencies are Moody's and Standard and Poor's. Below is a chart showing how each of the two rating agencies grade bonds. Know that investment grade bonds have a higher probability of repayment of principal and payment of interest, with non-investment grade bonds posing a much greater risk to the investor. This is an excellent example of the classic risk and return tradeoff.

	Moody's	Standard & Poor's
Investment Grade		
High Grade	Aaa – Aa	AAA – AA
Medium Grade	A – Baa	A - BBB
Non-investment Grade		
Speculative	Ba – B	BB - B
Default	Caa - C	CCC - D

One could further classify bonds and fixed income securities into two major categories: short term debt and long term debt.

Short-Term Debt

Most investors are familiar with money market accounts. Money market holdings are short-term instruments that include Eurodollars, certificates of deposit, Treasury bills (T bills), repurchase agreements, and commercial paper. Money market accounts maintain a consistent price per share of one dollar and money market mutual funds usually provide the investor with the option of having a checkbook to access money from the account. While money market mutual funds are considered relatively safe, financial institutions are always very careful to point out that returns or a specific interest rate are not guaranteed and the account balance is not insured by the FDIC. This may be a good time to point out that if your IRA is funded with a money market mutual fund, you may not have the ability to withdraw funds using a checkbook.

Due to the possible 10% penalty for premature withdrawal of money from an IRA, mutual fund companies usually require the investor to complete an IRA withdrawal form to remove IRA funds. Fund companies want to make sure that the investor is completely aware of any penalties associated with an early IRA withdrawal and that is not possible if the investor is writing a money market check at the cash register in Sears.

We're going to take a brief look at the underlying instruments in your money market account.

T- bills or **Treasury bills** are issued by the United States Government. 13 week and 26 week Treasury bills are issued on a weekly basis and are considered to be free from default risk. Remember that we are talking about debt investments. As the investor, you have loaned money to a government or corporation. Default risk means there is a possibility that the borrowing entity may not repay the entire loan. It is no different than you defaulting on your automobile payment or your home mortgage. With Treasury bills, you do not have to be concerned with default risk.

Federal Funds. The Federal Reserve System requires commercial banks to maintain certain levels of cash on location or at the Federal Reserve System. Often, banks either have too much cash or not enough cash. Banks that find themselves with insufficient cash levels at the end of the business day can borrow funds from other banks that have an excess of cash. This overnight loan is at the Federal Funds rate.

Repurchase agreements are used by securities dealers to buy inventories of marketable securities for resale. These purchases by securities dealers are for very large quantities of securities. The seller agrees to repurchase the underlying securities at an agreed upon price and time frame. The repurchase price is higher than the selling price, thus creating the required return for the seller.

Eurodollars are deposits in foreign banks that are denominated in U.S. dollars. They are loans to foreign corporations that have the stability and financial ability to repay the debt. Intermediary banks will usually receive a small fee for handling the transaction.

Bankers acceptances. Banks can act as intermediaries between U.S. companies and foreign companies. In the process, bankers acceptances are securities that act as a line of credit from the bank. This is often utilized by companies that are too small to issue commercial paper.

Commercial paper is a private corporation's short-term unsecured promissory notes. Maturities are less than 270 days and in comparison to T-Bills have a slightly higher default risk. Because of the slightly higher risk, commercial paper usually has a slightly higher yield then T-bills.

Certificates of Deposit. Jumbo CDs or negotiable CDs are deposits greater than $100,000 and are placed with commercial banks. They are exchanged on the open market and pay a fixed interest rate. They usually have a higher return than T-bills.

Municipal bonds are government entities at the city, town, parish, county, and state levels. Municipal bonds can be 30 days to 30 years in term. The short-term municipal bonds are considered money market instruments.

There you have it. The above short-term debt instruments fund money market accounts. I wanted to briefly mention each type of instrument because so many people have money market accounts yet really do not know about the underlying holdings. We will continue our discussion of bonds, taking a brief look at longer-term government, corporate, and municipal bonds.

Long-Term Bonds

Corporate bonds and government bonds share some general characteristics. Interest payments are usually made annually or semi-annually. The coupon rate is the annual interest rate that will be paid each period for the term of the bond. As an example, a 7% coupon bond will pay $70 per year on a $1000 bond. If the bond pays semi-annually, it will pay $35 every six months.

Bonds can either be bearer bonds or registered bonds. Bearer bonds can be exchanged just like cash. The debtor will pay the person who has ownership of the bonds. Registered bonds will only pay income to the registered owner.

Some bonds are secured and some are unsecured. Secured bond investors have the right to make claim to assets in the event of default by the debtor. Mortgage bonds are secured by underlying real estate which would include buildings and real property. Additional debt may be issued against the same property but it depends if the mortgage bonds are open-ended, limited open-ended, or close ended.

Collateral bonds are secured by stock and bonds of securities held in trust. Call provisions may be included in the bond agreement, allowing the debtor to pay off the debt early and at a specified price. By contrast, debenture bonds are unsecured bonds and holders of these bonds have the same rights as general creditors. Debenture bonds will usually pay a higher yield than secured bonds. This higher yield is compensation for the investor assuming a higher degree of risk.

Convertible bonds offer the investor the ability to convert bonds to an equity or stock position. Zero coupon bonds do not make any interest payments during the term of the bond. Zero coupon bonds are sold at a discount and pay the face amount when they reach maturity. Zero coupon bonds are subject to interest rate risk but not to reinvestment rate risk.

While we usually view bonds as a conservative investment choice, it is important for you to know that there are certain risks that bond investors face. Even bonds that are safe from default risk remain subject to interest rate risk and purchasing power risk. Specifically regarding interest rate risk, as interest rates increase, bond prices will decline.

Let's say that we have a 10 year bond paying interest semiannually. The bond yields 10% and is currently selling for the face value of $1000. In our example, we'll say that interest rates increase to 12%. Investors will pay less than par value for the bond so that yield equals 12% because that is the current interest rate. Because of the interest rate increase. investors will only pay $885 for the bond. When interest rates drop to 8%, the price of a bond yielding 10% would increase to somewhere around $1137.

I know all of this is tediously boring, but I think you will be well-served by knowing about bonds. Remember that bonds are one of the three major asset classes: stocks, bonds and cash. After finishing this section on bonds, you will know more than many people who claim to be financial professionals. This information is very dry and often overwhelming, but I assure you this is important information to be used by the astute investor. I never said this was going to be easy, but it will be worth it in the end. Know that we are discussing options for the most important investment account in the world--yours. We're going to discuss the various types of bonds, but remember . . .

> # There are no shortcuts to anywhere worth going.
> *Unknown*

Types of Bonds

Treasury Notes and bonds are offered through Treasury auctions. They are considered default risk free and make semiannual coupon payments. Notes have maturities of less than ten years, while bonds have maturities greater than ten years.

Treasury Inflation Protection Securities (TIPS) are indexed to the CPI or Consumer Price Index. The value of the bond fluctuates to reflect changes in the CPI. At maturity it is possible for the inflation-adjusted principal to be less than initial par value. This could happen in an environment of disinflation. The U.S. Treasury has structured TIPs so that the bond is redeemed at the greater of the inflation-adjusted principal or par value.

They provide an investment vehicle for investors seeking protection from purchasing power risk and interest rate risk. Indexed Treasury securities are eligible for STRIPs which we will discuss next.

Separate Trading of Registered Interest and Principal (STRIPs) Don't you just love all the acronyms? Investors can trade the interest as one security and the principal as another using eligible Treasury notes and bonds. Certain broker dealers and financial institutions separate the original security into its component parts, principal and interest. When this happens, each payment of interest or principal is treated as a separate security and can be traded individually.

U.S. Savings Bonds include series E, H, EE, HH savings bonds. Recently issued was the I bond. The first savings bond was issued in 1932 after being introduced by Congressman James Bond. That's not really true. I was just checking to see if you were paying attention. Bonds never really get me excited. This stuff is boring to write, so I know it must be boring to read. But bear with me.

I don't want to go to deep into U.S. Savings Bonds. Just remember that the maturity periods are usually 20 to 30 years depending on the type of bond. Series E, EE, and I bonds have thirty year maturities while the Series HH bonds have 20 year maturities. Series E, EE, and I bonds can be purchased with cash but HH bonds can only be acquired by exchanging E or EE bonds for HH bonds. I know that right now you're on the edge of your seat. I could write five more pages on U.S. Savings Bonds, but the term TMI or "too much information" comes to mind. Let's move on.

U.S. Government Agency Issues are issued by different governmental arms to finance certain types of activities. These types of bonds have a very low default risk. Some have the backing of the federal government. The Resolution Funding Corporation, the Federal Home Loan Bank, the Federal Land Bank, and the Farm Credit Assistance Corporation are all such entities.

Municipal Bonds are debt instruments issued by local governments. This would include governments at the county, city, parish, town, and state levels. Municipal bonds can be further broken down into two basic types, general obligation bonds and revenue bonds.

Revenue Bonds are municipal bonds that are issued for a specific project. A new baseball stadium, football stadium, or toll road could be financed by revenue bonds. The debt will be repaid from the revenues generated by the specific project. Revenue bonds are usually not backed by the local government and, because of this fact, bear a higher default risk than a normal general obligation municipal bond.

General Obligation Bonds are municipal bonds that are backed by the full faith and credit of the issuing government. and they are repaid by taxes collected.

Municipal bonds may be term bonds or they may be serial bonds. At maturity the principal for term bonds is paid in full. Serial bonds are required to retire a certain amount of the debt each year. Municipal bond interest is free from federal income tax and is also exempt from state taxes in certain states. However, capital gains resulting from the price increase of bond holdings are subject to federal taxation.

Private Activity Bonds are municipal bond issues that allocate more than 10% of the bond issue to be used for private commercial use. Also, more than

10% of the payment is secured by private business property and more than 10% of the principal and interest payments are results of payments used for private business use.

Municipal Bond Insurance can be purchased to insure against default risk of the issuing governmental body. As we learned earlier, default risk is the risk that the debt may not be repaid. This type of insurance can be purchased from the Municipal Bond Insurance Association (MBIA), the American Municipal Bond Assurance Corporation (AMBAC), or the Financial Guaranty Insurance Company (FGIC).

Corporate bonds are debt instruments used to create funding and create a debt relationship between an investor and a corporation. Bondholders of a corporation have senior repayment status, ahead of stockholders of the same corporation. Bonds are one source of corporate capital and interest payments are tax deductible for the corporation. Dividends paid to shareholders are not deductible. The legal document that defines the promises and repayment schedule is called the indenture.

On the other hand, debentures are unsecured bonds. Investors in debentures do not have any rights to corporate assets. Investors in debentures are treated just like any other creditor.

Convertible Bonds allow the investor the option to exchange bond holdings for shares of common stock in the corporation. Similarly, **warrants** are often attached to corporate bonds and allow an investor to purchase shares of company stock at a specified price.

Mortgage-backed securities (MBS) and **Collateralized Mortgage Obligations (CMO)** are securities that are invested in a pool of mortgages. The originating lender will turn around and sell the mortgages to investors. This may have even happened to your mortgage on a home that you own. You financed your new home and then six months later, you receive a notice telling you that your mortgage company has sold the debt to another company. When a large institutional investor buys a block of mortgages, they have purchased an income stream collateralized by real estate. When a mortgage is sold to investors and turned into an investment, it is known as securitization.

Many mortgage-backed securities are backed by the full faith of the federal government. This is effective in reducing the credit risk or default risk.

However, they are still subject to interest rate risk. One type of risk that is unique to mortgage-backed securities is the risk that the individual borrower might repay principal earlier than scheduled. Mortgage pre-payments have a negative impact on the total return of a mortgage-backed security.

Mortgage back securities are issued by three federal agencies. You might have heard the term Fannie Mae. That is a nickname for the Federal National Mortgage Association (FNMA). The acronym explains how the nickname was earned. Two other agencies are the Federal Home Loan Mortgage Corporation (FHLMC) and the Government National Mortgage Association (GNMA). The GNMA is often referred to as Ginnie Mae and is the only mortgage-backed security backed by the full faith and credit of the United States government. They are default risk free.

Collateralized Mortgage Obligations (CMO) Private investment companies decided to get into the act and created collateralized mortgage obligations. CMOs and mortgage- backed securities are similar in that the underlying securities are mortgages. Mortgage cash flows are segmented into different groups known as tranches. Mortgage-backed securities and CMOs repay principal differently from each other. A CMO investor will receive repayment of principal based on a particular tranch or repayment period.

Managed Money
A Solution to Consider

Earlier we looked at an example of an investor very heavily invested in Enron. In a different scenario your portfolio is comprised of three mutual funds. The total number of stocks in the portfolio is 550 and the number of investment grade and government bonds is 189. You have some Enron in your portfolio, but it is only about 1.2% of your entire investment account. You have been out of town on vacation and return from Cabo San Lucas to find that Enron is in severe financial difficulty and even under investigation. To make matters worse, the entire domestic stock market is reacting negatively to the news and it seems the broad market is in a downturn. The analysts at *MSNBC* and *Bloomberg* are saying pretty much the same thing; there is a mass exodus to bonds and fixed income investments.

A few weeks pass and you receive your quarterly account statement and it actually looks pretty good. You call your financial advisor and he/she explains that while the stocks in your mutual fund portfolio did take a hit, the bonds took the heat and increased in value. Welcome to the world of broad portfolio diversification! Financially ready to retire? Maybe not just yet, but you didn't lose your shirt (or your shorts) in one of the worst corporate debacles in U.S. history. Workers at Enron were not quite so lucky, seeing their retirement accounts go from millions to nickels in a matter of days. And you can't help but wonder how your plumber is doing in his Ameritrade account.

Knowing the difference between systematic and unsystematic risk is the first step in gaining a true appreciation for portfolio diversification.

In order to build a portfolio we have to consider the many financial options available to the prudent investor. Earlier we briefly discussed options and individual stocks but now we will turn our attention to what I refer to as managed accounts or managed money. We will look at the benefits of mutual funds, separately managed accounts, and also variable annuities. We'll consider how passive index funds and exchange traded funds can be utilized and you will also learn how fixed income vehicles can be allocated with equity investments to help create broad investment diversification. In our discussion of fixed income investments we analyzed bonds and certificates of deposit.

Not only will we consider how different financial products perform but we will also discuss the tax ramifications of each of these vehicles. Last but not least, we will review the costs, commissions, and internal fees associated with each type of investment.

Mutual Funds

The first mutual fund was created in 1924 when the Massachusetts Investors Trust Fund was created. The founding company of that first mutual fund is still alive and well today, known as MFS Investments. MFS stands for Massachusetts Financial Services. Today, there are over 360 different mutual fund families totaling over 16,000 different mutual funds. There are mutual funds that invest in almost every conceivable type of underlying security. There are funds that invest in mortgages, precious metals, junk bonds, large cap stocks, China (not the dishes), Japan, small companies, and the list goes on and on. Beginning in the 1980s, more and more assets began to shift to mutual funds as American investors became more comfortable with the stock market. Growth in the mutual fund marketplace has been faster than anyone might have predicted and yet there remains much confusion regarding fees, commissions, and how to properly maximize the benefits of mutual fund investing.

It is certainly well-documented that over the last 75 years, long-term investments in the stock market have outperformed most fixed investments and money market accounts. Mutual funds are one way that an investor can participate in the stock market and yet mitigate much of the unsystematic risk that we discussed in earlier areas of the book. A diversified mutual fund portfolio can offer the best opportunity to success in equity investing, both domestically and abroad. The third quadrant of the Wealth Matrix deals with wealth distribution, creating income and cash flow from your investments to generate a lifetime income. Conservative dividend paying mutual funds can help you accomplish that goal. People are living longer today and conservative equity investing can help combat the effects of inflation (purchasing power risk).

A mutual fund is a portfolio of stocks, bonds, mortgages, or other securities actively managed by a portfolio manager. Many mutual fund complexes utilize the team approach to mutual fund management, dividing the portfolio of underlying securities between five or six portfolio counselors. In the team approach, the group of portfolio managers will come together in committee meetings to discuss their concerns and also their best ideas for their segment of fund assets. Mutual funds must be registered with the Securities and Exchange Commission (SEC) and must meet the requirements of the Investment Company Act of 1940.

Mutual funds are open-end funds. This means the investment company issues new shares as additional investors seek to invest in the fund. The investment company is also the entity that purchases back or "redeems" shares from investors liquidating fund holdings. In addition to professional portfolio management, one of the great benefits to the individual investor is the ability to invest in fractional shares of the underlying companies in the mutual fund portfolio. An investor can start a systematic monthly investment program for $100 a month and immediately be diversified in the stocks of 200 different companies!

Mutual Fund Fees and Commissions

Each day the mutual fund company will calculate the NAV or Net Asset Value of each fund. The NAV is the current value of fund shares based on the value of the underlying securities. Some mutual fund companies sell no-load funds and no commission is added to the Net Asset Value. Other funds charge a commission or a "load" and this commission is added to the NAV to determine the price that an individual will pay. If a mutual fund never liquidated any shares, the fund's NAV would closely resemble the total weighted costs of the underlying securities. There are fund company transactions that do affect the Net Asset Value. When the mutual fund sells stocks to liquidate positions, gains and losses are realized and passed on to the investor. Net capital gains are paid out to shareholders, or they can be reinvested to purchase additional shares. When these gains are paid out, the NAV decreases by the amount of per share distribution. As time passes it seems that mutual fund companies keep creating more and more sales load variations. We'll take a look at the three or four most common share classes used by mutual fund complexes.

A Shares are the upfront commission that comes right off the top of the initial mutual fund investment. The **A Share** investor benefits from breakpoints on his/her invested assets. That means that he/she will pay a lower commission on larger investments. A mutual fund may charge a 5% commission for any investment under $50,000 as an example. The investor may pay a 4.75% commission on investments from $50,000 to $100,000, and a flat 4% on investments from $100,000 to $250,000. This "wholesale" pricing continues as the investment gets larger and larger until at $1 million the investor pays no commission at all. These numbers are intended as an example only, but you will find your actual experience will match this fairly closely.

A Shares on fixed income and bond funds are typically a little lower, maybe in the neighborhood of 3% to 4%. Fund companies realize the yield on these types of investments are lower and that is reflected in the commission charged to the client.

B Shares are a type of share class that operates as a declining surrender charge on the back end of the investment. There are some benefits and some additional costs to **B Shares**. Actually there is only one benefit. If you invest $100,000 in a mutual fund your first account statement shows a balance of $100,000 with **B Shares**. Had you invested in A Shares your investment confirmation might have shown an investment of $96,000 after the deduction of the A Share commission. Remember A Shares charge the commission off of the initial investment and you will see it deducted on your very first piece of correspondence from the fund company. **B Shares** are taken out of the investor's account based on a declining surrender charge that is reduced each year as time passes. The declining sales charge is usually reduced to nothing by the seventh or eighth year. Rest assured that the actual charges on your mutual fund investments will be carefully detailed in the fund prospectus. A typical declining B share would look something like this . . .

Year 1	5.0%
Year 2	4.5%
Year 3	4.0%
Year 4	3.5%
Year 5	3.0%
Year 6	2.0%
Year 7	1.0%
Year 8	0%

B Shares look like a good deal. Especially if you're a long term investor and you have no intention of pulling your money out any time soon. But whoa there, cowgirl! You need to know that **B Shares** do not provide the same lower commission structure for larger investments like A Shares do. For larger investors, **A Shares** are the least expensive way to go. Also **B Shares** have something special, something called a 12b-1 fee. A Shares can also have a 12b-1 fee but it is almost always lower than a 12b-1 fee on a B or a C share.

SEC Rule 12b allows mutual funds to charge an annual fee for advertising and distribution costs. In effect, you are paying a fee to support the sales efforts of your mutual fund company, proving again, that America really is the land of opportunity. The belief is that with your sincere help in marketing and distribution, the fund will be able to attract more assets and clients will benefit from economies of scale. Actually, there is concern by the investment academia that many of America's most popular mutual funds are getting too big, too unwieldy. Most 12b-1 fees are in the neighborhood of 25 to 50 basis points. To put it another way, ¼ or ½ of 1%. It doesn't sound like a lot but for larger accounts over a number of years invested, it really starts to add up.

C Shares are very easy to explain and understand. C Shares are simply an on-going asset based commission or fee of 1% of assets under management. The registered representative selling C shares really does not make as much up-front commission as the salesman selling A or B shares. In one respect, C shares force the advisor to take a long-term view of the client relationship. Over a number of years C shares are the most expensive but what's interesting is that C shares may influence the advisor to continually provide first class service to you, the client. With A and B Shares, the registered representative's compensation disappears after he receives his initial commission check from your investment. Why should you care? One thing that I will encourage you to do is seek quality advice, and I believe the best people do not work for free. Later on we'll discuss your various options for quality financial advice and the commission and fee-based alternatives available to you as an investor.

R Shares are a type of share class used in retirement plans. You will often see R Shares in 401(k) plans, SIMPLE IRAs, and SEP IRAs. R shares usually have a lower up-front fee of .75% to 1%

I Shares are the same thing as a no-load fund class. I shares are usually offered through fee-only financial advisors. You can implement your investment program by investing in funds that do not charge any commission. In this scenario, you have signed a fee agreement with a Registered Investment Advisor. You are paying a fee for advice instead of a commission for a product. You may get the very same advice and end up invested in the very same mutual fund. A Registered Representative is compensated by a commission from a sale, while a fee advisor is compensated by a fee for advice.

XYZ Mutual Fund Company could offer the XYZ Growth Fund. As an investor, you could invest in the XYZ Growth Fund and have the option of A, B, or C shares or you could open a fee-based advisory account. Usually advisory accounts will have an account minimum. Some Registered Investment

Advisors will have a $100,000 account minimum and another firm may have a $25,000 account minimum. More and more investors are gravitating to fee-based investment accounts, and I must admit this is my preferred method of working with clients.

No-load mutual funds do not have a sales charge. No-load mutual funds are used by the investor who purchases the shares in his self-directed brokerage account, by dealing directly with the mutual fund company, or by using the services of a fee-only financial advisor.

In addition to sales charges, mutual funds charge an annual expense ratio. This includes management fees and administrative costs. The management of the mutual fund subtracts these fees from your account balance, usually on a quarterly basis. If the annual fee is 1.5%, the fund will withdraw .375% each quarter from your account. Earlier we talked about the professional management of your investments and this is where the money comes from to pay the salaries of all those Chartered Financial Analysts (CFA). Over the years expense ratios have crept upwards and now in 2006, we're seeing a trend downward again. When investing, ask your registered rep or financial advisor about fees and commissions. If there is any hesitation on the part of the advisor, run the other way and don't look back.

Mutual Fund Benefits

Professional Investment Management. Mutual funds are managed by some of the most talented financial minds of our time. Most fund managers are held accountable for the performance of the portfolios they manage. In addition, demanding investors vote with their feet if they do not see favorable results from a portfolio manager. Many mutual fund managers hold the Chartered Financial Analyst designation, the highest professional designation

> Ask your financial advisor about the fees or commissions associated with her recommendations.

available in the field of asset management. The Chartered Financial Analyst designation is achieved after a minimum of four years of industry experience and three rigorous exams. The average CFA exam pass rate for U.S. candidates is 34%. When other countries are factored, the total average pass rate drops to 12.6%.

Diversification. Just like you may have heard all your life, don't put all your eggs in one basket. A portfolio with as few as 15 stocks can greatly reduce the unsystematic risk that we discussed earlier. Mutual funds can have anywhere from 25 stocks up to 200 or 300 holdings in some of the larger funds. Some mutual funds hold a blend of stocks and bonds, creating diversification across asset types. In a diversified portfolio when some stocks are down, others may be up.

Operating costs are kept low. For literally pennies, you enjoy broad diversification and the knowledge that your investments are being professionally managed. How much would it cost to individually buy 200 different stocks, realizing that you would have to pay a separate commission on each stock purchase? Maybe you'd like to hire a graduate from the Wharton School of Business with a CFA designation to manage your investments. He is going to want a 401(k) plan with a match, health insurance and a good dental plan. With mutual funds you benefit from instant diversification and professional management for less than 2 cents on every dollar, assessed annually. Not a bad deal and you don't have to offer a benefit package.

Shareholder services. I remember overhearing an investor services person at one mutual fund company talking to a concerned investor on the telephone during the bear market of 2000. The client was evidently concerned about the drastic drop in his account value. He was told that he had the same number of shares: they were just worth less. It occurred to me that there is a fine line between 'worth less' and 'worthless'. That being said, the investor services departments at most mutual fund complexes are manned by people who are knowledgeable and concerned about the welfare of their clients. The world of professional money management is so competitive, fund company executives go to great lengths to make sure the right people with the right attitudes are manning the telephones.

Another great shareholder service is automatic reinvestment of dividends and capital gains. When you take advantage of automatic reinvestment, your wealth increases even faster.

Money at work.

Most mutual fund families also have systematic investment plans which can put your monthly investment program on auto pilot. Imagine investing $500, $1000 or even $5000 a month, every month, into a high quality diversified mutual fund with money moving electronically between your bank and your investment portfolio. Later we'll take a look at the benefits of one of my favorite investment strategies, dollar-cost-averaging. Another great benefit to retired investors is systematic withdrawals. Your investment account can be set up to send you a check every month or maybe every quarter, depending on what suits your needs. Your fund account can send out dividends and capital gains in the form of a check or they can be automatically reinvested back into your account, as mentioned earlier. And you will have access to your account 24 hours a day, seven days a week from anywhere in the world with an internet connection. All mutual fund companies have secure encrypted web access for investors and you can be at an internet café on the Baja Peninsula and safely log into your account and check your balance.

Different Types of Mutual Funds
Equity Mutual Funds

This section is very important because you will get a glimpse into, not only the makeup of various mutual fund types, but what you might expect in the way of performance. I have been a student of investing and investment vehicles since 1990. I have trained investment representatives, performed client investment workshops around the country and been known to pack mutual fund prospectuses in my suitcase when my family goes on vacation. I know it is sad, but it's true.

Let's dig in and learn about mutual funds. We'll consider what funds might be appropriate for a particular type of investor and we'll also see how blending different types of funds together can create a diversified portfolio. Our discussion will enable you to have realistic expectations regarding volatility, performance, and how mutual fund blending can possibly reduce risk and enhance your overall return. We'll take a look at some of the most common types of mutual funds but you must know that there are currently over 16,000 different mutual funds. There are so many variations that there is not enough paper in this book to do a correct explanation justice.

Also be advised that we will be discussing active portfolio management in the next few pages. If you will remember, Modern Portfolio Theory embraces the concept that no one person can outperform the market and one should simply invest in funds that mimic market indexes. By contrast, active portfolio management holds the belief that one can outperform the market through the use of technical or fundamental analysis. In the case of mutual funds, fundamental analysis is the method of choice for analyzing potential holdings for inclusion in a mutual fund's portfolio. Technical analysis is security and market research based on the interpretation of price movement as reflected in stock charts and other indicators like trading volume, stochastics, and other terms that would really bore you. As we get started, please remember that even as we are having this discussion, someone is out there inventing a new mutual fund investment objective that will be outside the realm of anything we have discussed in this book. That almost certainly guarantees an updated edition of this book at a later time. It's a little like Star Wars. Even though you may not want to go and see the sequel, you know they're going to produce one. Oh well. Let's take a look at the various types of stock-based mutual funds available. I am convinced that when you have finished this section, you will have a better comprehension of mutual funds than 90% of our population.

Equity Income Funds are populated with stocks that usually pay substantial and reoccurring dividends. I love equity income funds for conservative investors seeking retirement income. Many equity income funds pay a monthly dividend and can be a great source of income for retirees. They usually have low volatility and hold up fairly well in down or bear markets. As indicated earlier, these mutual funds will be invested in large low-growth or no-growth stocks. Most profits from the underlying companies will be paid out to investors in the form of income. Over a 75 year period almost 40% of the total return in the S&P 500 was the reinvestment of dividends. Dividend paying companies were not very attractive in the 1990s when investors were enamored with high-octane internet and technology growth stocks, but after the bear market of 1999, investors are once again interested in predictable dividends from low-volatility companies. One of the few benefits of a bear market is investors can look back and see what types of investments held their ground during the lean years. Many equity income funds were in that group, generating consistent dividends while other investors were watching their technology funds lose ground. During the bear market, which began at the end of 1999, the typical equity income fund did lose a little ground regarding share price but the dividend yield helped compensate for much of the price decrease. I like equity income funds for conservative investors seeking retirement income. They can be blended in a portfolio with other types of conservative funds like balanced funds and income funds which we can discuss further down the road.

Balanced Funds usually have holdings in each of the three major asset classes, stocks, bonds, and cash. One of the benefits of balanced funds is that the client achieves asset diversification from the very first dollar invested. An equity fund can diversify an investor's money among two hundred different stocks, as an example, but a balanced fund diversifies the investor across stocks and bonds. Bonds are a valuable addition to a portfolio because there are periods of time when there is an inverse relationship in the performance of stocks and bonds. In times of stock market turbulence, many investors seek refuge in fixed income vehicles, like bonds, CDs and annuities.

Because of the asset diversification of stocks, bonds, and cash, balanced funds are more conservative than their equity-only brethren. They are good choices for conservative investors and people who have smaller amounts of money to invest. It is not uncommon for balanced funds to have as much as 50% of the fund assets in bonds, but the average is usually closer to 20% to 40%. One of my favorite balanced funds typically holds 55% domestic stocks, 5% international stocks, 30% bonds, and 10% cash. A benefit to investors and their advisors is that professional financial analysts are managing the balanced fund portfolio and constantly evaluating the percentage balance of stocks to bonds. A common debate among financial professionals is when one should own stocks or bonds, how much, and when to adjust the weighting of each. The balanced mutual fund takes all of those concerns and transfers them to the professional fund portfolio manager. Balanced mutual funds can be used in almost any portfolio. A balanced mutual fund is conservative by design but can also be used in the portfolios of aggressive investors.

Asset Allocation Funds are very similar to balanced funds. They usually provide diversification into bonds, stocks, and usually cash as well. Both balanced mutual funds and asset allocation funds can also be described as hybrid funds. Earlier we talked about stock funds and bond funds. Asset allocation funds and balanced funds invest in both stocks and bonds, thereby earning the hybrid moniker.

Many mutual fund companies have developed what they refer to as target mutual funds. These are asset allocation funds that are created with a specific target time frame in mind. For example, a mutual fund company might offer what they refer to as the 2020 Asset Allocation Fund. This fund might be a good choice for someone who wants to retire in the year 2020. The 2020 Mutual Fund will have an asset allocation that will be slightly more aggressive than the same company's 2010 Fund which is a fund designed for people interested in retiring in the year 2010.

Growth Funds hold stocks whose earnings are expected to increase. Stocks of companies that are in a growth mode usually do not pay dividends to investors. Earnings from the company are reinvested in infrastructure, production facilities, technology and other components that can improve the company's productivity and profitability. Investors in these types of mutual funds benefit from capital gains. Growth mutual funds are not the correct choice if an investor is income oriented. Growth funds can be aggressive or they can be conservative in nature. A large cap (capitalization) mutual fund might experience less volatility than a small cap growth fund.

The fund's prospectus is the best source for information to help you determine the level of risk for a specific mutual fund. Growth funds are usually best suited for the investor with a longer time horizon. Since growth funds typically do not pay a dividend, the growth fund investor may experience a few more ups and downs in his growth fund investment. Growth funds can be added to almost any portfolio to provide a component that can possibly help battle the effects of inflation and the loss of purchasing power.

Growth and Income Funds will try to achieve capital appreciation, income, and dividend growth. The focus is usually on growth or capital appreciation with dividend income being a secondary consideration. Growth and income mutual funds will usually exhibit less volatility than a growth fund. The dividends are a smoothing factor, adding to total return even in a down market.

Aggressive Growth Funds These types of funds are not for the faint of heart. While they possess the ability to achieve much higher returns, the potential for substantial loss also exists. They may invest in companies you have never heard of. They may invest in companies that are overvalued but show great promise due to some new product or service. Aggressive growth mutual funds usually fall farther in value than the overall indexes in a bear market. To put that in perspective, remember the S&P 500 dropped 22% in 2002. An aggressive growth fund might have dropped 30% to 40%. Likewise, when the S&P 500 rose 22%, the aggressive growth fund might post an even greater return over the same period. Wear your seatbelt on these types of funds. The highs can be higher, but the lows can be much lower. You might want to review the risk and recovery chart that we looked at in an earlier chapter. Skydiving looks like great fun until they tell you it's your turn to step out of the airplane.

Small Cap Funds Again, here the word cap is an abbreviation for capitalization. As the name implies, this type of mutual fund is predominantly invested in the stocks of smaller companies. Often these are companies that may have gone public in just the last one or two years and they may have great potential but also an unproven track record. Small cap funds over a period of 75 years, ending in 2002, averaged a little over 12% a year. But just like aggressive growth funds, they achieve that 12% return with a very high amount of ups and downs. Small cap funds and also aggressive growth funds can be valuable additions to an investor's account but I would recommend using them sparingly in portfolio design. A smaller allotment of these high volatility investments can offer your account a component for growth but you may be best served by building a core portfolio of solid blue chip stocks that have a proven record of earnings success.

Mid Cap Funds are funds that invest in stocks that fall somewhere between large and small companies. For years, mid-size capitalized companies were not widely tracked as a separate asset class. As the number of mutual funds has grown, so has the variation on mutual fund types. In 2003, 2004, and 2005 mid cap stocks had great returns, so many of the mid cap mutual funds were solid performers. This asset class should not be ignored and could be a valuable addition to a diversified portfolio. The definition of what constitutes a mid-size company will vary from one mutual fund company to the next, but a general approximation would be between $3 billion and $10 billion of capitalization. Small cap would be under $3 billion and large cap would be in excess of $10 billion.

Large Cap Funds are invested in well-established companies with assets usually exceeding $10 billion. Most of the companies are household names and may fall into the categories of blue chip stocks or income producing companies that pay shareholder dividends. One of the benefits of investing in larger well-established companies is that their leadership teams and management style are well-established and documented. As an investor, you have a better idea of what you're buying into. Occasionally, the wheels do fall off and examples would be Lucent Technologies, Enron, and WorldCom. These three companies are examples of unsystematic risk that can be eliminated with proper diversification. Large cap funds can be a core holding of an investor's account but to clarify your options, let's take a look at large cap funds defined by specific fund objective.

Large Cap Growth Funds are funds invested in the stocks of large companies that exhibit the potential for future earnings growth. This is one way that a moderate or conservative investor can add a growth component to their portfolio and do so with household name companies. Most of these companies are still re-investing profits in the growth of the company. The main benefit to the investor is the capital gain resulting from the price per share increase as the company grows in value.

Large Cap Value Funds are undervalued stocks that meet the definition of a large company due to their asset size. A company may have a value per share of $100, but the price per share may be only $80. This disparity in price and value can happen for several reasons. Certain industries can go in and out of favor; certain businesses may be cyclical. A company in the business of producing natural gas may experience a decrease in price per share in the summer, but as winter approaches price per share can increase. Many people use natural gas as a source of heat in the winter months. In times of economic recession, the demand for Lexus automobiles may drop, resulting in less profit for the corporation. During economic downturns, luxury items are often the first types of products to see a reduction in demand. These are examples of opportunities for an investor to buy stocks at a value. The types of mutual funds we have covered up to this point are examples of active asset management. The Efficient Market Hypothesis endorses the concept that there are no values in the stock market, that all stocks are worth their current price.

International Funds are invested in non-U.S. stocks. These funds may invest in companies on several continents, all within the same mutual fund. One well-known mutual fund family has a fund named EuroPacific. I think the name says it all. Broad based international funds usually use the MSCI EAFE as a benchmark. MSCI EAFE is an abbreviation for the Morgan Stanley Capital International index which tracks Europe, Australasia, and the Far East all in one inclusive index. Just in case you're wondering, the word "Australasia" is not a typographical error. It is a term created to include Australia and Asia into a singular geographic description.

Global Mutual Funds Global funds can also invest in U.S. stocks, as well as foreign companies. When investing in global or international mutual funds, be sure to read the prospectus and determine the country weighting in the portfolio. One reason to invest overseas is to find opportunities that do not have a positive correlation to the U.S. stock markets.

Sector Funds are funds that invest in a specific industry and have a very narrow investment objective. Sector funds are often referred to as specialty funds because of their focus on a tightly defined business segment. Sector funds can offer great opportunity but the investor must be aware of the risk associated with an undiversified mutual fund. An example that may not need much explanation is the technology industry. Had all of your money been invested in technology at the end of 1999, your 401(k) might have turned into a 101(k) and that is precisely what happened to hundreds of thousands of investors. One mutual fund company trotted out their newly minted technology fund in 1999 at an opening price of $10 per share. Two years later the NAV, or net asset value, of that fund was $2.80 per share resulting in a loss of approximately 72%.

As I mentioned earlier, sector funds can provide profit opportunities for investors willing to take a little risk. In my opinion, sector funds should be peripheral investments that are minor players in the diversified portfolio of the prudent investor. Examples of popular sector objectives include healthcare, financial services, communications, utilities, technology, and pharmaceuticals.

Some of these sectors hold great promise. In the first few pages of this book you learned that an estimated 77 million people will be retiring in the next several years. More and more Americans will be living longer but their need

> Sector mutual funds should probably be peripheral investments built around a diversified portfolio.

for quality healthcare will increase. Healthcare is a sector that may deserve a second look by the astute investor but it might be unwise to place more than 5% of assets in one specific industry or sector.

By contrast, in the 1990s the communications industry over estimated the need for band width. Band width is the capability for telephone and cable lines to carry volumes and volumes of data. Band width is what drives your cable TV, cable computer modem, or internet DSL. In addition, improvements in technology have reduced the need for thousands of union employees at telephone companies and employee reductions will continue over the next several years. Communications may not be a good sector play.

Technology is here to stay but may be a gamble for the prudent investor. The consumer costs for electronic equipment seems to drop with every new day. Notebook computers with 40 gig hard drives are selling for under $400, a 15 inch wall mountable flat screen TV can be had for under $200, and kids in junior high school carry cell phones that weigh less than an ounce. Technology is here to stay, but fierce competition is resulting in razor thin profit margins for product manufacturers.

Conservative and moderate investors might consider creating diversified core portfolios of large cap stock funds, equity income funds, balanced funds, and income funds. Sector funds can then be added to the portfolio, but you should probably not have more than 5% of your invested assets in any one sector. Look at industry sectors as more of a speculative risk. An overweighting in technology in 1999 guaranteed that many investors will spend their golden years working at the golden arches. Don't let that be you. Diversify over several asset types and classes, adding sector investments as a minor component.

Real Estate Funds hold underlying investments in different types of real estate. Certain real estate mutual funds will be invested in REITs or Real Estate Investment Trusts. A REIT invests in various types of income producing property where someone is paying rent or a mortgage. There are real estate investment trusts that specialize in apartment buildings, strip centers, and high rise office buildings. Earlier in our discussion of sector funds, we discussed the potential of health care investments as 76 million Baby Boomers age and become qualified AARP members. To cater to the needs of this ever-increasing elderly population, there are REITs that are invested in nursing homes, assisted living facilities and long-term-care facilities.

Real estate mutual funds can usually be counted on to be a dependable source of income for investors. REITs are required to return 90% of income back to investors. While the dividend income can often be very dependable, there is the possibility that the value of the underlying real estate could drop in value. This is one type of investment where all of us have some level of experience. As mentioned earlier, income is earned from real estate when an individual or company is paying rent or a mortgage. If you are a renter, has your rent gone up or down in the past few years? If you own your home, has the value gone up or down? If you have ever owned or rented any type of real estate then you should have a fairly accurate idea of the potential benefits and pitfalls of real estate ownership.

Real estate is a viable option for investors seeking reliable dividend income. Often, real estate will have an inverse relationship to the stock market. A study done in 1999 by Boston University determined that over the next 50 years approximately $41 trillion in assets would transfer from one generation to the next. This massive wealth transfer is a result of 76 million baby boomers entering senior citizen status, subsequently transferring remaining wealth to children, grandchildren, and institutions. After the recent bear market ended, researchers at Boston University were concerned that the $41 trillion wealth transfer would be substantially reduced due to one of the most severe and prolonged stock market drops in recent U.S. history. They discovered that retirement plans, 401(k) plans, and brokerage assets plummeted in value over the period between 1999 and 2002. Their research also indicates that, while stock market assets decreased in value, personal real estate holdings increased in value. In fact, real estate value increases more than made up for stock market losses. It is now estimated that the generational wealth transfer taking place over the next 45 years will be in excess of the $41 trillion originally predicted. The increase above and beyond the original $41 trillion is directly attributable to real estate value increases. A word of caution. All markets can experience a peak, a point where it just seems illogical for prices to go any higher. The real estate market is no different. A good example to consider is the performance of the NASDAQ 100 from 1999 to 2002. I like real estate as a portfolio option but you may be best served by owning a little of it, not a lot of it.

One final thought on real estate. If you calculate the value of your home and the percentage that your home value contributes to your total net worth, you will find that you are already heavily invested in real estate. When considering diversification, look at what percentage different types of assets contribute to your total accumulation program. For many Americans, a personal residence is one of their largest investments.

Precious Metal Mutual Funds hold stocks that are involved in the production of gold, silver, and platinum. You would incur substantial fees if you were to buy precious metals individually. You would experience a certain amount of inconvenience in the storage and handling of the actual product. Mutual funds offer the investor a way to invest in precious metals without those inconveniences. Gold funds invest primarily in gold mining companies but some investments might actually invest in gold bullion. Some mutual funds have invested specifically in South African stocks and other mutual funds invest in gold producing companies around the world. While gold is usually the precious metal of choice, some funds also invest in silver and platinum. Gold mutual funds usually perform as a defensive investment. As stocks head into a bear market, gold and precious metal funds are attractive to many investors seeking a stock market alternative. Gold can perform well in times of political uncertainty and often moves inversely to the price of bonds and stocks. Like sector funds, gold and precious metals should be considered peripheral investments that compliment a well-rounded diversified portfolio.

We have discussed most of the major mutual fund types that are funded with common and preferred stocks. Realize that in a universe of over 16,000 mutual funds, variations of the above fund types do exist but there are simply not enough pages for us to accurately describe each mutual fund option.

Bond Mutual Funds

Earlier, we learned that stocks, bonds and cash are the major building blocks of diversified portfolios. There are some differences between investing directly in bonds and investing in bond mutual funds. A bond mutual fund's dividends are not as predictable as the fixed interest rate on an individual bond holding. The dividends generated from a bond mutual fund are influenced by investors entering and leaving the fund portfolio and also changing interest rates can have an effect on mutual fund dividends. Bonds have a maturity but bond mutual funds usually do not. Bond fund portfolio managers are constantly trading bonds for the funds, generating profits and losses. One disadvantage of bond mutual funds are the expenses associated with fund portfolio management. Management fees and total expense ratios can negatively impact your investment results.

Bond Mutual Fund Advantages

There are some advantages to bond mutual funds. Smaller investors investing a modest amount each month can certainly benefit from bond mutual funds.

Advantages to bond fund investing are numerous. Your shares in a bond mutual fund are easily accessible should you need to access funds from your account. Transaction costs for individual bonds are considerably higher compared to investing in bond mutual funds. Also, most bond mutual funds generate a monthly dividend which is very important to investors seeking income from their investments. Individual bonds only pay dividends every six months.

Professional management is another key benefit of mutual funds. Actively managed bond portfolios can outperform more passive bond strategies. As we mentioned earlier, bond mutual funds can pay dividends as frequently as each month. One mutual fund benefit is the ease with which dividends can be sent to the investor to create a monthly income or dividends can be automatically reinvested in the fund. Reinvestment of dividends and capital gains can lead to account growth. Liquidity is another key advantage of bond funds. The investor can remove funds with just a telephone call and will not incur the price consequences and transaction costs associated with an individual bond holding. Bond mutual fund benefits are . . .

1. Monthly dividends to supplement income or reinvest into the fund.
2. Accessible to the smaller investor.
3. Professional portfolio management.
4. Diversification
5. Investor can liquidate fund assets with fewer negative consequences than with individual bond holdings

Bond mutual funds can be divided into two main categories: taxable and non-taxable. Remember that not all bonds are safe investments. Earlier we looked at the rating systems used by Standard and Poor's and Moody's. Let's take a look at taxable bond mutual funds.

Taxable Bond Mutual Funds

U.S. Government Bond Funds are invested in U.S. Treasuries. U.S. Bonds are issued by the federal government to raise money. They include Treasury Bills, Treasury Notes, and Treasury Bonds. U.S. Government funds can also include mortgage-backed holdings as well.

Mortgage-Backed Bond Funds Mortgage-backed bonds are referred to as pass through securities. High income is possible because not only is interest being paid, but each payment also includes a portion of principal unlike an ordinary bond. The Federal National Mortgage Association (Fannie Mae) and the Federal Home Loan Mortgage Corporation (Freddie Mac) have little or no credit risk because the government implies a guarantee. In the case of the Government National Mortgage Association (Ginnie Mae), the government guarantees payment of principal and interest.

Corporate Bond Funds are funded with debt instruments from corporations. Like all bonds, the investor should be cognizant of the credit risk of the underlying securities. The quality of bonds will be detailed in the fund prospectus. High-quality corporate bonds will be invested in strong well-known companies. Bond rating agencies like Standard and Poor's and Moody's perform significant due diligence when evaluating credit quality, so you can feel confident in the quality of the bond ratings. Investment grade bonds will have a rating of BBB or better.

High-Yield Bond Mutual Funds are invested in bonds that have less than a BBB rating. Another term for high-yield bonds is junk bonds. I guess "high-yield" has a little more of a ring to it. The very lowest rated high-yield bonds could be in very serious danger of default. Financial risk is one of the risks we can significantly reduce by broad diversification.

Global Bond Mutual funds can provide additional diversification for the investor seeking to build a portfolio of securities that do not have a positive correlation. When the U.S. dollar weakens, global bond funds can outperform. Likewise, if the dollar appreciates, global bond funds will usually lose value. Foreign currency gain can lead to capital appreciation in global bond funds.

Tax-Exempt Bond Mutual Funds

Based on the highest current tax bracket, many Americans will work into the month of May each year just to pay their income taxes. Americans love the concept of tax-free investments and municipal bonds provide that opportunity. Municipal bonds are coupon-bearing securities issued by local governments to fund projects and improvements to infrastructure at the county, city, parish, and state level.

If you are in a higher tax bracket, you will be attracted to the obvious tax benefits of municipal bonds. Interest income avoids federal taxation. If the bonds are issued in your state and you live in a state with a state tax, municipal bond income would also be exempt from state tax. There are fewer legitimate tax shelters than there were many years ago and, because of that, municipal bond mutual funds are very popular with high tax-bracket investors.

Private activity bonds issued after August 7, 1986 can be subject to the alternative minimum tax or AMT. AMT applies to individuals earning substantial income from what the IRS refers to as tax preference items. The AMT or the alternative minimum tax usually has the greatest negative impact on wealthy Americans.

Our discussion of the tax ramifications of municipal bonds is a good time to mention that munis are not entirely tax-free. Capital gains on your municipal bond mutual funds would be taxable. It is the income that is tax free. Losses can also be deducted.

It is important to note that there are two basic types of municipal bonds: general obligation bonds and revenue bonds. General obligation bonds are backed by the full faith, credit, and taxing authority of the borrower. Remember that the borrower is usually a city, county, parish, or state government. When you invest in municipal bond mutual funds you are investing in your community. You are investing in roads, bridges, schools, and infrastructure to improve or maintain the quality of life and services in your community.

In contrast, revenue bonds are bonds that are repaid from the revenue of a specific project. Bridges, toll roads, sports stadiums, and hospitals are examples of projects that are often funded by revenue bonds. Revenue bond investors earn their income from the revenue generated from the completed project. Most revenue bonds have maturities up to 30 years.

A private activity bond is a specific type of revenue bond. Private activity bonds usually carry a higher credit risk or default risk than general obligation bonds.

Municipal Bond Mutual Funds invest in the types of securities mentioned above, resulting in income that is free from federal tax. If you live in a state that has a state tax and you invest in a state specific municipal bond fund, your investment income will be free from state income tax as well. A resident of California who invests in a California municipal bond mutual fund will pay no federal or state tax on the income generated from his investment. If a resident of California invests in a New York municipal bond mutual fund, the income will be free from federal income tax but will be taxed at the state level in California.

National Municipal Bond Mutual Funds invest in municipal bonds across the nation. They provide broad geographical diversification to the investor. This is a benefit since some states have riskier bonds than other states. Since this type of mutual fund invests in municipal bonds across the nation, the investor will be taxed at the state level on income earned from bonds not specific to their state of residence. Of course, some states do not have a state income tax and, in those states, the concept of state taxation is irrelevant.

State-Specific Mutual Funds are limited to municipal bond issues from a single state. This is a benefit to investors who wish to invest in bonds from their state. These municipal bond investors would enjoy income free from state tax and federal income tax. Also, a resident of one state could certainly invest in the municipal bonds of another state and fund income would be free from federal taxation. For instance, the state of Texas does not have a state tax. But if a Texas investor wanted to minimize his federal income tax liability, he could choose the best municipal bond mutual fund from any of the 50 states. New York and California investors make up the two largest groups of state-specific municipal bond investors in the nation. I think this is true for three reasons:

1. High state taxes in New York and California
2. High population density
3. High-net-worth investors seeking to minimize their tax liability

Single state mutual funds do not offer the same level of diversification that national municipal bond mutual funds do, resulting in a greater level of state specific risk.

Insured Municipal Bond Mutual Funds are a great way to invest for the conservative investor seeking income and capital preservation. These mutual funds are guaranteed by an outside insurance company specializing in this marketplace. The insurance company is waiting in the wings to guarantee, not only the principal but the income as well. This guarantees that the investor will receive all payments as scheduled.

High-Yield Municipal Bond Mutual Funds - Earlier we discussed junk bonds from a corporate standpoint. Even municipalities can issue junk. High-yield municipal bond funds invest in municipal bonds with a very high degree of credit risk. They also exhibit liquidity risk. Because of their low quality,

.it may be difficult for you to find someone interested in taking them off your hands. Municipal bond mutual funds are a solution to this dilemma

That covers everything available in bond mutual funds. If you live in a state with a high state tax and you are in a high tax bracket, you may be well-served by investing in a municipal bond fund specific to your state. You would enjoy income free from state and federal income tax. If you live in a state like Texas with no state tax, you are free to shop for the best municipal bond mutual funds from across the nation. How do you define "best?" Well, you have heard me talk about diversification ad nauseam. Municipal bond mutual funds are best suited for high net worth investors seeking to reduce tax liability. If state taxes are not an issue, you might want to seek a fund that invests in bonds from many different states. Remember that the more accurate term for high-yield bonds is junk bonds. Limit your exposure to junk bonds.

Stock and Bond Mutual Funds – In Closing

You have been very patient as we have drilled down into the building blocks of portfolios, stocks and bonds. We have also taken a thorough look at the main types of stock and bond mutual funds. I mentioned earlier that every new day brings a new mutual fund variation to the market. There are mutual funds that invest in "sin" stocks. Yes, it's true. These mutual funds invest in companies that derive their primary revenue from alcohol, tobacco and gambling. I guess you could look at these as defensive investments. I am not sure if there is any economic situation that would have a negative effect on the sales of alcohol and tobacco.

At the other end of the spectrum are mutual funds that are socially or ethically conscious. Some mutual funds exclude companies that derive their primary revenue from alcohol or tobacco. Some mutual funds are green funds, funds that only invest in companies that are friendly to the environment.

The simple fact is that there is a mutual fund for every type of investor. There are funds designed for Muslim investors and also funds for conservative Christians. The development of investment products is a constantly changing landscape. But this landscape benefits the specific needs of each investor. Investors in 2006 are not only concerned about their investment returns, they are also concerned about their world. They are concerned about the world they will leave to their children and their grandchildren and this is reflected in the choices in their lives.

The investment objective of each mutual fund will be clearly explained in the prospectus and you should know mutual fund companies can change the investment objective of a particular mutual fund. The fund company must go through a process but it can be done. I recommend at least an annual review with your financial advisor. There are several reasons for this, but one good reason is to re-evaluate your goals and make sure that your investments are still on task to meet your financial objectives. A mutual fund that has deviated from its original investment objective should be re-evaluated to make sure it is consistent with your goals.

Mutual funds provide many benefits to investors as we mentioned earlier. Professional management, instant diversification, automatic reinvestment of capital gains and dividends, and the ability to purchase fractional shares are just a few of the many benefits.

But mutual funds can be very inefficient. Some mutual funds are more tax efficient than others. It is possible to get a 1099 at the end of the year for capital gains or dividends even though your account lost money. Also, mutual fund investors have no flexibility regarding the underlying stocks in the mutual fund account. Your mutual fund may force you to hold Wal-Mart stock even though you may resent Wal-Mart for shutting down local mom and pop retailers in your small town. And your mutual fund does not offer the ability to remove highly appreciated stocks from your portfolio and gift them to a charity or family member.

Is there a way for an investor to enjoy a professionally managed tax-efficient account and also have the flexibility to make choices concerning individual stocks held in the account? Are there managed accounts that provide investors with customized portfolios and strategic tax management?

Separately Managed Accounts (SMAs)

Separately managed accounts first entered the financial landscape back in the mid 1980s when E.F. Hutton introduced the first wrap program. Since then, asset growth in SMAs has been growing at an overwhelming pace. An interchangeable term is Private Managed Account, and that is exactly what investors get. SMAs have a specified investment objective, as do mutual funds, but one key difference is that the client/investor actually owns the individual shares in the portfolio. For example, let's say that you are interested in a separately managed account that has an objective of income and capital preservation. But you may notice some stocks in the portfolio that you have a negative bias towards. You can request that the portfolio manager remove those securities.

Separately managed accounts offer an incredible amount of flexibility but they are not for everyone. SMAs have much higher investment minimums to be able to participate. In the past, an investor would be required to invest a minimum of $250,000 to open an account, but advances in technology have made it possible for account minimums to drop as low as $100,000 for some accounts. Managed mutual fund wrap accounts can be opened for as little as $25,000.

As a rule, separately managed accounts or private managed accounts are not for the small investor beginning a monthly investment program. SMA money managers are registered with the Securities and Exchange Commission (SEC) as Registered Investment Advisors. Private account managers direct accounts under a well-defined investment objective and strategy. Remember that we are talking about active portfolio management. An investment firm can have several portfolio models available with varying investment objectives. In addition to portfolio managers, analysts support managers by performing research and individual security analytics.

As we mentioned earlier, these portfolios are usually funded with individual securities held in a custodial account. The manager has discretionary control over portfolio holdings. Investment accounts are customized to accurately meet the needs of each individual investor and this level of portfolio customization is not available with mutual funds. For instance, a SMA manager can exclude particular investments from the portfolio if the investor already has substantial holdings in those securities.

Since the private account investor owns the individual securities, he also owns the tax basis. The portfolio manager and the client can choose to sell certain portfolio holdings based on their tax ramifications. This places the manager and client in control of the timing of gains and losses. Mutual funds simply do not allow this level of flexibility. Earlier we talked about mutual funds generating capital gains even when your account might have lost money. This occurs when the mutual fund is forced to sell assets because some fund investors want to redeem shares. A separately managed account is your account alone, so you do not have to suffer financial consequences imposed on you by others. Mutual fund investors do not have the same autonomy that private account investors enjoy.

Because the investor actually owns the underlying securities she may dispose of them as she wishes. She might want to gift certain appreciated holdings to a charity or transfer certain securities to children or grandchildren. Flexibility is the order of the day, making separately managed accounts the perfect choice for the wealthy and high-net-worth investor.

Improved tax efficiency and money management tailored to the specific needs of each client make private accounts an obvious consideration for clients seeking personalized wealth management.

Even though more and more investors are enjoying the benefits of privately managed accounts, it is more difficult to find performance data on them than it is to find comparative analysis of traditional mutual funds. *Money Magazine* ranks mutual funds. *Forbes* ranks mutual funds. Your neighbor probably has his own top 100 list of hot mutual funds, but it is a little more challenging to research SMAs. One contributing factor is that returns are not as standardized due to the level of account customization available with each new SMA investor. You and I could open individual accounts with the same firm, and my portfolio would have some underlying holdings that were different than yours.

Just like any other stock or bond portfolio, privately managed accounts should be considered long-term investment vehicles. In earlier pages we learned about asset allocation and Modern Portfolio Theory. Those same concepts are applicable to separately managed accounts as they are with mutual funds. A trusted and experienced financial advisor can help you define your proper asset allocation and then work with you to select professional money managers to implement your investment program.

If you are an investor in the wealth distribution and preservation quadrant, you should consider separately managed accounts as an investment option. SMAs may also be a good choice for clients starting to consider their wealth transfer options.

Variable Annuities

I have included a discussion of variable annuities in the actively managed section of the book. If you will remember, earlier we discussed two different schools of thought regarding investment management, active and passive. Most variable annuities will have 30 to 40 investment options. Usually one of those options is an S&P Index 500 sub-account and the other 29 or 39 options are actively managed sub-accounts. "Actively managed" indicates that there is a portfolio manager who believes he can outperform the market or possibly minimize market volatility, as in a balanced fund.

The other 29 to 39 investment options in the variable annuity look quite a bit like what we have discussed in earlier chapters. You might notice small-cap, mid-cap, and large-cap investment options. You would probably also recognize an equity income investment option or a growth oriented investment option. Variable annuities usually provide a broad number of investment options, enabling you to develop an account diversified across several asset classes.

Variable annuities are securities products and are regulated by the NASD and the SEC. A contribution or investment in an insurance company contract is called a premium. In fact, they would shudder if they saw that I used the term contribution. Let's say you invest $100,000 in a variable annuity. You can allocate your premium among the 30 to 40 investment options. It is important that you know that the underlying investment options look and taste like mutual funds but they are definitely not mutual funds. They are often referred to as sub-accounts, or variable investment options.

Annuities have two basic phases, an accumulation phase and a distribution phase. An investor can place money in an annuity and let it earn income over a number of years. Withdrawals prior to age 59 ½ usually incur a 10% penalty tax. In addition, most annuity contracts have a surrender period. The surrender period is a number of years when the investor will pay a surrender charge if he/she removes funds from the annuity contract. Do you remember B shares in our earlier discussion of mutual funds? Annuities work in much the same way. Let's take a look at an example of a declining surrender charge schedule for an annuity.

Sample Annuity Surrender Schedule

Year 1	7%
Year 2	6%
Year 3	5%
Year 4	4%
Year 5	3%
Year 6	2%
Year 7	1%
Year 8	0%

There are a few caveats to the surrender charge schedule. Most annuity companies offer some exceptions to the surrender charge. Usually a contract holder can withdraw up to 10% of the surrender value of the contract without incurring a surrender charge. The annuity contract owner can usually withdraw this amount for any reason. Some insurance companies allow the contract holder to withdraw 10% of the total account value each year without penalty. It is extremely important to understand the fine print before placing your hard-earned money in any financial vehicle.

As an example, if I have invested $100,000 and the first year surrender charge is 7%, I could withdraw 10% of $93,000, or $9,300. One thing to remember is that if I am under age 59 ½, I will incur a 10% penalty tax on that $9,300 withdrawal. It will cost $930 to access my own money, but I will have the satisfaction of knowing that I am making a personal contribution to the federal government.

The insurance companies have also devised a few other ways for annuity contract owners to avoid surrender charges. Most insurance companies will waive surrender charges under certain conditions related to health: disability, terminal illness, or a long-term-care situation. Many fixed annuities have surrender periods exceeding 10 years, so you must realize that an annuity investment is a long-term proposition.

What are the benefits of investing in a variable annuity? Probably one of the most important benefits is tax deferred growth. There are no limits on variable annuity contributions as there are in IRAs, so an investor is only restricted by the contract size limitations imposed by individual insurance companies. Variable annuities usually have higher internal fees than a mutual fund investment and the NASD discourages investors from funding IRAs with variable annuities. The NASD's stance is that investors already benefit from the taxed-deferred growth potential inherent in an IRA, so there is no reason for them to pay the higher associated fees of variable annuities.

Assets in annuities grow on a tax deferred basis. You will not receive a 1099 on an annuity while you are in the accumulation phase of the contract. However, if you pull money out of the contract prior to age 59 ½ you will incur a 10% penalty. You should also know that money withdrawn from a non-annuitized contract comes out "lifo". Lifo means last in, first out. Withdrawals are understood to be profit first, principal last. If you invested $90,000 and then the account grows to $100,000 (ignoring any surrender charges) a withdrawal of $10,000 would be taxed because profits are removed first, principal last.

Let's use that same example and say that you invested $90,000 with after-tax money and now the account is worth $100,000. In this scenario you withdraw $15,000. Ignoring any possible contract surrender charges, $10,000 of your withdrawal would be taxed at your ordinary income tax rate while the remaining $5000.00 would not be taxed because it constitutes a return of your principal.

It is very important that you know that gains removed from any type of annuity will be taxed at your current income tax rate. By contrast, qualified dividends and long term capital gains in mutual funds and stocks are taxed at a maximum of 15%. How would this impact you if you were a 31% tax bracket?

$10,000 gain taxed at ordinary income tax   31% = $3,100
$10,000 gain taxed as a long term capital gain   15%= $1,500

Withdrawn gains on annuities and most other tax-deferred financial vehicles are taxed at your current income tax rate at the time of withdrawal. This also applies to IRAs, 401(k)s, and 403(b) plans.

Withdrawals from IRAs, annuities, 401(k)s and other tax-deferred plans can be taxed up to 100% more than non tax-deferred investments!

Also since any income growth in your tax-deferred annuity is not taxed until funds are withdrawn, annually earned annuity income is off the radar screen for purposes of current income taxation. This is especially important for retirees.

In 1935 Franklin Delano Roosevelt said,

"There will never be a tax on social security benefits".

But today social security benefits can be taxed if your income surpasses certain thresholds.

50% of Social Security benefits are taxable if…
A single taxpayer earns over $25,000.00
Married filing jointly earns over $32,000.00
85% of Social Security benefits are taxable if…
A single taxpayer earns over $34,000.00
Married filing jointly earns over $44,000.00

Annuities have some other benefits. An annuity owner will name one or more beneficiaries on the contract. This is beneficial because annuities can pass outside of probate directly to the named beneficiary(s). If the contract owner named his estate as the beneficiary on the contract, then annuity assets could be at the mercy of the probate court.

In several states, annuities are protected from creditors and liability claims. Currently in the state of Texas, I could be sued, but the money in my annuities would be protected. That is something to consider for people with assets to protect. I recently had a discussion with an 87 year-old woman who was still driving and had $750,000 sitting in bank CDs. I had a duty to advise her that if she rear-ended someone at an intersection, her entire bank account could be cleaned out in a matter of months.

One benefit we will discuss in a later section is that annuities can pay a lifetime income, but we will cross that bridge when we come to it.

Fixed Annuities

Fixed annuities are the conservative siblings of variable annuities. Fixed annuities are not securities products and are not currently regulated by the NASD. As their name implies, fixed annuities pay a fixed interest rate over the life of the contract. But to be exact, fixed annuities often pay a higher interest rate in the first year and then in later years, drop to a lower guaranteed interest rate. Fixed annuities are a viable consideration for conservative investors interested in capital preservation. If a fixed annuity starts off paying 7% or 8% interest in the first year and then drops to 3% in subsequent years, the investment return will probably not keep pace with inflation.

One of the issues investors must consider with all annuities is the surrender period associated with the various contracts. We just looked at a sample surrender period schedule for a variable annuity and fixed annuity surrender charge schedules function in the same manner. It is not uncommon to see a fixed annuity offer a bonus interest rate or bonus deposit for investors willing to accept longer surrender periods. Longer surrender periods can cause a planning problem for some senior citizens. At a time in their life when they may want or need to access lifetime savings, the provisions of their annuities may tie their hands and put a lock on their hard earned assets.

Fixed annuities offer the same or similar withdrawal provisions and tax considerations as variable annuities. When evaluating any annuity there are several important items you need to consider. The following checklist may be helpful when comparing various annuity contracts.

Fixed Annuity Checklist

The annuity checklist can also be helpful when evaluating variable annuities. Just ignore the first two items concerning interest rates. As a consumer, you deserve to know anything that might influence the annuity recommendations of your financial professional. If a particular annuity generates a 10% commission for the salesperson and another annuity generates a 5% commission, the higher commission could influence product recommendation.

1. Interest Rate The First Year	
2. Interest Rate Following Years	
3. Surrender Period Years	
4. Surrender Period Schedule	
5. Early Withdrawal options	
6. Hardship withdrawal options	
7. Company Financial Ratings	
8. Optional living benefits	
9. Commission paid to agent	

As we mentioned earlier, variable insurance products are funded with investment options associated with the stock and bond markets. While variable insurance and annuity contracts frequently offer guaranteed or fixed interest options, variable products are usually more suitable for investors that are comfortable with accepting some of the risks and benefits that are encountered in market investing.

In summary, we have discussed several investment options. We examined Modern Portfolio Theory and then drilled down into the building blocks of investments, stocks and bonds. We looked at how stocks and bonds are used to create diversified mutual fund portfolios and separately managed accounts.

Billions of dollars are flowing into annuities as millions of Baby Boomers grow older and approach retirement. We reviewed the benefits and limitations of both fixed and variable annuities and provided you a checklist that should prove helpful when evaluating annuity contracts and insurance companies.

Many pages ago we discussed the differences between active and passive investing. We looked at actively managed mutual funds and separately managed accounts. Actively managed accounts are supervised by a portfolio manager or team of managers who believe they can out-perform the market. Sometimes they do and sometimes they don't. The next leg on our wealth management journey takes us to passive investing, using one of my favorite investment vehicles, exchange traded funds.

Passive Investing

Passive investing is the antithesis of active portfolio management. In its purest form, the Efficient Market Hypothesis states no one can outperform the markets over any substantial period of time with any consistency. If you will remember, earlier we discovered that over 90% of success in your investment portfolio is due to asset selection, not market timing or individual security selection.

But are there really any statistics to back any of this up and, if there are, why would anyone still use active portfolio managers? Well, in sideways markets, active managers have been known to outperform passive index investing. And some active management styles have been known to reduce risk in portfolios, a great value to older or conservative investors with capital preservation as a key investment objective.

By analyzing returns over a ten year period, we can get a snapshot of how active and passive investing measure up against each other.

Actively managed funds that underperformed their corresponding Russell index over a 10 year period. Between 12/31/1994 and 12/31/2004

Large Cap Value Before tax 87%	after tax 96%
Large Cap Blend Before tax 81%	after tax 94%
Large Cap Growth Before tax 54%	after tax 80%
Mid Cap Value Before tax 82%	after tax 91%
Mid Cap Blend Before tax 67%	after tax 84%
Mid Cap Growth Before tax 57%	after tax 78%
Small Cap Value Before tax 43%	after tax 94%
Small Cap Blend Before tax 17%	after tax 44%
Small Cap Growth Before tax 16%	after tax 29%[i]

---

[i] Morningstar. US equity mutual funds. Returns reflect 10 year annualized figures. Funds are categorized by their Morningstar objective. Past performance is no guarantee of future performance.

You'll probably notice that an extremely high percentage of actively managed mutual funds underperformed their corresponding index. You might also notice that fewer actively managed small-cap funds underperformed their indexes, specifically the small-cap growth and small-cap blend funds. An investor could build a portfolio using low-cost index funds for the large and mid-cap portion of the portfolio and use active managers for the small cap value and small- cap blend allocation. I guess there is more than one way to skin a cat? When I first heard that phrase, I had to ask myself, why would anyone want to skin a cat? And why would a person need more than one way to skin a cat? I digress. Where were we?

Exchange Traded Funds (ETFs)

An avenue for the passive investor is one of my favorite investment vehicles, the exchange traded fund. Exchange traded funds, or ETFs as they are often referred to, are no-load passive investments that trade like a stock during regular market hours. ETFs are unmanaged funds that track a particular index such as the S&P 500 or the NASDAQ 100. Over the past few years exchange traded funds have proliferated to the point that there is an index and an ETF that tracks every country or region of the world. There are exchange traded funds for just about every major sector of the economy as well. There will be a ticket or transaction charge but usually never as large or onerous as the A or B share commission on actively managed mutual funds that we discussed earlier. Even if you invest in actively managed no-load funds, their internal fees and expense ratios would be much higher than the management fees of exchange traded funds. As of the writing of this manuscript, an investor with TD Ameritrade could buy 5000 shares of an exchange traded fund for a grand total of $9.99! While the average actively managed fund might have an on-going expense ratio of 1% to 1.5% of assets under management, the typical ETF might have an expense ratio of .20 to .60.

Benefits of Exchange Traded Funds

- Exchange traded funds have lower minimums. They are sold in shares and an investor could buy just one share. However, the commission on a smaller investment would reduce the possibility of a favorable return on your investment. If we bought an ETF share in our Ameritrade account that cost us $21.00 a share but we paid a $9.99 commission, then we have paid a commission in excess of 45% of our purchase price. Since we can buy up to 5000 shares for $9.99, larger investments become very cost effective.

- Exchange traded funds are no-load investments with much lower operating costs. In comparison to actively managed mutual funds, exchange traded funds can have operating costs that are often as much as 80% lower than actively managed funds.

- Traditional mutual funds frequently force an investor to pay capital gains even while the particular investment might have lost money. Exchange traded funds are more tax-efficient and usually only generate a capital gain when the investor sells their ETF holdings.

- Exchange traded funds can be traded instantaneously during the day. Traditional mutual funds are traded based on forward pricing. Forward pricing means that if I place an order to buy a mutual fund at 1:00 CST, I will purchase shares at the closing price when the market closes for the day.

- Exchange traded funds have less paperwork than a traditional mutual fund.

- ETFs can be traded like a stock. With a click of your mouse, you can open a position in an exchange traded fund in a matter of seconds. Exchange traded funds can be sold short, and you can also place stop or limit orders.

- Because exchange traded funds track specific indexes, there is very little (if any) slippage in investment objective. This characteristic makes it easier to create diversified allocated portfolios.

To really understand how exchange traded funds work, we need to revisit the concept of asset allocation. Asset allocation is based on the belief that asset classes with a negative correlation can perform inversely to each other. If your stocks are down, your bonds might be up. If your foreign assets are taking a hit due to the valuation of the Euro, your U.S. domestic holdings may be trending up. Rather than trying to predict what asset class will out-perform, you can be invested in several different asset classes simultaneously.

One of the problems with traditional mutual funds is that it is often difficult to accurately peg an asset class for a specific mutual fund. Some actively managed funds can invest in many different types of companies and bonds within the same fund. Some active funds have been guilty of style slippage. They might have started out as a small-cap fund and a few years later the managers or executives decided they also wanted to invest in mid-cap stocks. Some portfolio managers find themselves chasing fads and short-term returns to the detriment of their investors.

The best place to learn more about exchange traded funds is the internet. Barclays Global Investors has probably created more exchange traded funds than any of its competitors. Barclays has more than 100 ETFs and you can learn more about their offerings at www.ishares.com. The iShares website is very user friendly and can be an educational resource for investors interested in utilizing exchange traded funds in their portfolio. As of the first quarter of 2006, nine out of ten of the fastest growing ETFs were iShares funds. Some of the most popular exchange traded funds are shown below.

SPDR (Symbol SPY) Spiders, as they are called, follow the S&P 500. SPDR is an abbreviation for Standard and Poor's Depository Receipts. The S&P 500 is comprised of 500 stocks that equal approximately 78% of the market value of all domestic stocks. These stocks are listed on the NASDAQ, NYSE, and AMEX exchanges.

Qubes (Symbol QQQ) The Qubes track the 100 largest stocks on the National Association of Securities Dealers Automatic Quotation system, or the NASDAQ. This is known as the NASDAQ 100 and is heavily weighted in technology stocks.

Diamonds (Symbol DIA) Sponsored by the American Stock Exchange, the Diamonds track the Dow Jones Industrial Average (DJIA). The Diamonds have the third largest trading volume of all the exchange traded funds. The expense ratio is under .20% per year and the fund pays dividends monthly.

An entire book could be written on exchange traded funds, but I wanted to provide a general and very brief education on ETFs and how they might fit into your financial program. With their low fee structure, they are a viable option for the long-term investor. With one purchase, an investor can buy a basket of stocks encompassing a narrow sector of the market, a broad asset class, or an entire global region like the Morgan Stanley Capital International Europe Australia/Asia Far East index (MSCI EAFE).

Wealth Accumulation
A Game Plan

Over the past several pages we have looked at the building blocks of diversified portfolios, stocks and bonds. We also examined managed accounts, mutual funds, and annuities. We wrapped up by discussing the benefits and virtues of passive investing.

So where do we go from here? What are some effective strategies for accumulating wealth? Should you invest in actively managed funds or passive investments like exchange traded funds? To quote Nick Murray, "Investor performance is as important as investment performance." This means that a disciplined investor in an actively managed mutual fund will probably have better investment results than an undisciplined investor in an exchange traded fund. I can personally see the benefits of both passive and active strategies. But let's take a look at what history shows us.

The Benefits of a Buy and Hold Approach

Between 1972 and 1982 the S&P 500 was basically flat.
Between 1982 and 1999 the S&P 500 was trending up.
Between 2000 and 2002 the S&P 500 dropped like a rock.

In an earlier discussion we learned that markets only do three things. They go up, down or sideways. Knowing markets perform in these three ways, we need to know how markets have performed for investors over a similar period in time.

Between 01/01/1974 to 12/31/2003

Stocks -	**Avg. Annual Total Return**	**12.2%**
Bonds -	**Avg. Annual Total Return**	**9.4%**
Cash Equivalents -	**Avg. Annual Total Return**	**6.4%**[22]

What we can learn from the time periods illustrated above is even though there were tumultuous years in the market over a 30 year period, investors who hung in for the long-term experienced solid growth in their investment portfolios.

It is not always recommended for an older investor in the wealth distribution phase to stay invested as his/her life savings drop in a prolonged bear market, but younger investors who can weather the inevitable market downturns can profit from a buy and hold strategy. For investors in the wealth accumulation phase of their life it is important to remember that investor performance is as important as investment performance.

Any stock or equity investment can be risky when held for the short term, but as your holding period increases, risk is reduced. Equity investments are most suited for investors who can accept the commitment to a long-term investment program. But what does long-term mean? There is no hard and fast rule but most investment advisors define long-term as ten years or longer. When we measure investment returns in the S&P 500 during 1, 5, and 10 year periods we find some interesting statistics.

> # Investor performance is as important as investment performance.
>
> *Nick Murray*

When we dissect the thirty year period into separate one year holding periods we find that 77% of the time investors had a positive return on their investment, had they stayed invested for any one year. As a one year investor you had a 23% chance of experiencing a negative return on your investment.

When we take that same thirty year period and look at five year holding periods we find that five year investors had a positive investment return 92% of the time.

Investors that were invested in any ten year period had positive returns on their investment 100% of the time!

Dollar Cost Averaging

An important strategy for those in the wealth accumulation phase of their life is a systematic investment program known as dollar cost averaging. Dollar cost averaging is a gradual way to invest in the market, by investing a fixed dollar amount on a regular schedule. Regular investing encourages discipline and keeps you investing in down markets. As a matter of fact, as your investment is deposited into your account each month, you will find yourself hoping the stock market drops on the day your investment is deposited. Let's take a look at an example.

Date	Price/Share	Shares	Cost
Jan 15	$3	100	$300
Feb 15	$5	100	$500
Mar 15	$10	100	$1,000
Apr 15	$4	100	$400
	Total	400	$2200.00
	Avg. Cost Per Share		$5.50

Investing $450.00 per month			
Date	Cost/Share	Shares	Cost
Jan 15	$3	150	$450
Feb 15	$5	90	$450
Mar 15	$10	45	$450
Apr 15	$4	112.50	$450
	Total	397.50	$1800.00
	Avg. Cost Per Share		$4.53

In the previous example the average price over a four month period was $5.50 per share. Obviously a person would want to buy shares when the price per share was the lowest but it would have taken a crystal ball to know which months would have been the best months to invest.

As you can see, an investor allocating a fixed dollar amount per month automatically bought more shares when prices were low and fewer shares when prices were higher. Our monthly investor sent $450 each month to his account. In January, when prices were at an all-time low, he purchased 150 shares. In March when shares were at a high of $10, our monthly investor only purchased 45 shares. While the average price per share was $5.50, our systematic investor paid an average of $4.53 per share, almost a dollar less. Systematic investing does not guarantee a profit but it can substantially reduce the average price per share paid by the investor.

Systematic monthly investment programs are an excellent way to instill discipline in your investment plan. If you get into the habit of paying yourself first, you will be surprised at the results you can achieve by investing a fixed dollar amount each month.

As an investor, you have the choice of utilizing an active or a passive investment strategy. Investing in index funds is probably one of the best ways to implement a passive strategy. Since we're discussing dollar cost averaging, let's see how a monthly investment in an S&P 500 index fund might have performed.

If you invested $200 per month in the S&P 500 over a thirty year period encompassing 01/01/1974 to 12/31/2003, your account balance at the end of ten years would be $50,401. Your account balance at the end of thirty years would be $755,000!

Money At Work From 01/01/1974 to 12/31/2003

Investing $200 a month in the S&P 500 Index with dividends reinvested.

After 10 Years account total = $50,401

Principal invested during 10 years = $24,000

After 30 Years account total = $755,000

Principal invested during 30 years = $72,000

The investor who stayed the course in the S&P 500 for thirty years amassed an account of $755,000 but only invested $72,000 of principal. 90% of the ending account balance was the result of capital gains and dividends reinvested! Of course, this illustration does not factor taxes into the calculation. A patient strategy of paying yourself first through dollar cost averaging can put your wealth accumulation program on auto pilot.

Build A Diversified Portfolio

One of the biggest concerns I hear when I mention the buy and hold theory of investing is the horror stories about people losing large sums of money during the bear market between 1999 and 2003. The simple fact is that many investors who were well diversified between stocks, bonds, and other asset classes did not experience the large account draw-downs like their undiversified counterparts.

144

Investors who were invested in both conservative stocks and bonds had good experiences during the recent bear market. In addition, a controlled exposure to global securities can actually decrease portfolio volatility and possibly increase long-term returns.

But only investing in a mutual fund that holds 300 large cap domestic stocks is not well diversified. You should consider investing across asset classes and across international borders. By holding small-cap stocks, mid-cap stocks, large-cap stocks and possibly some bonds in your portfolio you will be able to minimize the inevitable systematic risks that face all investors.

> I have never had a married couple tell me that over the past year they had invested or saved too much money! You'll never go wrong by saving money for a rainy day.

The best way to create an optimal portfolio that matches your risk tolerance and time horizon is to find an advisor that will help you determine your risk tolerance and create an allocation using Modern Portfolio Theory and the Efficient Frontier. This is accomplished by a short risk tolerance and investment objective interview. Usually you will need to answer no more than ten or fifteen questions and then the investment professional enters your responses into the allocation software. A proposal is instantly generated, providing you with a roadmap for the development of your new investment account. The result is the familiar pie chart, a snapshot of your recommended asset allocation. The main goal is to help you reach a balance between investing for maximum potential returns and the ability to sleep soundly each evening knowing that you have made prudent financial decisions regarding your investment dollars. Three keys to successful wealth accumulation are . . .

1. **A properly allocated portfolio.**
2. **Invest for the long haul.**
3. **Pay yourself first with systematic investing.**

Challenges To Wealth Accumulation
1. **Debt.**
2. **Taxes.**
3. **Inflation.**
4. **Paying yourself last.**

Debt

Debt is one of the greatest hurdles to wealth accumulation. Over the years we will face some issues that are merely speed bumps, but some of the problems along our journey will be of greater magnitude and consumer debt is one such problem. Currently, there are approximately 185 million credit card holders with an average of eight credit cards per user! In 2003 the average balance per family was a little over $9000, with typical interest rates for credit cards ranging from 18% to 25%. On average, 40 to 60 million people are close enough to insolvency to consider filing bankruptcy. Bankruptcies reached a record high in 2003 with more than 1.66 million people filing, a 5.23% increase from 2002.

In many instances, younger Americans want to acquire the same possessions their parents have: a large home, nice cars and expensive vacations. Many younger consumers forget that it may have taken their parents years of sacrifice to earn the privilege of their current standard of living. Professionals and young couples in their 20's and 30's do not want to wait. As you acquire assets using debt, you must realize that most of the items that you purchase are depreciating assets. Most of us are forced to use debt to acquire a home or maybe our personal automobiles. But the home is an appreciating asset and probably one of your best and largest lifetime investments. On the other side of the coin, your cars lose value the very minute you drive them off the dealership's lot.

Debt is a huge obstacle to wealth accumulation. Earlier we showed what a $200 monthly investment in the unmanaged S&P 500 could have accomplished. Over a thirty year period, $200 a month would have grown to over $755,000! Imagine what you could accomplish if you could invest $400, $600, or even a $1000 a month. If you look at the reasons that you are not investing more money on a monthly basis, I think you will find debt is a major obstacle. Debt sneaks up on you. It can be as innocent as going out for dinner on a weeknight when you're too tired to cook supper. You may not have any extra cash in your wallet or purse, so just this once you'll make an exception and use the credit card.

Managing Debt

- **Pay more** on your credit cards than the minimum. If you just pay the required minimum payment, the card may never be paid off.

- **Create a list of your debts**, with the smallest debt balances at the top of the list. Let's say the debt at the top of your list is a small debt of $500 and your minimum monthly payment is $75. The next debt on your list has a minimum payment of $75 also and a total balance due of $1500. Start to send in $100 instead of the minimum $75 payment to the $500 debt at the top of your list. The extra $25 a month will accelerate the debt payoff. When the $500 debt is paid off, accelerate the next smallest debt. You will now increase your monthly payment on the $1500 debt. As mentioned earlier, on this debt your monthly minimum payment is $75 also, but now you will start sending in $150 per month. Remember, you just paid off the $500 debt, improving our cash flow by $75 a month Start to send that extra $75 to accelerate the $1500 debt payoff. The key here is to accelerate debt payments, chopping off the smallest debt balances first, then moving on to the next smallest. In addition to the financial rewards, there is also an emotional benefit from reducing the number of bills you have to pay each month.

- Search for the **lowest interest rates** on your credit cards but also be very careful to read the terms. Some cards may offer a very low interest rate for balance transfers, but the rates may go up in six months or a year. Read the terms very carefully.

- **Never, never, never, be even one day late** on a credit card payment. Most credit cards have the ability to double or even triple your interest rate if you are just one day late on your payment. This interest rate increase is forever. It's like saying a cuss word in front of your mother. Once you say it, you can't take it back! If your payment is 30 days late then it goes on your credit report as a late payment. Protect and improve your credit report at all costs.

- If you buy something on a "12 month same as cash" agreement, be sure to **pay the balance in full before the 12 months is over**. In most instances, if the debt is not paid in full, the fine print in the contract states that the lender can back charge the total interest over the previous 12 months!

- **Keep the number of credit cards to the very minimum** because you want to keep the number of monthly bills you pay to a minimum. I have counseled people who go into depression each month when they pay their bills. Remember that debt takes both a financial and an emotional toll on your family's well-being.

- **Live beneath your means**. The best status symbol is the one no one sees-- your bank account.

Taxation

Benjamin Franklin once said, "In this world nothing is certain but death and taxes." We're going to take a few moments and address the effects of taxation on your wealth accumulation plans. In later areas of the book we will look at the effects of taxation in your retirement years and we will also look at the effects the estate tax could have on wealth transfer at your death.

According to the Internal Revenue Service, roughly 132 million tax returns were filed in 2004 and almost 134 million returns were filed in 2005. You were probably one of those 132 million tax filers or, if not, you are now a fugitive from the law. Taxation is certainly something that none of us can escape. But there are ways to legally avoid taxation or defer taxation on the growth of our investments. Later we will discuss strategies to minimize taxation when you transfer assets, either at death or while you're alive (inter-vivos).

If you are being taxed at 31%, it is easy to understand that for every dollar you earn, 31 cents is going to support the federal government. We are going to focus our attention on the federal tax and how to legally utilize the system to our advantage, but many of us must also deal with state taxes. In our discussion of federal taxes, you must know that there are tax considerations when placing money into investments and also tax considerations when money is removed from certain types of investment accounts. As we discussed earlier, in most cases

> I am proud to be paying taxes in the United States. The only thing is – I could be just as proud for half the money.
>
> *Arthur Godfrey*

money withdrawn from tax-deferred investment accounts will be taxed at current income tax rates. Money withdrawn from non tax-deferred accounts can often be removed at a maximum tax rate of 15%. As of the writing of this book, qualified dividends and long-term capital gains are taxed at 15%. By contrast, money removed from an IRA at retirement is withdrawn and taxed at the client's current tax bracket. The client being taxed at a 31% tax bracket would pay 105% more in taxes that the investor only paying 15%!

There are some benefits of tax-deferred investing. Assuming your tax-deferred investment enjoys a favorable return . . .

1. You earn interest on the principal.
2. You earn interest on the interest.
3. You earn interest on the money that you would have paid in current taxes.

There are two ways to contribute to tax-deferred investment plans. Many employer sponsored plans allow the investor to invest into the plan with pre-tax money. Some individual IRA investors may be able to deduct their contributions to a traditional IRA from their annual tax return. Also investors can contribute to an IRA with after tax money. Almost anyone can have a traditional IRA. The only question is, are the contributions deductible or not? Bill Gates can have a traditional IRA but he cannot deduct the contributions. Before we go any further I should explain that the term IRA is actually an abbreviation for Individual Retirement Arrangement. If you ever have specific questions about the tax code, a great resource is www.irs.gov.

We have already discussed how tax–deferred growth can benefit your retirement account. But what about pre-tax contributions? Some employer sponsored retirement plans allow salary deferral or pre-tax contributions. SIMPLE IRAs, 401(k) plans and 403(b) plans are employer sponsored retirement plans that allow employees to contribute with pre-tax income. Pre-tax salary deferral contributions to retirement programs can lower your current income tax liability. Employee salary deferral plans provide two great benefits to the investing employee, tax-deferred growth and the immediate benefit of reducing the employee's taxable income for the year of contribution.

Pre-tax investing lowers income taxes due. Let's say that an employee earns $50,000 a year. The employee is in a 25% tax bracket so the employee's federal tax liability for 2005 is $12,500. If the employee decided to invest 10% or $5000.00 of pre-tax contributions to the company 401(k) plan, her taxable income would be reduced to $45,000. If her $45,000 income is taxed at the same rate of 25%, her income tax liability is reduced to $11,250. This is an annual income tax savings of $1,250.00.

Pre-tax investing allows you to invest more. Let's say that the employee mentioned above pays the 25% tax due on her $50,000 income. Her tax bill for the year is $12,500 leaving our employee an after-tax income of $37,500. If she invested 10% of her after-tax income, she will be investing $3,750. If she had invested 10% of her pre-tax income she would have invested $5000. If she contributes before-tax money she can put away an extra $1,250 per year into her retirement plan.

Common Employer Sponsored Retirement Plans

What kinds of plans allow pre-tax contributions? All of the plans that allow salary deferral contributions are employer sponsored retirement programs. Let's take a look at some of them.

401(k) Plans allow employee pre-tax contributions. Another term you will hear me use quite a bit is salary deferral. Pre-tax and salary deferral are the same thing, basically enabling the investor to postpone taxes until some point in the future. Many companies offer 401(k) plans and the chances are good that you may have a 401(k) plan at your place of employment. In most instances you cannot withdraw funds from your 401(k) plan until age 59 ½. Usually a withdrawal prior to age 59 ½ will force the investor to incur a 10% penalty in addition to the income taxes due on the amount withdrawn. The premature distribution rule as it relates to age 59 ½ is applicable to almost all of the retirement plans. There are some exceptions to this rule and there are ways to avoid the 10% penalty. We will consider retirement plan withdrawal options in a later section of the Wealth Management Manual.

403(b) Plans are very similar to 401(k) plans. However, 403(b) plans are only available to certain types of non-profit entities and their employees. Public schools, charities, and hospitals are examples of organizations that qualify for 403(b) plans.

A **SIMPLE IRA** plan is an employer sponsored retirement plan for companies with 100 or fewer employees. SIMPLE plans are very inexpensive to administer and are basically salary deferral IRAs with much higher contribution limits. The SIMPLE IRA is a low-cost alternative for the employer seeking to offer a salary deferral retirement plan to his employees. For a small company, the SIMPLE plan is almost always more cost effective than a 401(k) plan. SIMPLE IRAs do not have the same administration costs and ERISA concerns that 401(k)s have to deal with. The employer does have to make a small contribution match, usually a maximum of 3%, but in two out of five years, can go to a 1% match. The employee is immediately 100% vested in the account but if the employee withdraws money within the first 24 months of the account opening, the IRS will assess a 25% penalty! Ouch!

A **SIMPLE 401(k)** is a variation of the SIMPLE IRA, but the SIMPLE 401(k) has more reporting requirements. The company size limit is also 100 or fewer employees. One of the benefits is that employees can make loans from their 401(k) account or take hardship withdrawals.

SEP IRAs are very popular retirement plans for small businesses as well. SEP is an abbreviation for Simplified Employee Pension and like the SIMPLE, employee accounts are funded with individual IRAs. What makes the SEP unique is it is not available for employee salary deferrals. In fact employees cannot make contributions at all. All of the contributions into a SEP are made by the employer. If an employer decides to contribute 20% of his income to his own personal SEP account, he must also contribute 20% of each employee's income to an account in their name. An employer must really love his employees to implement a SEP plan, since he will be making 100% of their account contributions. SEPs are a good option for the self employed person with no employees. It is also a good option for a business comprised of close family members. The Simplified Employee Pension is a way to transfer dollars to family members/employees of your closely-held business.

Individual Retirement Arrangements

Traditional IRAs are available to all U.S. citizens, regardless of income or if the investor participates in a employer retirement plan or not. As we learned earlier, Bill Gates and Donald Trump can have traditional IRAs. The only issue that comes into question is the deductibility of contributions. I am fairly confident that Bill Gates and the Donald cannot deduct their traditional IRA contributions. Deductibility is based on two factors, income and participation in an employer sponsored retirement plan.

To be eligible to contribute to a Traditional IRA an individual must have an earned income and be under the age of 70 ½. Also, unemployed spouses of people who have earned income qualify for a Traditional IRA. This is referred to as a spousal IRA. Maximum contributions for 2006 and 2007 are $4000 per each employed person. In 2008 the contribution limit is increased to $5000.

For people age 50 and older, there is an additional $1000 catch-up provision for 2006 and each year thereafter.

As we mentioned earlier, anyone can have a Traditional IRA but not everyone can deduct their contribution each year. If the investor does not participate in an employer sponsored retirement plan, he may deduct the full contribution to his Traditional IRA. If a couple is married and one spouse does have an employer sponsored retirement plan, the other spouse may still deduct his full IRA contribution if he does not have an employer sponsored retirement plan and the adjusted gross income (AGI) is less than $150,000.

Spousal IRAs are available to spouses that have no earned income, but their spouse does. Even if your spouse participates in an employer sponsored retirement plan, you can still contribute to a spousal IRA. Your family's income level and participation in an employer-sponsored retirement plan will influence your ability to be able to deduct any contributions.

Distributions from Traditional IRAs prior to age 59 ½ would incur a 10% federal tax penalty. There are certain distributions prior to age 59 ½ that would avoid the 10% penalty: death, permanent disability, IRS levy, higher education expenses for dependents or participants, first-time home purchase ($10,000 limit), medical bills that exceed 7.5% of adjusted gross income, medical insurance premiums for unemployed people, and a qualifying rollover or the timely removal of excess contributions. An investor can also avoid the 10% early withdrawal penalty by removing IRA funds in substantially equal periodic payments for five years or until age 59 ½, whichever is later. This is accomplished by taking advantage of IRS rule 72(t).

The cutoff date to open a Traditional IRA for the previous year is April 15th of the current year, with no extensions. Here is a word of caution. When sending a check in to your IRA account, make sure to note in the check memo section your account number and also the year that you would like the contribution to be credited for.

You are required to start taking distributions from your IRA after you turn age 70 ½. The formal term is Required Minimum Distribution or RMD. The government wants you to start using the money you have accumulated in your IRA. The truth is they actually want you to start paying income tax on your Traditional IRA money and the only way they can make you pay taxes is when you withdraw money from your account.

What if you don't remove the money? Uncle Sam will charge you a 50% penalty tax for not complying with the required minimum distribution rules. This penalty is assessed against any dollar that should have been distributed but wasn't. Here's how it works.

As an example:

Required Minimum Distribution (RMD)	$2500
I only remove $1500 from my IRA	$1500
Money that should have been distributed	$1000
50% Penalty on $1000 **PENALTY**	**$500**

As you can see with the 50% penalty, the federal government has a way of getting your attention. Distributions from IRAs are taxed as ordinary income.

Roth IRAs are one of the best vehicles for long-term retirement planning. Roth IRAs are always funded with after-tax income but the great benefit of the Roth is that in retirement years, all funds can be removed from the account without any tax due. Roth IRAs grow tax-free, not tax-deferred! Another great benefit of the Roth IRA is that principal can be removed without penalty for any reason at any time. Funds are removed from the Roth as 'fifo' which means first in, first out.

To be able to participate in a Roth IRA you must have earned income or be a spouse of someone who has earned income. As with the Traditional IRA, the maximum contribution for 2006 and 2007 is $4000 per individual. In 2008 the maximum increases to $5000. In 2006 and each year thereafter the catch-up provision for people age 50 and older is $1000.

The Roth is a fantastic retirement planning vehicle. I love the Roth because of tax free growth and the ability to access your principal without penalty. Not everyone can contribute to a Roth IRA. If you are single, you can contribute to a Roth IRA as long as your adjusted gross income (AGI) is under $95,000. Contributions for single investors gradually phase out between AGI of $95,000 and $110,000.

Married couples filing jointly begin to phase out of Roth contribution at $150,000 AGI and cannot contribute any amount to a Roth once they reach $160,000 in adjusted gross income.

In a traditional IRA, premature withdrawals would be subject to a 10% penalty and come out as 'lifo' or last in, first out. Withdrawals from a Traditional IRA are presumed to be comprised of growth first and then principal. Unlike the Traditional IRA, not everyone can participate in a Roth IRA. Gross income over $160,000 for joint filers or $110,000 for single filers would cause a taxpayer to be unable to contribute to a Roth IRA.

A Roth IRA can be set up as late as April 15 of the current year, with contribution credit given to the previous year. Tax filing extensions do not affect the deadline on opening a Roth for the previous year.

As I mentioned earlier, you have access to your principal anytime that you need it without penalty. In order to be able to remove any gain from the account, the withdrawal must be qualified. For a distribution to be qualified, the account must be at least five years old and one of the following must take place:

- First time home purchase with a $10,000 lifetime limit.
- Death
- Permanent Disability
- Attainment of Age 59 ½

In our earlier discussion of Traditional IRAs we discussed the Required Minimum Distribution that must take place once the participant reaches age 70 ½. There is no Required Minimum Distribution for Roth IRAs. An investor could leave funds in their Roth IRA until death, allowing the account assets to pass to the beneficiary. The Roth IRA is a unique investment accumulation vehicle that also has an estate planning benefit, allowing the account to pass outside of probate to a named beneficiary.

Inflation

Let's zoom forward in time twenty years from now. You are attending a party where a group of your closest friends have gathered to celebrate your retirement. If you had to guess, what do you think gasoline now costs per gallon? How much does a postage stamp cost or a gallon of milk? How much does a house cost? How much does it cost to run the air conditioning system in your home twenty years from now? These are very legitimate questions that you should be asking and you should be asking these questions today, not twenty years from now.

A postage stamp cost 3 cents in the 1950s and today's cost is 39 cents. That is equivalent to a 1300% inflation rate! An ice cream cone cost 5 cents in 1950 and today it costs $2.50, an increase of 4,900%.

Average home prices have increased 1800% since 1959. I know you're probably thinking that 1959 was a long time ago, that a little inflation is expected. Hey, I know 1959 was a long time ago. I was born in 1959 and I feel ancient, but that's another story for another time. Did you know that between 2004 and 2005 residential property values in Las Vegas increased by 48% in one year?

> **If your money is safely earning 3% in a savings account and the Consumer Price Index is increasing at 5% per year, you are "safely" losing 2% each year.**

Inflation is measured by the consumer price index. What is the consumer price index? It is an index made up of 95,000 items surveyed from 22,000 stores as well as 35,000 rental units. Basically, it is a way to measure if the cost of living is going up or going down. And it is also a way to measure how much the cost of living is changing. Housing makes up 41.4% of the consumer price index (CPI). This is appropriate since housing is one of the largest investments and cash outflows for the average American.

What does inflation have to do with your wealth accumulation program? Simply this: if your money is "safely" earning 3% in a savings account and the Consumer Price Index is increasing at 5%, then you are "safely" losing 2% each year. Your money must grow at a pace that exceeds inflation for you to be able to maintain a standard of living on par with your current lifestyle.

We have covered quite a bit of ground. You have learned the differences between active and passive investment strategies and you may be wondering what strategies and vehicles would be best for your situation. You deserve a program tailored to your risk tolerance, obectives, and particular situation. Let's ask our panel of experts to share their thoughts on wealth accumulation.

Wealth Accumulation
Advisor Roundtable

MARK DIEHL:
If you were counseling a younger couple just beginning an investment program what suggestions might you give them?

What are 4 or 5 key components of a successful wealth accumulation program? Please feel free to elaborate. I think readers are interested in your opinions regarding wealth accumulation.

Randy Smith, CFP®, MBA: There are many challenges to wealth building today. The complicated stock market, economics (national and international), political climate and terrorism all add to the challenges. But I think the major challenge for building wealth has been and still is the investors themselves. It is very difficult, in this country, to get people to save first and live from the remainder. In general, money and saving has such negative connotations. In most Americans minds and emotions, saving is like dieting, it just isn't fun.

Matthew Tuttle, CFP®, MBA: Here are the key components:

1. Get clear on what you want and why. Most people understand goals; your goals are the "what" you want in your life. Your values are the feelings, states, and emotions that are most important to you; they are the "why" you want to achieve your goals. For example, you may want to retire at age 65 with $100,000 per year income, this is the "what" you want. The reason "why" might be that it gives you a sense of security, freedom, and peace of mind, these are your values. Before you can start a wealth accumulation plan you need to know what the target is, you cannot aim for a goal that you do not know. Your values will help inspire you to take action to achieve your goals. To get clear on your values regarding any area of your life you just need to ask yourself "what is important about (area of your life) to me?" Since this book is concerned with your money the question is "what is important about money to me?" If you ask yourself this question and give it some serious thought you will come up with your values regarding money. Some examples might be freedom, security, independence, happiness, peace of mind, etc.

Once you know your values you must then set goals. Some rules for goal setting include:

    a.   They must be in writing.

    b.   They must be specific and measurable. What is the exact day you want to retire? What is the exact dollar amount you want as income?

    c.   They must be inspiring to you. This does not mean that you must have the goal of accumulating millions of dollars, just that whatever goal you have must be inspiring to you.

2. Get clear on your current reality. Once you know where you want to go you must figure out where you are now. This means getting organized and having a clear understanding of where you are in a couple of key areas: Assets set aside to fund your goals, cash reserves, debt, risk management, and estate planning.

3. Control what you can control and don't worry about what you cannot. Don't get hung up on retirement planning calculations telling you that you will never have enough. Don't get hung up on the gloom and doom that you might hear in the media. You cannot control what happens in the market, the economy, or the world. You can only control your actions. Come up with a plan and stick with it.

The one main area you can control is how much you save. Get clear on where your money is going and realize that you are probably wasting money in a number of areas. Make the commitment to have money automatically deducted from your salary or savings account every month and put into your savings.

4. Find an advisor who you are confident can handle and coordinate all of your finances so you have time to do the more important things. Money is not the most important area of your life. For many people health, family, and other areas of their life are more important. The difference is that money can be delegated while health and family cannot. You only have 168 hours per week and the quality of your life is directly related to how you spend those hours. By delegating your finances you have more time to spend on the areas of your life that are more important.

We follow an investment strategy called Risk Controlled Investing. It involves planning for the worst and hoping for the best. There are four bad things that can happen to a traditional portfolio: The market can go down, interest rates can go up, oil prices can go up, and inflation can go up. We use mutual funds and try to have at least one fund in every portfolio that should go up if something bad happens. To do this we use mutual funds that follow hedge fund like strategies---long/short, commodity linked, merger, distressed securities, non-traditional asset allocation, bond arbitrage, etc. We combine funds together that have a low correlation to each other with the goal of creating a portfolio that produces stock market like returns with bond market like risk. The key is to create stable returns and avoid the big gains and the large losses that can come from traditional investment strategies.

Wayne Starr, CFP®, ChFC: An investment program is not an end in itself. It is a means to an end, usually multiple ends. Even before we could begin to discuss where and how to invest, the goals for the funds must be established.

Even before the goal discussion can occur, focusing on their income(s) and lifestyle is critical. People need to understand the importance of saving and how to use debt wisely.

My most successful clients have embraced a definite attitude about saving and debt that has worked well in our consumption oriented world. I consult with three doctors who make substantial incomes now but definitely did not upon graduation from medical school. Two of the three graduated with significant debt.

Doctor A decided that the only way to create wealth was to adopt a simple plan: save a third, spend a third, and pay federal state and local taxes with the remaining third. When I began working for him well over 10 years ago, he and his wife had saved $1 million in CDs and money markets. Today his net worth is approaching $4 million.

Doctor B is a specialist but not in an area that is highly compensated. Whenever she has wanted something like new windows in the house, she borrowed the funds, set a specific target for paying the debt and did so before incurring any new debt. Together, we also planned how she could take full advantage of retirement plans sponsored by her employer. While she does not drive the latest model car, or dress like she just stepped out of Vogue, she is debt free, has assisted nephews with college, and is well on her way to financial independence.

Doctor C, upon graduation from medical school as an orthopedic surgeon, was faced with a mountain of debt. He and his wife made a decision before the first practice paycheck arrived. They set a goal of paying all of the medical school debt as quickly as possible and before beginning to acquire things. They rented a residence and drove an old Volkswagen until the school debt was gone.

Normally I will divide goals into short, intermediate, and long term goals as time is a critical factor. A typical short term goal could be to create liquidity for emergencies such as the loss of a job. This goal is normally defined by the amount of after tax income multiplied by a time factor such as six months. Since liquidity is the goal, safe investments such as CDs would be recommended.

Depending on the ages of the children, an education goal could be short, intermediate, or long term. Retirement/financial independence will normally be the goal with the longest time frame.

Besides goal setting, defining time frames, making savings a priority, and controlling debt, a fifth component of a successful wealth accumulation program is asset allocation.

A well defined asset allocation plan creates discipline and a method to fight the fear-greed cycle that afflicts many investors. It helps one to avoid buying high and selling low. Market timing does not work.

Dana Sippel, CPA/PFS, CFP®: For a younger couple just beginning an investment program, my initial and most important piece of advice, would be to "pay yourself" first. What I mean by this is to figure out a way to set aside a portion of your paycheck into a 401(k) or other savings vehicle before the remainder of the check gets spent on discretionary items. If you follow this principal you are investing in your future financial security by sacrificing some immediate gratification wants.

Secondly, I would advise a younger couple to invest their portfolio aggressively since they have a longer investment time horizon. Their portfolio should consist of a higher percentage of growth investments such as domestic and international equities, real estate and commodity investments.

Next I would advise them to protect themselves against catastrophic losses. An unexpected death, disability, casualty losses, loss of a house or a lawsuit can have a devastating effect on your financial health. Insurance policies cannot protect you from the emotional losses, but having the proper insurance in place can offer protection from financial losses.

I firmly believe investing in your own personal knowledge is the most important and lasting investment a person can make. I would encourage everyone to make this investment. Increase your knowledge and professional skills whenever possible. In addition to making you a well rounded individual, it will make you more valuable and marketable in the future.

Seriously consider any entrepreneurial opportunities. The time to start a business is when you're young and not locked into a certain company, salary or family. It becomes much harder as you get older.

My last piece of advice to a young couple or anyone who is trying to increase their wealth would be to always live below your means. I will tell you a personal story about my wife and me. We were a young couple, both working full time and married a few years when we purchased a townhouse. We were barely scraping by but we were proud of our real estate investment. A year later our daughter was born. So now we had a new house, a new baby and a lot of new bills. Our debt was starting to accumulate. We had to face the hard cold facts. We were living beyond our means and we needed to do something about it. One night my wife and I sat on the floor of our living room to discuss our financial situation. We both agreed that we needed to continue saving for our future. There was only one choice. I told her it was time to cut up all the credit cards except for one, which would be used for emergencies only. I remember the tears rolling down her cheeks when I told her we needed to go to a cash basis. If we didn't have the cash to purchase it, then we'd live without it. To make a long story short, the bottom line is that we learned to do without the "stuff" that we didn't really need to begin with. It's true we didn't have new furniture, a new car or take expensive vacations like some of our friends, but we also didn't have debt. We made a choice that day to invest in our financial future. It is a choice that neither one of us regrets.

Cary Carbonaro, CFP®, MBA: I enjoy working with young couples. I often get couples starting out in their 20's or 30's who make very high incomes in excess of $200,000, but who have no net worth. They come to me and say we make all this money but we have nothing to show for it. They are smart to come to me now! I put them on a plan towards financial freedom and it is not difficult at all!

1. Look at your budget! Everyone that walks in my door has to give me a budget. I have waited up to a year in some cases before the client completes it. I can't do financial planning without it! You must spend less than you make

and I don't believe in debt except college, autos at zero percent and housing with a fixed payment in most cases.

2. Max out your 401k. This is really painless. You are taking it out before you see it! It reduces your taxable income and in most cases it gets matched. If they think that is too drastic, I tell them start with 3-6% and up it 2-3% each year. Due to compounding and the time value of money, the sooner they start the better. I even give them a chart of what it will look like if they wait. The numbers don't lie.

3. Always spend less than you make! This is very difficult in our consumer driven society. Delaying gratification by staying within your means is the surest way to wealth accumulation. It doesn't matter if you make 30K or 300K.

4. Use debt wisely I was taught by my father, the late Paul F. Carbonaro, who was a lender at JP Morgan Chase, to pay off my credit card bills monthly no matter what. I didn't even know what finance charges were. It is a slippery slope you can go down with credit and if you develop bad habits early, you can spend your life trying to dig yourself out of a hole. Consumer debt is skyrocketing – in the neighborhood of $2.16 trillion as of year-end 2005. I recently read a quote by the president of the National Foundation for Credit Counseling, Susan Keating: "There is no doubt that American consumers are amassing more debt than ever with little thought towards how they will repay it."

5. Protect your Earning Power At a young age your biggest asset is your earning potential. So never stop learning, going to school and upgrading your skills. You also need disability income you can get from most employee benefit plans. I would also tell them to read the book, "Think and Grow Rich" by Napoleon Hill.

Jim Reardon, JD, CFP®: Take 10% of everything you make right off the top for one or more of your buckets described below. Use up to 10% of your additional resources to further your values, support your church, your schools, your community, your friends and those less fortunate. Over time, this will be your most rewarding investment.

The Money Game begins with the "five buckets," a concept I learned from Dr. Donald Guess--a dentist who was on a mission to save other doctors from their foolish habits:

1. <u>Bucket one is your emergency money</u>. Most people live from paycheck to paycheck. As a consequence, most people are only one paycheck away from insolvency and bankruptcy. For this reason you must save your money until you have 3 to 6 months of your salary put away in certificates of deposit or Series I bonds. This emergency money will protect you in case of illness or you experience a lay-off from your work.

2. <u>The second bucket is your protection money.</u> Protect the people and things you value most with insurance such as life insurance, (if you have a mate and children) health insurance, disability income, and property insurance.

3. <u>The third bucket is for your home.</u> As soon as you can afford to do so, invest in a home. "Rent money is spent money." A suitable home is much more important than a car that deteriorates in value as soon as you get it off the lot. There's nothing wrong with a starter home. Start with what you can afford. (About 2 ½ times your yearly take-home pay, maximum). As your income improves you can trade the equity in your home for another home or fix up and enlarge the starter home.

4. <u>Bucket four is for your retirement</u>. Always put enough money from your salary into your 401(k) plan to maximize your employer match. This is like making 100% on your money in one year. Next, invest in Roth IRAs. As a young person who will never pay tax on the income and gains, you should be able to compound your returns many times over before you begin to draw on this asset. Finally, if you have additional money to invest, consider a 529 plan for your children or max out your 401(k) plan for yourself or your spouse.

5. <u>Your wealth building bucket is the fifth bucket.</u> Learn to invest a little money into a variety of investments such as mutual funds which allow for small and periodic investments. Learn to master all different types; bonds, large, medium and small cap stocks, real estate, natural resources and real estate. Always start investing in what you know and understand best.

Diana Grossman Simpson, MBA, CFP®: First of all, I would encourage them to discuss their goals in detail. Each partner needs to know where the other one is coming from financially. That is, they need to understand each other's priorities and "hot buttons". Hiring a professional financial planner can facilitate this process, because the advisor knows the important questions to ask, like "how many children do you plan to have?", "is it important to you to save for college for your children?", or "when do you want to retire – and what will retirement look like?". I know how tough it is for a couple with kids to even have a conversation at all, much less take the time to discuss future plans. But a couple has to get on the same page, financially speaking. If one partner is thinking early retirement at the lake and the other sees them living in a loft apartment downtown so she can volunteer at the art museum, there's a conflict. Or maybe Mom's thinking about a local college close to home but Dad's saving for Harvard Medical School. Until you get everybody headed in the same direction, it's hard to motivate people to save.

I generally will encourage a young couple to build a "foundation for financial security" first. This usually involves establishing some sort of budget, building a cash reserve, and paying down debt – especially short-term debt. I look at how they work together to manage their finances, and make recommendations regarding spending and saving habits. The running joke with my clients is that I spend half my time doing marriage counseling. Because sometimes that's what it takes to get a financial plan together!

John Scherer, CFP®, CLU, ChFC: I use what I call 'The Five Fundamentals of Fiscal Fitness' to help my clients start on the path to building wealth. Those principles were developed by Bert Whitehead of the Alliance of Cambridge Advisors (ACA) and are one of the pillars of the "Cambridge System" which I use extensively in my practice. In the interest of full disclosure, I am a member of ACA and currently serve on its Board of Directors as Treasurer. These five fundamentals are:

1. Save no less than 10% of gross income.

2. Eliminate credit card debt, auto loans, and any other consumer debt except school loans and your home mortgage.

3. Take full advantage of employer pension plans (401k, SEP) – this is integrated with #1 (e.g., the 10% can and should be into retirement plans first, then outside of that once maxed out).

4. Have enough liquidity – 10-20% of annual income in cash reserves in checking or money market accounts; 20-40% of annual income in fixed vehicles inside of 401(k) or IRA plans.

5. Have the right amount of home – meaning fair market value of the home is 2-4 times one's income.

If a younger couple starts on the five fundamentals and invests in a diversified portfolio and rebalances yearly they are guaranteed to achieve incredible financial success.

Randy Smith, CFP®, MBA: When beginning a wealth accumulation program, the earlier the better. The time value of money is extremely important but is still a secret to the masses. Next, save through your employer's plans (401(k), SIMPLE plan, etc.). Tax deferral and company matches are very helpful to wealth building. Equally as important is keeping your family's overhead low. It is very easy to over spend your earnings when you are young. When the children arrive, one parent usually decides to stay home. You have an increase in outbound cash flow with children and a loss of revenue from the stay-at-home spouse, thus the credit cards bills increase and saving rate often goes to zero. Big mistake. Very simply, avoid "lifestyle creep" if at all possible.

Kathy Stepp, CPA, CFP®: The most important aspect to wealth accumulation is patience. The successful wealth accumulators save consistently, even if the incremental amounts seem small. They are not discouraged by the rate at which their money grows.

Someone beginning an investment program should first look to his or her employer to determine what retirement plans are available. Many employers offer salary deferral plans, which are beneficial in many ways. First, the contributions are tax-deferred, saving current taxes. Second, employers often match some of the employee contributions, which is just 'free money' to the employee. Finally, the contributions are made directly from pay consistently, which takes the temptation to spend the money away. And because the contributions are invested consistently over time, the employee takes advantage of market downturns by buying more shares of the chosen investment when its price is down.

Beyond a company retirement plan, IRAs are attractive vehicles for long-term wealth accumulation. Contributions to IRAs may be deductible or not, but the earnings on the investments within IRAs are always at least tax-deferred. In the case of Roth IRAs, the earnings are never taxed. IRA contributions can be made all at once or in portions throughout the year.

Finally, creating a personal investment account outside of retirement plans is also important. It is possible to start with a small amount of money, so long as you agree to continue to add to it on a regular basis. Specifically, we recommend using no-load mutual funds that offer regular investing programs. The actual investment choice should be made to coordinate with the investment choices made within the company retirement plan and/or IRA. Always choose the best options offered in the company retirement plan, where the options are likely limited, then build a diversified portfolio around them with the IRA and personal investment accounts.

I would encourage a young couple starting out to investigate these options, then set forth a plan for regular monthly savings. They should be patient and allow their investments to accumulate and grow. If they set up the savings to be automatic, they can establish their household budget around the savings. Even if the savings amounts seem small at first, they should be patient and let the money work for them. They will be astounded at the results over time.

June Schroeder, CFP®, RN: First of all it is good to see that younger people are interested in planning and investing. We have seen a shift as we now get more calls from those under the age of 50 in a year than we did the first 20 years of our business! The problem we see for them is there are more "must haves" now than ever before, i.e. cell phones, internet and cable can add $300 to a budget line that was $50 just a few years ago.

Thomas M. Wargin, CFP®, CFA: We tell them that the sooner they start saving the better off they will be. It gets tougher the longer you wait. Our first piece of advice is: "Spend less than you earn!" And get used to it! That's what allows them to have money to invest. Sit down together and make a spending plan - choosing where the dollars go. This plan should include cars and vacations, and buying a home. Not to mention how many children they want - my wife and I have 4 sons. So we incorporate short and long term goals often trying to blend financial opposites! Then take advantage of opportunities for payroll deduction with possible matching (That's a no- brainer!). It's often easier to save when you don't see it in the first place. Since we can't foretell the future, we can only guess that Social Security will be very different so a target of saving 15% of their income is probably a good goal.

June Schroeder, CFP®, RN: I have actually done pre-marital financial counseling for some couples - a gift from their parents. I remember doing two

in one week several years ago. One couple got married and another did not!
It was apparent at the sessions which couple had the better chance of financial
compatibility. And since financial stress is one of the chief causes of health
problems not to mention marital discord, I guess you could say I was happy to
have been of service!

Thomas M. Wargin, CFP®, CFA: One other point for young people is that
"bad things can and sometimes do happen." We have a client whose husband
died at the age of 35. One of the first things I did in this business was to hand
her a check from the insurance company for his term life insurance. It was a
safety net for her and their two children.

Chad Starliper, CFP®, CLU, ChFC, EA: The toughest and most important
lesson to learn is save…and save some more. There really is no magic formula.
In order to create wealth, you have to start with some.

Our society has created a buy-now-pay-later mentality, and it's tough to get
much done that way. For those that learn to delay gratification, they will
become much more successful. This level is all about behavior and how they
manage money.

Talking about some targets within the family and what is important is an easy
first step—which you'd probably just call communication. The gist is that
randomness never produces much progress unless they just make so much
they don't have time to spend it all.

It always helps to lay out everything you own, owe and spend. Too many
people try and run or hide from reality.

In an earlier section of the book I mention that debt is one of the killers of a
wealth accumulation program. I think author, Dave Ramsey, does great work
in this area. One of the first things I always like to look at is their after-tax
income compared to their spending. There is a figure we like to arrive at in our
planning called "net income remaining to fund objectives." This tells us—and
them—what money will be available to accomplish goals. So that is how I
would start: (1) lay out every fact we know about their money; (2) see how
much money they will have to work with after living expenses; and (3) make
any necessary adjustments to spending.

Debt, for starters, is the enemy of growth, particularly credit cards and cars. It pays to get aggressive with those areas, which are essentially like having holes in your boat.

At the end of the day, accumulators need to be very purposeful with their savings and spending. If they need to allocate $500 per month to a car replacement fund, then set up some traceable method of doing that; so that in 3 years when the money is needed, it's there.

The last really important thing is not getting caught up in the perception game of keeping up with your neighbor. There is an old saying that we kill ourselves trying to get things we don't need in an attempt to keep up with people we don't like. Not letting other people define what is normal should have been put at the top of my list.

A British psychologist coined the phrase the hedonic treadmill, which basically illustrates how people quickly adapt to new things and redefine the new status as normal. It creates a perpetual cycle of always wanting more to fill some materialistic vacuum. So don't get on that treadmill if you want to accumulate wealth!

Mike Busch, CPA, CFP®, CEBS: The first thing I would do is try to motivate them to spend less than they make by illustrating the incredible opportunity they have to harness the time value of money. I would coach them that "it's not what you make, it's what you save" so they understand how they can actually become more wealthy than others who earn substantially more than they do. I would advise them to invest more aggressively while they are young. If they have workplace 401(k)s, I would counsel them that the minimum they should contribute is the amount it takes to capture the employer's matching contribution. Otherwise they are just leaving money on the table. I would encourage them to consider making it a policy that they always save ½ of every raise they receive. This helps them avoid developing a spending lifestyle, disciplines them to save, and will help them grow their nest egg very quickly. Finally, I would advise them to beware the impatience of youth. I want them to understand what they have going for them is time, and if they just let time and the markets do their work, they will be in good shape. The real challenge to accumulating significant wealth is the temptation to try and rush the process and constantly change their investment approach based on short-term market movements.

Types of Investments

MARK DIEHL:
What types of investments do you recommend for your clients? I know you make recommendations based on risk tolerance and time horizon but do you favor individual stocks, mutual funds, exchange traded funds, or wrap accounts? Do you usually recommend active or passive management, or some combination of both?

Mike Busch, CPA, CFP®, CEBS: I typically recommend a combination of individual stocks and no-load mutual funds. Owning individual stocks has several advantages including the ability to manage your tax liability. And if you are a long-term oriented investor, the cost of owning individual stocks is less than mutual funds. Stocks also can accumulate large un-taxed gains, which qualify for a step-up in basis for your heirs at your death. That means that some of your gains will escape taxation entirely. Mutual funds have some nice attributes as well. They allow us to diversify the portfolio. They also allow us to access managers who specialize in certain segments of the market.

I believe the best approach is to be active in philosophy but passive in style. By that I mean that I advocate using active management to beat the indexes, but I also believe that by holding positions long-term and reducing portfolio turnover, the trading expenses and tax drag on the portfolio can be minimized, further enhancing return. It is not too difficult to find managers who have performed better than the indexes on a relatively consistent basis. Much of the conventional wisdom that says most managers do not beat the index is correct, but misses the point. The argument for active management should not be whether the average manager beats the index, but whether there are **some** managers who exhibit the ability to outperform the indexes.

Wayne Starr, CFP®, ChFC: The Investment Committee at BKD Wealth Advisors has developed a list of approved investments that cover four asset classes: stocks, bonds, commodities, and real estate. Within those broad classes we utilize:

Individual stocks
Actively managed equity mutual funds-domestic and foreign
Exchange traded funds (ETF)

Index equity mutual funds
Separate managed accounts
Bond mutual funds
Individual bonds—agency, treasury, municipal, corporate
Certificates of Deposit
Real Estate Investment Trusts
Money Markets

We will employ the vehicles that fit the investor's profile and that we feel will best achieve his or her goals. Equity mutual funds and individual bonds and CDs make up the majority of my clients' investments.

Generally we utilize active management in our portfolios. We believe that quality, consistent, active managers are identifiable. There are instances, based on investor preferences, when we will use an S&P 500 Index fund while allocating mid cap, small cap, and international positions to active managers.

Dana Sippel, CPA/PFS, CFP®: I favor an appropriate diversification of mutual funds and exchange traded funds. I do not believe individual stocks are the vehicle of choice for most investors due to the increased risk of investing in the potential failure of a single company. In order to diversify this risk away you would need a whole basket full of individual companies to cover all market sectors, small and large companies, and a variety of industries and businesses.

The use of mutual funds and exchange traded funds give immediate diversification, professional management and continuous oversight at a very reasonable cost. Mutual fund managers are paid to keep an eye on the stocks within their funds on a daily basis. If any developments occur that might affect a stock either positively or negatively, adjustments are made to the portfolio to insure the highest returns. It is virtually impossible for the average individual investor to dedicate the time necessary to monitor a collection of individual companies on a daily basis. Additionally, because mutual fund managers have financial clout behind them, they have access to information about company management, company financial position and the ability to use this information to make informed decisions on individual stocks within their funds.

I advocate a combination of active and passive management. I believe this is the best approach to building a diversified portfolio. There have been numerous studies done on both styles of management and so far the results have been inconclusive in showing that one is better than the other in any or all market conditions.

The advantages of the passive management style, sometimes referred to as indexing, include lower management costs, increased tax efficiency, non-subjective decisions and market tracking performance.

The advantage of the active management style is that the manager or management team will make active decisions for the portfolio based on research and analysis of different companies and varying market conditions. It is a "hands on" approach.

Cary Carbonaro, CFP®, MBA: It completely depends on the person. I base it on their goals, risk tolerance, time horizon, etc. I use a few risk tolerance questionnaires that let me really gauge how they feel. One of the questionnaires uses behavioral finance questions to gauge the investor's point of reference.

I don't invest in individual stocks because I don't believe in taking single position risk. If I am hiring a money manager, they will use stocks since that is their full time job to manage the client's portfolio. They can monitor, put stop losses, hedge, etc. Their job is to analyze and add alpha. Within our comprehensive investment management plan, we detail our recommendations relative to constructing a portfolio consistent with the client's investment goals, objectives and risk tolerances. The core part of our investment philosophy concerns identifying, evaluating and mitigating the risks associated with the markets, as well as the investment vehicles we select. When constructing and managing a portfolio, our models seek to find the asset classes and investment vehicles which add the most value to our portfolio—i.e., highest risk adjusted rate of return.

Generally, to evaluate whether an "active" manager adds value, we search for portfolios with a high degree of alpha and R2, coupled with a low degree of beta. Value vs. Growth is a principal we favor. We believe the Efficient Market Hypothesis. We use exchange traded funds or ETFs for the market core, large cap, bonds, and individual laddered bonds. These have the lowest fees. We use ETF's and actively managed mutual funds with low expense ratios for small, mid and high yield bonds. We also add natural resources, gold and hedge funds. I am a big fan of exchange traded funds because you get a basket of stocks similar to a mutual fund yet it trades on an exchange like a stock. Stocks are better than mutual funds for tax loss harvesting and being able to predict income and capital gains. ETFs don't have capital gains where mutual funds often do. You could get a tax bill on a mutual fund that lost money. The expenses are also much lower on exchange traded funds. We don't use any wrap accounts

Jim Reardon, JD, CFP®: For accounts that are tactically managed (see below) or if internal costs of funds are the major concern to the client, we will sometimes use exchange traded funds. For clients who like to have "name brand" funds they can follow in the newspapers we will use no-load and load-waived funds. For non-profit organizations and foundations we often use funds that are specially created for them by prominent money managers who specialize in managing institutional funds. For accounts over $750,000 we like to use a cross section of individual stocks and bonds for at least a portion of the portfolio.

We describe *passive* management as "buy and hold." While this strategy works well during secular bull markets it can be a bad idea during secular bear markets--particularly for people with short time horizons. All of our portfolios are *actively* managed with the intent to reduce or minimize downside risk.

There are two basic types of managed portfolios; *tactical* and *strategic*. Tactical managers will set a target asset allocation strategy based on a client's risk profile. As market conditions warrant, the tactical manager will respond to the market by making measured changes to the allocation strategy. During extreme market conditions, the allocation strategy in a tactically managed portfolio may differ substantially from the target portfolio.

When the market for stocks is *overvalued* you may find the portfolio strategist reducing the exposure to stocks and reallocating the money to other types of investments such as real estate, natural resources, money market funds or bonds which may be undervalued. When the broad market for stocks is considered to be *undervalued* you may find that the portfolio strategist has over weighted the portfolio allocation to stocks.

Tactical portfolio managers use a variety of proprietary methods to determine how much exposure each asset class should be given at a particular time. *Market trend analysis* and *relative strength analysis* are often components of a tactical allocation strategy. The portfolio goal during strong rising market trends is to maximize market exposure and to reduce it during prolonged falling market trends.

Strategic portfolio managers maintain a rigid allocation strategy. They will periodically rebalance the portfolio in order to maintain the allocation strategy. Strategic managers focus close attention to the relative performance of the underlying mutual funds in a strategic portfolio. When a fund's performance lags for a significant period of time in relationship to other funds with similar objectives, it will be considered for replacement by the portfolio strategist. We employ both types of actively managed portfolios.

In the early days, my radio show was carried on WIBW AM Radio the "farm voice of Kansas." It was natural that several of my first clients were farmers. During one of the first conversations I was told by a farm couple that they kept all of their assets in certificates of deposit because they were not risk-takers. Now I can't think of a more risky enterprise than farming. It wasn't until later that the importance of what they had said dawned on me.

To them, farming was not the same risky enterprise that it is to me. Despite all of the unpredictable events that could occur, they had learned to manage the risks of farming to the point that they did not consider it to be as risky as other investments. I realized that learning to manage market risk was one of the most important elements of success.

Our clients can't afford to lose a large portion of their assets so we are continually studying methods of risk management that will best prevent sustained loss. Risk management became a regular topic for my radio guests. One of the most profound guests was David L. Smith, editor and publisher of *Cyclical Investing Comment* newsletter. From David, I learned that all investments have cycles and being able to read the cycles is critical to your success in portfolio management. From Mark Hulbert a newsletter publisher and columnist for *Forbes* and the *New York Times,* I learned that contrary to every thing I had read--you *can* time the market. From Walter Rulowe at *Growth Fund Guide* I learned the value of using charts to determine market cycles and market momentum trends.

All of these things have served us well as we continue our quest to preserve capital and make it grow.

Diana Grossman Simpson, MBA, CFP®: Since our clients are generally younger with less than $1 million in investable assets, we focus mostly on mutual fund investments and exchange-traded funds. I believe these investments offer the best opportunity for return with the least amount of risk.

We offer active, discretionary investment management to those clients who want full service, but will also provide advice on 401(k) accounts or passive investments if the client is so inclined. We work closely with the clients to determine the best strategy for their situation. Often, the client will have a 401(k) account at work that provides limited investment options, but will also be saving outside of the 401(k) (in an IRA or other account) for retirement. In this situation we will generally make "passive" recommendations within the 401(k) on what we call "core" holdings and then "actively" manage their other investments in an effort to enhance returns.

John Scherer, CFP®, CLU, ChFC: I recommend no-load mutual funds almost exclusively. Mutual funds have an inherent diversification benefit, and most investors do not have enough zeroes in their net worth to be able to make owning individual stocks advisable. Also, with all the low-cost choices available today, there is no reason to ever use funds with loads or surrender charges.

I'm in the passive management camp. There is no reliable evidence that active management provides any real long term value. Academic research tells us that passive, index-type investing is most prudent for consumers.

Randy Smith, CFP®, MBA: I personally like I Shares, ETFs, overseas funds, bond funds and REITs. It is easy to diversify using this methodology. These assets have lower overhead costs which flow through to more profit for my clients. I will often use a wrap account, with a lower percentage fee as well.

Kathy Stepp, CPA, CFP®:   After we develop an individual investment strategy for each client, we make specific investment recommendations to complete the target portfolio. We typically use no-load mutual funds because we believe they are the best vehicles for achieving diversification in portfolios under $2 million.

Within each investment category, we identify the mutual funds we feel are best managed, and we use those. However, it is not uncommon for a client to come to us with a portfolio of individual stocks or a large position in a single company. We analyze the stocks and recommend whether to keep or sell them. Likewise, some clients have a particular interest in a company, and we research that company to make a recommendation to buy or not. If the client ends up holding individual stocks, we will incorporate them into the portfolio design and choose mutual funds that complement them.

We favor active management over passive management, because we believe good fund managers can add value by picking good stocks and avoiding bad stocks. Passive management does not allow for the avoidance of bad stocks. To us, the key is to find the fund managers who excel in a certain style or niche, and invest with them.

Thomas M. Wargin, CFP®, CFA: We use them all but the choices can vary according to the price we have set as a good buy, the past performance, income needs of the client, and when the investment is made. Not all of our clients own the same things.

Exchange traded funds are gradually replacing mutual funds due to their low cost structure and one of the ways we enhance returns is to manage the costs. Will they replace all the mutual funds? That I don't know.

June Schroeder, CFP®, RN: We discuss our investment philosophy with the clients. Sometimes what the client wants is not the best choice in our opinion so education is the next step. But are they open to it? If not, perhaps this relationship is not a good fit. Over the years we have learned that if we buy something they want and it goes up they take the credit, but if it goes down they blame us for buying it. If we don't buy it and it goes up they blame us for not buying it, but we do get some thanks if it goes down!

Thomas M. Wargin, CFP®, CFA: We are active managers. We use individual stocks, bonds, in addition to actively and passively managed funds. We like individual stocks from the cost benefit standpoint - no ongoing expenses except for the trading, but we buy with the intent of holding for at least 3 years, maybe longer. We like to have a core portfolio of good franchise companies someone could hopefully own forever. We balance risk with a reasonable price tag.

Chad Starliper, CFP®, CLU, ChFC, EA: This is quite a large topic, and an interesting one. But without getting into some harangue about this age-old debate, we are firmly entrenched in the passive management camp. The research we have looked through is fairly conclusive that active management is not advantageous. Once you adjust for size and valuation risk factors, most all alpha from the supposed top money managers disappears. That holds true whether we've looked at small caps or emerging markets. We don't buy the notion that only the largest cap areas are efficient and that the others can be exploited. Moreover, the evidence suggests that there is little if any correlation between top managers in one period being the same top performers in successive periods. That means it's random—or luck.

We've got mounds of technical evidence on this issue, but clients really don't need all of that. We just explain why we believe markets are efficient, how the world processes information in a free market, and that our time is better spent elsewhere. Even picking all great managers is like picking up dimes in front of a bulldozer—a lot of work for very little benefit. And that's assuming you can do it across the board and consistently, which we don't think we can.

For us, it's all about portfolio structure. Once we see what we want, it's a matter of costs and execution. The cheaper we can build it, the more money the client makes and the happier they are with us. Incidentally, a passive asset class portfolio is more easily designed to match their cash flow goals and other objectives because there isn't this ambiguous notion of what to buy or what's hot. Active management creates a lot of unknowns that have less reliable distributions of returns.

We use a mixture of ETFs and mutual funds, which allow us ample diversification within an asset class. Because we design portfolio strategies using many global asset classes, we look for those vehicles that get us the most efficient exposure to the areas we think add value.

Individual stocks are never considered for several reasons. Aside from the fact that we aren't in the business of doing that, and that we don't think anyone else is successful at it either, there just aren't any compelling reasons for them. (unless it is within a passively managed separate account in lieu of a mutual fund, which would normally be for tax purposes).

Positions in a few stocks create concentration risk and non-systematic risk, neither of which compensates the investor. Modern finance theory, espoused by such prominent folks as Fama and French, essentially says that the expected return of a security should approximate the expected return of the asset class to which it belongs. That being true—more or less—it then holds that a diversified basket of holdings with the same characteristics would make more sense than owning a single name. Why own one, with all of the risks, when you could own 1,000?

Mutual funds offer the best way to capture the returns of an asset class, diversify within an asset class, and do it cost effectively and with minimal day-to-day micromanagement.

Employee Benefit Analysis

One of the biggest mistakes people make today in their personal financial planning is not taking advantage of employer benefits. The following analysis is provided by Dana Sippel, CPA/PFS, CFP. I want to thank Dana for making this available to the readers of *The Wealth Management Manual*.

Dana Sippel, CPA/PFS, CFP®:   Any employee who is not saving enough dollars into the retirement plan to obtain the full employer match is leaving part of their compensation on the table. Most of us can not afford to leave money on the table yet people do it everyday. Another under utilized employer benefit are the cafeteria plans that allow you to pay for unreimbursed health costs as well as dependant care expenses using pre-tax dollars.

Let me illustrate with a common scenario. John is employed by ABC, Inc. with a $75,000 annual salary. ABC, Inc. offers a 401(k) that matches dollar for dollar on the first 5% of salary contributed into the 401(k) plan. ABC, Inc. also offers a flexible spending account for medical expenses that allows employees to set aside $2,500 annually for unreimbursed medical expenses. ABC, Inc. also offers a Dependent Care Spending Account (which can be used for care expenses of children or elderly parents) that allows employees to set aside $5,000 annually. Let's look at what happens when John utilizes all these employer provided benefits and when he uses none. The following table illustrates the effects of both.

	Utilizing no Employer Benefits	Utilizing all Employer Benefits
John's Salary	75,000	75,000
Deferral to Health Care Spending account	0	(2,500)
Deferral to Dependent Care Spending account	0	(5,000)
Income Taxable for Social Security and Medicare Tax	75,000	67,500
Deferral to 401(k) plan	0	(5,000)
Income Taxable for Federal and state taxes	75,000	62,500
Employee Social Security Tax and Medicare tax @ 7.65%	(5,738)	(5,164)
Federal Income Tax @ 20%	(15,000)	(12,500)
State Income Tax @ 5%	(3,750)	(3,125)
Net take home cash pay for John	50,513	41,711
401(k) plan balance at year-end - John's contribution	0	3,750
401(k) plan balance at year-end - ABC, Inc. contribution	0	3,750
Total 401(k) plan balance at year-end	0	7,500
Pre-Tax Dollars for Unreimbursed Health Care Expenses	0	2,500
Pre-Tax dollars for Dependent Care Expenses	0	5,000
John's total after-tax compensation	50,513	56,711

By using all of the employer provided benefits, John ends the year with $7,500 of contributions in his 401(k) plan, of which $3,750 was paid by ABC, Inc. Who wouldn't take $3,750 for free? By using all of the benefits, John ended up with an increase of $6,198 or 12% of his total after-tax compensation.

Wealth Accumulation
Action Plan

1. Diversify across asset classes and reduce or eliminate unsystematic risk by minimizing the use of individual stocks in your portfolio. If you feel you must invest in individual stocks, place 95% of your money in mutual funds, index funds, or wrap accounts. Use the remaining 5% of your investment money to invest in individual securities.
2. Invest in a manner consistent with your time horizon and risk tolerance.
3. Invest frequently and regularly. Pay yourself first. Take advantage of dollar cost averaging. We're talking about the most important investment account in the world, yours!
4. Don't obsess on the stock market. Invest your money and then go out and live your life. Spend time with your wife and kids. Go fishing or play golf. If you are properly allocated across different asset classes and across international borders you can ignore 99% of what you see on the news about the markets and the economy.
5. Invest for the long-term. Any stock held for the short- term can be risky.
6. Invest with inflation in mind. If you think the price of gas is going up, maybe you should be sure to have some oil stocks in your portfolio.
7. Debt is your enemy. Reduce or eliminate your debt.
8. Invest in tax-deferred and tax-free accounts for your retirement. 401(k) plans and IRAs.
9. Build an account equal to at least six months of income in a vehicle like a savings account, short-term CD, or money market account for emergencies.

Section 3
Wealth Distribution

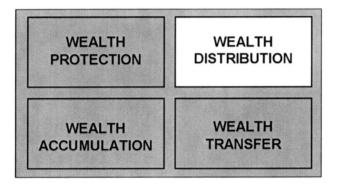

WEALTH PROTECTION	WEALTH DISTRIBUTION
WEALTH ACCUMULATION	WEALTH TRANSFER

Wealth Conservation & Distribution

Well, you finally made it. You're at a point in life where you have accumulated substantial assets. When you were younger, you might have been willing to take a little more risk that you are today. You still want to enjoy a good return on your investments, but you really don't want to lose what has taken years to accumulate. And yet you are challenged with the idea that you might live another 30 years of your life in retirement. If you invest your money "safely" at 3%, you might outlive your money. If you invest too aggressively, you might lose your money.

These are dilemmas each of us will some day have to face. In a recent Fidelity Investments report on retirement issues, Farrell Dolan, CFP® and Van Harlow, CFA reached the following conclusion:

" America faces a complex challenge: securing incomes that last a lifetime for a rapidly growing population of retirees. Both retirement and employee medical benefit programs are placing more and more reliance on individual savings and wealth management. And a multi-trillion-dollar decline in stock values has sharply impacted the finances and psychology of retirees and those to retire soon. The market correction highlights the increased urgency of investor education and planning for lifelong income in retirement."[23]

There are so many issues that have to be considered at this phase in our lives. You may remember very early in the book, I pointed out there are only two ways to make money:

1. PEOPLE AT WORK.

2. MONEY AT WORK.

You may be at the stage in life where you would like to quit working or possibly do something that you have always had a passion for, but maybe you could never afford to follow that passion. If you were a $300,000 a year corporate executive with a $320,000 a year lifestyle, you might not have been able to afford to leave your penthouse office to pursue your dream of becoming an artist. Maybe you want to spend six months of every year building homes for Habitat for Humanity or maybe you would like to do mission work in

Guatemala. I recently read a story of a 98 year-old man moving to Hollywood to pursue an acting career.

We are re-defining retirement and, as we move into our 50s 60s and beyond, we are re-defining our lives. But to have that luxury to create a life not dictated by earning an income, not dictated by having to work, you must have money at work. If you want to quit working for money, you must have money working for you. I want you to notice that I am not saying to simply quit working. That's your call. I would like for you to have the option to quit working for money. It's your retirement, after all. But after age 60 many people will work for reasons other than money. You may work to better your world, to serve God, to follow a dream. You may decide not to work at all because you finally want to use those golf clubs that have been gathering dust in the garage all those years. This book is a message of choice, helping you get to a point in life where you are not dictated by financial or employment responsibilities, but directed by your passions and vision. The third and fourth quarter of your life should be about fun, travel, time with family, and contribution to the ideals and organizations that make a difference in the world.

> # If you want to quit working for money, you must have money working for you!

If you're like most of us, the first two quarters of your life were preparing the canvas and laying out the drop cloth. You had to find a good window with plenty of sunlight and you placed the easel to full advantage. But now things are really starting to get fun. At this stage in life, we actually bring out the paints, applying color to the canvas.

We are going to focus on three main areas in the capital preservation and distribution quadrant:

1. Investing for income and capital preservation. We'll consider income producing stocks and bond investments, with goals of income, conservative growth, and market defensiveness. We will also take a look at the possible uses of annuities at this stage in your life.
2. Withdrawing money from your IRAs and retirement plans in the most effective way possible. Proper steps must be taken to maximize income,

avoid penalties, and use current tax law to your best advantage. Another consideration is the beneficiary designations in your retirement plans.

3. Planning for long term health care. While modern science is helping many of us live longer, the increased expense of declining health in your later years will have to be factored in your planning. Prescriptions, doctor visits, and the costs associated with long term care will have a major impact on your standard of living in the fourth quarter of your life.

We will also look at how your existing life insurance can provide financial leverage for your retirement assets in later years. You will need to be confident that adequate assets remain to provide for the comfortable lifestyle of a surviving spouse and your existing life insurance is one way to guarantee those funds. So, let's get started.

Income in your retirement years will probably come from three major sources:

1. Employer Pension Plans
2. Social Security
3. Your personal savings plans (401k, IRAs, Annuities)

Defined Benefit Pension Plans

Preceding generations had a social security system they could count on and many employees before us had a defined benefit retirement plan provided by their employer. Defined benefit plans guarantee a defined monthly retirement benefit that is payable to the retiree for the remainder of their life.

The employee and spouse could also choose a survivorship option. By utilizing the survivorship option, the employee could take a permanent reduction in benefit, say 30%, and when the employee passed away, his/her spouse would receive an income for the rest of their life. As you can imagine, these plans are very expensive to maintain. It can be quite costly to guarantee an income for the lives of two people. Actuarial calculations are used to attempt to predict exactly how long a person might live.

Another challenge for the administrators of defined benefit plans is that the employer bears the investment risk. The pension plan must invest the money so that needed funds will be available for retirees. Over the years, defined benefit plans have been in decline for several reasons.

1. Unpredictable investment returns.
2. Retirees living longer.
3. Thinner corporate profit margins.
4. Workforce mobility.
5. Regulatory complexity.
6. Employee perception – lack of appreciation.

Many companies still maintain defined benefit plans, but each new year brings additional plan dissolutions. The defined contribution plan became the wave of the future. The rise of the 401(k) heralded a new era in retirement planning. As an employee, maybe you are making pre-tax contributions to your 401(k) plan. Maybe your employer is matching some of your

> The number of defined benefit plans decreased from 114,396 in 1985 to 32,231 in 2002, a decline of almost 72%.
>
> *American Benefits Council,* May 2004.
> "Pensions at the Precipice"

contributions. But the main difference between a defined benefit plan and a 401(k) plan is that in a 401(k) plan you are bearing the investment risk and you are making most of the contributions to the plan. There is no guarantee of a defined benefit amount at your retirement. The ball is truly in your court. If you retire with $1 million dollars in your 401(k) it's your job to make sure that it lasts your lifetime, and a million dollars doesn't buy what it used to. In fact, some of that $1 million may also need to be there for your spouse after you're gone.

Social Security Retirement Benefits

As we have already determined, you may not be able to count on Social Security or a guaranteed monthly lifetime income from your employer. According to Karl Border, professor of financial economics at the University of Nebraska, "the government's own actuaries predict the Social Security system will go bankrupt by 2030, but could face financial crisis as early as 2014."[24]

> A recent Gallop Poll found that Americans, for the first time, list Social Security as the No. 1 domestic issue, ahead of the economy, healthcare, and terrorism.
> *The Washington Times*, March 28, 2005

You have the option of receiving benefits as early as age 62, but according to socialsecurity.gov, if your full retirement is at 67, the following permanent reductions can be anticipated for those workers requesting early benefits:

Age 62 = approximately a 30% annual benefit reduction.

Age 63 = approximately a 25% annual benefit reduction.

Age 64 = approximately a 20% annual benefit reduction.

Age 65 = approximately a 13 % annual benefit reduction.

Age 66 = approximately a 6.7% annual benefit reduction.

As you can see, your monthly retirement benefit will increase if you can wait until full retirement age. For those workers born after 1959, the full retirement age is now 67. Back in the early days of the social security system, there was speculation regarding the eventual taxation of social security benefits. In 1935 Franklin Roosevelt said, "There will never be a tax on social security benefits." We live in different times now and social security retirement benefits can be taxed.

50% of social security income is taxable if a single taxpayer earns over $25,000 in taxable income or married taxpayers, filing jointly, earn over $32,000 in taxable income in a year. If you think about it, those thresholds are very easy to exceed. But the plot thickens.

If a single taxpayer earns over $34,000 of taxable income in a year or a married couple, filing jointly, earns over $44,000 in taxable income, then 85% of the social security benefit is taxable.

The responsibility for a secure comfortable retirement has been placed squarely in your hands.

There used to be an unwritten code stating that the difference between your current age and age 100 should be the amount of money you should have in stocks, with the remainder being held in bonds. A 65 year-old person would have 65% of their money in bonds and 35% of their money in stocks. As they got older they would reduce their stock holdings and increase their bond holdings. Statistics show that most of us will live longer than our grandparents and fixed investments may not be able to keep pace with inflation and provide the income that we'll need to last into our 90s.

The challenge is to balance the need for growth with the desire for predictable retirement income. Over the years, I have counseled many investors approaching retirement. I took their questions to our advisor panel.

Retirement Investing Advisor Roundtable

MARK DIEHL:
What are your thoughts regarding appropriate investments for retirement income? A recent paper by Fidelity mentioned that aging Baby Boomers will be concerned about the possibility of outliving their money. What solutions do you feel have value for retirement income?

Mike Busch, CPA, CFP®, CEBS: Mark, what I see is retirees becoming too conservative too quickly. Medical advances have translated into longer life expectancies. Many individuals will be "retired" for upwards of 30 years. Retirees' biggest risk used to be the market volatility of their investments. Increasingly, the risk that their portfolios will not keep up with inflation is the bigger risk. The other problem I see, which is related, is that retirees often think that their portfolio has to produce dividend or interest income to cover their living expenses. They forget, or don't realize, that they can spend capital gains just as easily as they can spend interest income. Because they don't understand this, they feel compelled to devote much larger portions of their portfolio to fixed income than may be prudent.

Chad Starliper, CFP®, CLU, ChFC, EA: The distribution phase of retirement and investment planning is quite different than the accumulation phase. The reason is that portfolios react very differently once withdrawals begin depending on the direction, sequence, and magnitude of returns. People who retired in 2000 thinking life was so good found out the hard way what bear market withdrawals can do. So it's very important to look at how the investment strategy will line up with the client's plan over a very long period. We use Monte Carlo Simulation to test various investment and income strategies in terms of the probabilities of accomplishing their goals.

We've found that the types of income streams, the size of their assets, the amount of income they want, and the time frame all play large roles in making everyone's plan very different.

But getting to what is appropriate, we don't think that the investment methodology changes just because someone retires. We believe that income should come from total return of the portfolio. The issue is back to designing the proper globally diversified mix.

There are two commonly held views that we don't subscribe to. One is the notion that retirees should gradually reduce their exposure to stocks. Retirement plans often last over thirty years—which means that retirement money lasts longer than it took them to save it. We're talking about very long time frames for 60 year-old people.

The other is that you should design the portfolio to live off of the income and interest. This may be a simple idea to administer, but it is not a good way to treat the assets. It misses the entire point, and lets the tail wag the dog. It really is this: what investment strategy and other tools will give me the highest probability of sustaining the income I want for my lifetime? Anything other than that seems a bit reactionary.

The one specific tool that gets a lot of attention around our retired or retiring clients is the immediate annuity—basically a self-settled pension fund. Fixed income streams that are not market-related can have a very beneficial effect on portfolio longevity for many clients. Annuities make it easier to build an income base, even if just for some low expenses, they take a lot of the strain off of the investments to perform a certain way, and they add a good deal of security because they are guaranteed by an insurance company. A variable version of this concept can also be played, or perhaps an inflation-indexed fixed annuity.

But at the end of the day, products and tools do not correct under-funded asset bases and do not replace planning. The first thing is getting them enough money; the second is what to do with it. Number two is sort of irrelevant without number one.

June Schroeder, CFP®, RN: According to a recent AARP survey, nearly 80 percent of Boomers are planning to work into their 60's and 70's-- full or part time for income. This bodes well for putting off the need to tap into retirement savings. We are already seeing that trend. Tom and I are Boomers and we plan to keep on doing what we love to do-- our business.

Tom Wargin, CFP®, CFA: When we view working as an asset, it can be central to the plan. We currently have several clients in their 80's who are still vibrant and involved and they are certainly not Boomers. Today's Boomers at 60 are reportedly like the 40 year olds of before. They are healthier and don't view themselves as nearing the time to go out to pasture. Younger Boomers still are anchored on 65, but that will probably change as they age.

June Schroeder, CFP®, RN: So, in summary, work longer, stay healthy, plan for the worst and hope for the best.

Kathy Stepp, CPA, CFP®:   We spend a lot time educating our retired clients about cash flow in retirement. Many clients were taught that they must use only earnings, or specifically interest, from their investments in retirement. We encourage our clients to consider the total return, and not just the yield, as the earnings available in retirement. It is actually the cash withdrawal rate that is key to financial independence, not the portfolio's yield.

The target rate of return dictates the portfolio design. The rate of return is a total return, which means that it includes interest, dividends, and appreciation. As interest rates are at relative lows and dividend rates for the market as a whole are also low, most of the total return these days comes from the appreciation. In other words, much of the portfolio's earnings become principal, which many clients try to avoid using. However, if they do so, they will see their purchasing power shrink over time while their investment portfolio grows, unused!

The appropriate cash withdrawal rate from an investment portfolio in retirement should be determined by reducing the target rate of return for a reasonable inflation rate and a reasonable 'cushion' rate for defense against portfolio downturns. For example, if the portfolio's rate of return is 9%, then an appropriate cash withdrawal rate may be 5%, after allowing 2% for inflation and 2% for a 'cushion'.

Randy Smith, CFP®, MBA: As stated earlier, a retirement cash flow analysis based on the clients' desired lifestyle is very helpful. Retirees must often manage their personal expectations and budget to not outlive their assets. The market and the investor can only build a certain amount of wealth. The retiree must shoulder most of the responsibility for not depleting *their* assets. If they have saved sufficiently and efficiently, this is usually not a problem. If they have been less than frugal before retirement, retirement budget counseling will be needed. The "in retirement" budget counseling meeting is never fun.

John Scherer, CFP®, CLU, ChFC: For my clients in retirement, I use a combination of stripped treasuries (zero coupon bonds) and a diversified equity mutual fund portfolio for the optimum combination of secure income and growth which will not be outlived. In generic terms, once "enough" money is saved for retirement, putting half into a ladder of treasury strips and half in equities will provide both guaranteed income for 8-12 years (depending on interest rates) backed by the full faith of the US Government and equity returns which have on average quadrupled invested dollars over rolling 10 year periods dating back to 1971.

While there are other options for providing retirement income, including preferred stocks and the immediate annuities mentioned before, this method provides the best combination of guaranteed income, growth potential, and flexibility.

Diana Grossman Simpson, MBA, CFP®: We have a very specific retirement income strategy called "Growth with a Safety Net™" that was created and trademarked by my partner, Stewart Welch, III. The strategy involves using laddered bond or certificates for immediate income needs and mutual funds for growth within the portfolio. The balance between stocks and bonds will vary depending on the client's annual withdrawal amount and their risk tolerance, but the strategy is tax efficient and generally works well for our clients psychologically, as well.

The whole transition into retirement can be emotionally stressful, especially for those who are accustomed to saving a portion of their income. It is hard to wrap your head around the idea that you don't have to work any more, and that your money will work for you. It can be uncomfortable to be that dependent! And investors who have been through bear markets can be understandably cautious. Our strategy allows the client to maintain a "Safety Net" of investments that are far less subject to market fluctuations – usually for five or more years – so that the client can sleep comfortably at night, knowing that his portfolio can withstand the ups and downs that are inevitable with an equity portfolio. It is always our goal to maintain a client's lifestyle without spending principal. That way, no matter how long the client lives, there will always be income available.

Tom Wargin, CFP®, CFA: It is important to remember that we have to deal with inflation so we need growth in the portfolio. With increasing life expectancies and health care costs, spending needs could more than double or even triple during retirement. My father-in-law is 96 and was convinced he would die at 80.

We would recommend dividend paying stocks, inflation indexed bonds, exchange traded funds or even an annuity, if appropriate. What vehicles we use would vary according to the type of account-- taxable or deferred-- and the age of the client--are they 55 or 75. Actually the investments are the same as saving for retirement, just the asset allocation could change.

If appropriate, a guaranteed income from annuitizing one of their accounts could form the base or core of their income needs. However, under IRS rules, if you annuitize money in an IRA, the amount paid is deemed to be the Required Minimum Distribution (RMD) amount even if it exceeds the calculated amount using the Uniform Table. Therefore, you cannot consider the extra amount above the RMD calculation to offset other IRA RMDs. This is the negative to annuitizing money in IRA or retirement accounts.

June Schroeder, CFP®, RN: Health history can be a factor in the decision. For example, poor health can result in an increased payout making an immediate annuity attractive. We have clients who have out-lived their life expectancies like Tom's dad has and they can beat the odds. If they don't, they win anyway because they increased their income when they needed it.

Cary Carbonaro, CFP®, MBA: First, I think you need a plan that factors in inflation and has a life expectancy of 100. This plan should factor in your current spending, lifestyle, etc. I think it should be updated annually. As we discussed a minute ago, I think you should use an immediate fixed annuity for 10% of your investable assets. This guarantees that a portion of your assets will provide an income you can't outlive.

After calculating total income from the client's social security, pension and other income sources, I will use a properly asset allocated growth portfolio to cover any shortfall. You can't stick you money in CDs because you could be in danger of outliving you money. If you have $5 million and spend $25,000 a year, you are in no danger of outliving you money. What you spend is just as important as the size of your nest egg!

Laddered bonds work well for income, as does a mix of preferred and closed end funds. I use an outside professional money manager to manage everything but the laddered bonds. I also think you should have a percentage of your money in growth. I know some advisors say you will always have a top performing asset class and that is where you should take the income.

Wayne Starr, CFP®, ChFC: The same investments we have discussed earlier are appropriate investments in retirement. The issue is in what proportions and in what asset allocation.

When one retires, a switch in emphasis occurs from accumulation of assets to the consumption of assets. Risk tolerance will usually change. Am I willing to put as much at risk when the time has come to depend on the accumulated assets for an income?

We find that aggressive allocations will become more conservative and that already conservative allocations will stay about the same. For example, the business owner who sells close to retirement tends to be conservative in the investment of the proceeds. He or she has spent many years with the majority of their assets tied up in the business. Now two things occur, they sell the source of their livelihood and are now without a pay check other than the one that can be generated by the "proper" investment of the after tax sales proceeds.

We employ Monte Carlo analysis to test the viability of different withdrawal rates. Our goal is to show the client a safe rate of withdrawal that will allow him or her to not outlive their assets.

We seek solutions that will allow the client to consume assets in a manner that makes them last as long as possible and may even, hopefully, allow for inheritances. Solutions can incorporate charitable remainder trusts, asset allocations that do not disregard the return potential of equities, and bond ladders that generate income and allow for larger periodic distributions based on maturities. We may even employ the use of immediate annuities.

Kristi Sweeney, CFP®: It's key that people have a plan. If you estimate how much you'll spend in retirement, then factor in inflation and a modest growth of assets, properly structure your income and growth assets to keep up with inflation, you just may make it. But it's tough to plan for thirty or forty years of retirement. If you need help, get advice from a planner. Realize that your retirement may have different phases:

- Stage 1--active, healthy (this is a time when you may be traveling or pursuing hobbies and interests so you are spending portfolio income and even find that you are dipping into principal).

- Stage 2--inactive, still independent but health compromised (spending less on travel, clothes and entertainment... but more on medical care).

- Stage 3--Loss of independence, loss of health (spending income and often principal on medical care and long term care).

At a recent Financial Planning Association meeting, outliving assets was a subject of much concern. Thanks to medical technology, we can expect to live longer, on average, than our parents and grandparents. Accommodating this trend, Social Security income retirement age is inching up so many people will be working longer. But many people will plan on finding enjoyable work in their semi-retirement. Some will retire at the normal Social Security age (or even earlier) and then worry about outlasting their money. These people may end up going back to work after traveling and enjoying retirement for a few years.

Matthew Tuttle, CFP®, MBA: I believe in keeping this simple. We take systematic withdrawals from investment portfolios based on a client's age. For clients below 70 we use withdrawal rates of 5% annually or lower. Over the age of 70 we might withdraw more. Every year we would bump up the withdrawal by 3% for inflation. So for example, if we took out $100,000 in year one we would take out $103,000 in year two. By using risk controlled investing we believe that a client's portfolio should be able to generate enough in the way of interest and capital gains to sustain these withdrawals for as long as they live.

I do not believe investments have to be shifted over into bonds and other income producing investments in retirement. Capital gains and income are all green, to me there is no difference. The key is having an investment strategy that avoids large losses and has a sustainable withdrawal rate.

Dana Sippel, CPA/PFS, CFP®: An appropriate portfolio to provide retirement income would be a balanced, diversified portfolio. The portfolio would include both growth and fixed income investments. Many people think of a retirement portfolio as a portfolio that you would purchase a number of certificates of deposits or bonds at 6% and live off the income. Today, that strategy has a high probability of failure.

Most retirees can expect to spend 25 to 40 years in retirement based on today's life expectancies. Over this long period of time, a portfolio without growth investments will quickly lose purchasing power. This will result in an erosion of retirement income as the years pass, forcing a scaled back lifestyle in later retirement years. An individual needs to build a portfolio that includes both international and domestic stocks, real estate, possibly commodities and of course fixed income instruments. The specific allocation for a retiree's portfolio can vary dramatically depending upon their wealth, their spending patterns and other sources of income that are available during their retirement years. Most clients should target having about 60 to 70% of their portfolio invested in growth type securities throughout the retirement years. A portfolio allocated in this manner has been statistically shown to be able to provide annual portfolio withdrawals of 4% annually for an indefinite period of time.

Jim Reardon, JD, CFP®: Baby Boomers are going to need lots of money in retirement because they are going to live longer.

- Social Security benefits will be cut
- The official retirement age will increase
- Baby Boomers pensions and savings will not be adequate
- Many of them will end up going back to work.

Baby Boomers are not as bad off as they were expected to be. Recently a client emailed me about a report on PBS about the average Baby Boomer having about $150,000 in retirement assets. While that is hardly enough to sustain a Baby Boomer through 30 years of retirement, thanks to their provident parents who lived through the Depression Years and who hoarded money--over a trillion dollars in inheritances are expected to come their way over the next two decades. Don't expect Baby Boomers to be anywhere near as provident for their children.

At least the Baby Boomers have an expectation of some Social Security. Of course, it will be in a much different form than it is today. My concern is much more for the "Baby Busters" who are the current generation of working and professional people who have almost no chance of entertaining the thought of idle days and fulfilling activities in their old age unless they are truly good stewards of their assets

Craig Karpel's book, *The Retirement Myth* was written in 1995. Here's a passage:

> "Mass retirement is on its way to becoming a historical curiosity. With the fall of communism, it is no longer necessary for capitalism to compete by offering workers a pot of gold at the end of a rainbow; a longer rainbow will have to do. With the rise of global economic competition, it will be impossible for the U.S. public or private sectors to afford to compensate Americans with decades of later life leisure when this country's workers are already paid more in an hour than workers in Mexico earn in a day, more in a day than workers in China are paid in a month. Vast numbers of baby boomers are going to need to work part-time or full-time when they're older."

Craig S. Karpel, <u>The Retirement Myth,</u> Harper Perennial (1995), 235.

Does any of this sound familiar?

For years an analogy for retirement income security has been the "three-legged stool."

When each leg of the stool is strong, retirement income can be expected to be strong. The legs of the retirement security stool are:

- Social Security
- Pensions
- Personal Savings

<u>Social Security</u>. The notion of Social Security as providing anything more than "bare-bones" subsistence is an idea that began losing its wings when Congress reduced benefits to newly disabled workers in 1980. According to Karpel, politicians learned during the Carter Administration that cuts could be made in Social Security benefits without great political consequence and Congress has been whittling away at Social Security ever since.

<u>Pension Plans</u>. For the past two decades defined benefit pension plans have been giving way to defined contribution plans that offer far more modest retirement income expectations for most Americans. For years, the Urban

Institute economists have been predicting that half of all Baby Boomer retirees are likely to be without significant employer-provided pension benefits. Adding to the expected pension shortfall, is news that even the most stable companies have under funded pension plans. The number of under funded pension plans country-wide is estimated to be between 25%-50% of all plans in existence.

Recent news articles indicate that worker pension expenses add $1,800 to every General Motors automobile. This makes GM auto prices prohibitive in relationship to Toyota and Honda, their principal competitors. There is talk of a bail-out plan for both Ford and GM which would put these companies into Chapter 11 or some other form of bankruptcy. They would dump the pension plan liabilities on the federal government's Pension Benefit Guaranty Corporation (PBGC) and emerge with streamlined union agreements and no pension baggage.

Whereupon, every troubled corporation in America would likely follow suit and we would end up with a situation very similar to the savings and loan bail out. Behind the PBGC lies little more than an authorization to borrow a limited amount of capital from the U.S. Treasury. This means the federal government would have to increase the national debt by hundreds of billions of dollars if it had to fund every troubled corporate pension in America.

Personal Savings. These are almost non-existent. In fact, Americans have been spending more than they make for the past several months. According to Karpel, when the three legs crumble underneath the rickety stool, home values will plunge as aged Baby Boomers begin dumping their houses on a shrinking number of younger workers who can't afford their over-inflated homes, and the American stock market will soon have to follow suit, plunging us into a "Great *Depreciation"* which will throw large masses of "dumpies" (destitute, unprepared mature people) into the streets.

Of course, this is a doomsday scenario and not an absolutely irreversible situation but what impresses me most is how little this script--written ten years ago--has changed. One of the solutions to this potential train wreck is based on the relatively happy realization that Baby Boomers are healthier and smarter and more active than any previous generation and they are fully capable of holding their own in the workplace for a much longer period of time.

Karpel says: "If enough of us free ourselves from the retirement myth and embrace models of productive aging...the baby boom generation will be said to have at last outlived its narcissism and… We will be able to transcend the petty work of paying the rent and become engaged in the great work of healing the world."

It's interesting that Robert J. Myers who was considered to be the architect of the Social Security system continued to work into his 80s. Colonel Harland Sanders didn't begin to market his chicken recipes until he was 65 when he realized he couldn't live on social security. Two storied coaches, Joe Paterno and Bobby Bowden, continue on into their 70s. Pro football coach Marv Levey is 80. Peter Drucker, the dean of American management consultants, practiced well into his 80s. Justice Oliver Wendell Holmes served productively on the bench until his retirement at age 91, and Bob Dole can still deliver the goods at the age of 80.

My grandfather ran his newspaper until he was nearly 75 and my mother built a new store when she was 65 and ran it for ten years. As for me, I changed careers (again) at 58 and for the past six years have been doing what I have prepared for all my life. I intend to build a business (not a job) and "keep on trucking" for years to come--so Baby Boomers, I'll see you in the workforce.

Investing For Capital Preservation

MARK DIEHL:
At this stage in life, people have accumulated substantial assets. Maybe they have sold their larger home since they are no longer raising children. They also have accumulated significant dollars in 401(k) plans and IRAs. I think Americans know they need to stay invested but are concerned about having their life savings at undue risk.

Kathy Stepp, CPA/PFS, CFP®: We've seen clients struggle with maintaining wealth when they have no investment plan, or when their spending consistently outpaces their earnings, or when they have no surplus in their portfolio to act as a buffer against an extended bear market.

Our investment philosophy is to manage our clients' money in such a way as to maximize the probability of reaching a target return on average over time while minimizing investment risk. We accomplish this by diversifying the portfolio to a mix of assets that we believe will produce the target rate of return over the long run and then periodically rebalance to the desired portfolio mix. The rebalancing itself is a good strategy for guarding against making poor investment choices, because it takes the emotion out of the decision. When the portfolio is out of balance, something has gone up or down. When an investment or an investment class has gone up, its percentage of the portfolio as a whole has gone up, which means we want to sell some of it and reinvest the proceeds into something that is down. Doing so results in the desired 'buy low, sell high' strategy that is so often sabotaged by emotions, creating an obstacle for someone trying to maintain wealth.

Of course, a common challenge for someone who has retired with just enough investment capital to support a particular lifestyle is to keep spending in check. This is a common issue for newly retired people who are not used to having so much time on their hands to go out and spend money! It becomes especially important if their investments experience a downturn in the early years of retirement. These people must make an effort to manage their expenses responsibly.

Diana Grossman Simpson, MBA, CFP®: An investor with substantial assets today is going to be understandably cautious. There was so much wealth created suddenly in the late 1990s and then lost during the bear market…the term *wealth preservation* seems to have a much stronger meaning these days. Now, people are more likely to describe themselves as "conservative" investors, whereas several years ago everybody was "aggressive". As far as my advice goes, it really hasn't changed much since I started in the business fourteen years ago. I've always recommended implementing an investment strategy that has a high probability of achieving the client's goals without taking unnecessary risk.

Working with a professional investment advisor can be instrumental in making this strategy successful. People are so emotional about their money, and they tend to make irrational decisions based on either greed or fear. Good professional managers do not make investment decisions based on emotion – they make rational decisions based on experience and available information. In my experience, it is the bad decisions that individual investors make based on emotion that keep them from being successful – like buying an investment after it has already gone way up in value (greed) or selling out of an entire portfolio in a panic (fear). Ultimately, the strategy I would recommend would be dependent upon the client's circumstances. For example, I had some clients recently invest some money with me. They were young professionals, and the wife had come into some money from a trust. Our initial strategy was fairly aggressive; they did not need any income from the portfolio and wanted the money set aside for long-term growth. However, several months later, the wife was diagnosed with a chronic illness, and they were unsure how much longer she would be able to work. The decision was made to change the investment strategy to be more conservative until they had a better idea of what they would be facing.

Jim Reardon, JD, CFP®: If you have wealth and you want to maintain it, it is imperative that you develop a plan and work the plan. Every week for over five years I interviewed some of the best known names in money management on my radio program. Each of them had a different plan. For a long time, I wondered how so many people with such different plans could be so successful most of the time. The most valuable lesson I learned was that money managers understand their plan, they have faith in their plan, and they follow their plan. The plan, like the market, is never perfect but it works much of the time and it sustains and protects the investments--particularly in bad times.

Although I have over fifteen years experience in the financial business, I was out for a number of years while I was involved in local and state politics. My present business was begun on April 1, 2000 which was right at the beginning of the worst stock market crash in my lifetime.

I believed that most of the market losses that were occurring to prospective clients at that time were the result of poor risk management and over-concentration in highly inflated growth and technology investments. During the stock market's free-fall in 2001 and 2002, I was busy giving *panic-proof investing* workshops and diversifying new clients into alternative investments such as money markets, real estate, bonds, convertible securities and natural resources. We stabilized the portfolios and the accounts soon grew back to their original positions.

During the market crash, our business prospered and grew because of our dedication to preserving capital as well as making it grow. Given the conservative nature of our clients who are primarily seniors and non-profit organizations, we believe that protecting accumulations is our number one priority and growth of assets is second.

Wayne Starr, CFP®, ChFC: The major challenges to maintaining wealth, in my opinion, are the fear-greed cycle, the lack of discipline (absence of an Investment Policy Statement), a consumption driven economy, the burgeoning cost of healthcare, inflation, and yes, lawsuits.

The process that I follow for all clients begins with understanding what the client sees as the uses for the money. Simply, "What are your goals and where does this money fit?" We want to know about short, intermediate, and long term goals. We want to know how the assets were created and how it is held- retirement accounts, trusts, sole name or joint tenant. Where we end up as far as an Investment Policy Statement will be greatly affected by the answers to our questions.

Next, we will delve into risk tolerance to measure the capacity for risk as well as the tolerance. Does the client have enough money to "accommodate" the risk tolerance, the subjective side of the issue. For example, a retired person with $250,000 does not have the risk capacity to have 75% in the equity market. Conversely, someone with $250,000 all earmarked for retirement in twenty years does have the capacity to handle a 75% equity allocation.

Following the analysis, we are ready to develop the strategic asset allocation which is spelled out in a formal Investment Policy Statement. This statement is reviewed annually with the client to see if it is still appropriate for their goals. Are any changes needed because of taxes, goal revisions, consumption patterns, income, and gains/losses.

Cary Carbonaro, CFP®, MBA: Regarding investment management, the 2001-2003 bear market was the worst in history. It was even worse than the 1970s bear market. The lessons that should have been learned during the bear are the same as today. If you follow asset allocation and are properly diversified, your highs may be lower but your lows will definitely be higher. Most of our clients lost somewhere in the area of 20% over the entire bear market. It was made back by the end of 2003 and early 2004. I had potential clients come to me who lost 90% during the recent bear. How can you recover from that when you are 65 or over? The answer is you can't, because you don't have the time to make it up. It was pure greed, lack of knowledge and trusting a broker with blind faith that got them there in the first place.

Investing is a long term proposition. The stock market overall has returned 8-10% since the 50s. Do you know how many years it actually came in at 8-10? Less than three times in over 50 years. It is up 21%, down 11%, etc. and evens out. What is even more interesting is if you look at the performance by asset class type. All asset classes rotate. An asset class will be on top one year and on the bottom the next. If you are in each asset class you can smooth out your performance. I also like to benchmark my clients. This way they know how they did in each asset class and if they beat the benchmark.

John Scherer, CFP®, CLU, ChFC: With regard to capital preservation, the biggest challenge to maintaining wealth is to make sure that asset growth outpaces the increasing cost of living. A well diversified and annually re-balanced portfolio of US large, US small, foreign large, foreign small, and emerging market stocks really has no chance of losing money over long--and by long I mean 10+ years-- holding periods and is essentially risk free.

Tom Wargin, CFP®, CFA: Inflation and taxes--basically the "friction costs." They slow down and sometimes eliminate the ability to maintain and improve real spending power. Fees from investment managers and advisors should also be added into that equation. But remember, you either spend time or money. If you spend time, are you spending it productively? If you spend money, are you getting the value you expect from your advisor and do you even know?

June Schroeder, CFP®, RN: I view the challenges to maintaining wealth as the same old things with new twists: greed, fear, pride, complacency, procrastination, and change. It's also keeping up with the Jones's. People fail to determine the difference between needs and wants, aided of course by Madison Avenue advertising! We also have those who constantly make choices that prevent them from accumulating more or even retaining assets. A person might be unable or unwilling to change lifestyles after a divorce or death of a spouse. We had one woman who refused to accept that she would run out of money by age 62 if she continued to live as if she were still in a two income family. On the other hand, some people don't identify what really makes them happy and they have a decidedly undefined concept of what wealth means to them. Wealth is not just dollars-- it's also personal stuff. As the old adage says, "We only go around once."

Kristi Sweeney, CFP®: My practice does not invest or advise on investments, but I am well aware of the critical importance of avoiding unnecessary risk. Since not being diversified is one of the biggest threats to wealth accumulation, I think it is very important for most people to have an investment advisor who believes in diversification of assets, does not try to time the market and helps my clients rebalance their investments. We refer clients to fee-only or fee-based investment advisors who are CERTIFIED FINANCIAL PLANNER™ Practitioners.

Annuities

MARK DIEHL:
There has been a lot of talk recently about the suitability of annuities, both fixed and variable. Do your clients invest in annuities? When do you think annuities are appropriate and when are they inappropriate?

Matthew Tuttle, CFP®, MBA: I am not a big fan of annuities. I think a lot of annuity sales are driven by the large commissions and not the suitability for the client. When we use annuities it is usually to replace an unsuitable annuity with one more suitable when withdrawing money out of annuities all together would result in a negative tax consequence.

As of this writing fixed annuities in many cases are paying less than CDs. If we get into a higher rate environment and people can lock in 7-8% in a fixed annuity then this investment might be more suitable.

Equity indexed annuities can also be an interesting product as long as the client understands how they work. Unfortunately, due to the complexity of these it is rare that someone outside (or inside) the industry can actually understand how these work and have realistic expectations. I often meet people who were told they could expect some unrealistic return from an indexed annuity. If one looks at this investment as an alternative to other "safe" investments then it may be attractive.

Wayne Starr, CFP®, ChFC: Our clients rarely invest in annuities. When we begin to work with a client who owns an annuity inside of an IRA, we will routinely terminate the annuity and reinvest the cash proceeds using the vehicles mentioned earlier. We will not, however, terminate until the surrender charge period is over. In that situation we will review the investment options offered so we can select those that fit the asset allocation.

Clients who own annuities outside of a qualified plan pose a problem. Termination of the annuity could trigger a large ordinary income tax liability on the profits. Since we are all about wealth preservation we want to defer that tax. We will first analyze the investment options to determine quality and range of alternatives. Next we review costs—remaining surrender fees and insurance company based expenses.

When it is reasonable, we will recommend a tax-free exchange (IRS Code Section 1035) to an annuity with much lower insurance company based fees. We have found two companies that offer low cost, no commission, no surrender fee plans that provide quality investment options.

My comments so far may lead one to believe that we think annuities are inappropriate and that is correct. We are concerned about placing a tax shelter inside a tax shelter, such as IRAs. We are concerned about taxes—there is no way to take advantage of lower capital gain tax rates inside of an annuity. We are also concerned about the high expenses, commissions, and surrender charges associated with the majority of annuities. Many people have lost money in variable annuities when the technology bubble burst because no one called them to suggest re-balancing. I fear the advisors who sold those annuities were out selling new annuities to create new commissions.

There are times when an annuity may be appropriate. We have recommended annuitization of non-IRA annuities to create a guaranteed income flow from an annuity with large profits that, again, are taxable as ordinary income. Annuitization allows the tax to be spread out over a long period. But the "guarantee" of a stream of income that cannot be outlived is only as good as the issuing insurance company. Company quality has to be investigated thoroughly.

Another case of appropriateness can arise when a client has taken full advantage of all other tax effective investments. If the client still wants more tax deferral and is willing to forego capital gain tax treatment, a no commission, no surrender fee annuity may be advisable.

Dana Sippel, CPA/PFS, CFP®: Annuities, like any other financial vehicle make a better fit in some people's financial plans than others. Annuities can be appropriate for the very conservative client who wants to guarantee a secure income stream they cannot outlive. When used in this manner, annuities can be thought of as essentially an income insurance policy. Since many people will not receive a traditional pension, an annuity can be a way to provide regular income. An annuity can also make sense for someone who has a large sum of money and would like to secure a portion of it in a fixed income vehicle and leave the rest in a managed investment portfolio.

One of the biggest drawbacks of an annuity is the high contract costs. Because of the fact that these contracts are offered primarily through insurance companies, they have many layers of expenses built in which can easily approach 3% or more annually. These contracts also frequently have surrender charges if you exit the contract within the first five to ten years of their existence. These charges make it very costly to transfer a contract to another financial services provider if the owner's circumstances change. There are, however, some lower cost annuity contracts available through certain providers.

Cary Carbonaro, CFP®, MBA: One benefit of all annuities is you are in essence converting non-qualified money which means non-IRA, 401K etc into tax-deferred money. This means it gets to grow tax deferred until you take it out. When you receive payments, they are part taxable and part return of capital.

I think fixed annuities are often overlooked and underused. A fixed annuity is guaranteeing a portion of your money for a retirement income you can't outlive. If you have a history of long life spans in your family tree, a fixed annuity can guarantee that you don't outlive income generated from at least a portion of your assets . This is for a conservative portion. I use 10% of your investable assets. This money is not in the market, not at risk. If you annuitize at age 60 and live to 110, you will enjoy a fixed income for 50 years. It is based on mortality tables.

The guaranteed income is backed by the insurance company so you must use an insurance company that is financially solid. Independent rating companies provide an analysis of any company you might be considering. The most well known insurance rating organization is AM Best and their highest rating is A++.

I also recommend at least 10 or 20 years period certain depending on the age. That means if you die during the 10 or 20 year period the payments would go to your beneficiary. Jonathan Clements, a writer for the *Wall Street Journal* wrote an article on 07/27/05 titled "The Secrets to a Happier Retirement... Family, Friends and a Fixed Annuity."

You didn't mention index annuities. I have never used these and I will not. An article in *Investment News* from March 27, 2006 says that the leading equity index annuities "sell the sizzle and don't deliver the steak." Equity index annuities are complex and pay the person who sells them a very high commission. That alone should make you question it. There are always three parties in the equation, the advisor, the client and the insurance company. My husband says the insurance company is like the house and almost never loses. The advisor gets paid a large amount of money so he doesn't lose. You can see where I am going. I guess in financial planning you can't say always or never but I have just never seen any reason to use these.

Variable annuities are also very complex and they have good, bad and ugly in this category. I believe if you have already maxed out all pre-tax savings and you want your money to grow tax deferred, a variable annuity would be appropriate.
I am interested in what is referred to as the guaranteed retirement benefit. It is a rider that works as portfolio protection. The fees are high on this product so you have to make sure the performance can support it.

Jim Reardon, JD, CFP®: Most of the cases I have been involved with over the past two years as an expert witness have centered on the sale of variable annuities. I think it is safe to say that the press does not like annuities of any kind, state and federal regulators are leery of the motives of those who sell them, and annuity sales practices draw more litigation than most other financial products.

Having said all of this, I am surprisingly neutral toward annuities. Although the suitability issue is frequently raised, the real issue to me has always been the abhorrent sales practices and representations of the insurance agents who offer them. Over a fifteen year career, I sold many fixed annuities to people who had long time horizons, and who wanted competitive interest rates, principal guarantees and tax deferral. I have never had a premature surrender nor, to my knowledge, a complaint. Most of my clients have annuities that they have acquired over the years from me or from other sources. I consider them to be just one more tool that can be used to serve the client.

Lengthy surrender penalties and high internal costs have made variable annuities unattractive in many cases. I can tell you, however, that for certain clients, new benefits known as "living benefits" seem very attractive. While living benefits don't guarantee that a variable portfolio won't lose money, they do offer (at a price) riders that will mitigate losses and assure a substantial retirement income benefit option over a required time.

One of my friends refers to living benefits options as "guard rails." If the Golden Gate Bridge didn't have guard rails, people would drive 20 miles an hour across it. With the guard rails a driver feels comfortable driving at a higher rate of speed. These riders act as guard rails to protect against a fatal accident and to perhaps allow one to invest more freely and with less worry. While I would not advocate the purchase of one of these as an alternative to a mutual fund portfolio, I would consider one of these annuities as an alternative to an already existing variable annuity that does not offer living benefit features.

In cases where I find a client with existing annuities with no surrender fees, I will usually exchange these annuities into a no-load annuity that has half the internal costs of the existing variable annuity and no surrender penalties. We then assign a portfolio strategist to manage the sub accounts with the same active management methods we employ for our other platforms. We do not receive a commission for this annuity but we do receive our standard management fee for managing the portfolio.

Annuities that are used in retirement plans—particularly IRAs are called "qualified annuities" because they are part of a qualified retirement plan. Annuities that are not retirement annuities are called "non-qualified annuities. I have heard it said for years that annuities are patently unsuitable for IRAs and other retirement plans because the tax deferral feature in an annuity is "redundant" and has no added value inside an IRA. While it is true that they are generally more expensive than a mutual fund and the tax deferral feature is not necessary, there is nothing inherently wrong or unsuitable about an annuity, either fixed or variable acting as a retirement or quasi-retirement vehicle.

Since 1911, annuities have been the principal retirement program for millions of teachers, employees of hospitals and other health care non-profit organizations. An American teacher's annuity program is considered to be the biggest pension plan in the country and perhaps in the world. This annuity company provides 403(b) compensation benefits for thousands of universities and hospitals at very minimal internal costs. These investment vehicles are just as cost effective as mutual funds and they offer lifetime payout features not available with mutual funds or any other type of investment. We manage millions of dollars for clients who are in these no-load, no-surrender variable and fixed teacher annuity retirement plans.

Diana Grossman Simpson, MBA, CFP®: Unfortunately, most of the annuity products that I see prospective clients invested in are not particularly appropriate for their situation. I often see IRA annuities, which rarely make sense to me, or too much of an investor's money tied up in an annuity product.

I find that people do not understand annuities, and many times are in the dark about the conditions of their contracts.

Occasionally, an annuity will make perfect sense for a client. Annuities can provide a secure source of income over one's lifetime, which is appealing to those who are relying on their investments for income. There are also tax benefits with annuities, but I rarely recommend an annuity for tax benefits alone.

I guess the bottom line is that I know that commissions on annuities are very high, and so I sometimes wonder if the annuity sale was truly in the best interest of the client –or the salesperson?

John Scherer, CFP®, CLU, ChFC: Annuities are not advisable for the vast majority of people. I avoid them for my clients, as the same benefits can usually be derived by using other vehicles at a fraction of the cost of most annuities and without giving up the flexibility that is inherent in an annuity.

Where annuities can make sense is for those who are extremely risk-averse and insist on having some amount of guaranteed short term returns in their holdings. Other candidates for annuities are those who have a need for guaranteed income to pay for living expenses such as health insurance, property taxes, groceries, etc. In these cases an immediate annuity, which pays a set amount each year like a pension can be a viable option.

In either case, if a person does decide to utilize annuities they would do well to consider annuities which pay no commissions to the sales agents. Commission paying annuities typically pay agents 2-10% of the invested amounts as commissions. In order to recover those costs the insurance companies assess charges to the investor ranging from 1-2.5% yearly in addition to surrender charges for taking the money out of the annuity in the first 7-15 years of the policy. No-commission (also called 'low-load') annuities typically have annual charges of under 0.75% with no surrender charges at all if the investor decides to move their money to a different product or company. Several companies offer such no-commission products – they can be found with a simple internet search of 'commission free annuity'.

Randy Smith, CFP®, MBA: Annuities do have a place in the investor market but I very rarely use annuities of any kind. Some of my clients do have annuities but they already existed in their portfolio. Annuities are tools that are grossly over used. In the accumulation phase, they should be used as another tax deferred vehicle when an investor has exhausted *all* other tax advantaged plans and still has a large cash flow and savings need.

Kathy Stepp, CPA, CFP®: Some clients already own annuities when they come to us. When we ask them why they own annuities, the answer is almost always that they were sold the annuities by a broker whom they trusted but did not necessarily understand.

In general, we do not recommend annuities. The cost of combining an investment with an insurance product is too high, in our view. The typical annuity sales pitch argues that the tax deferral of the annuity outweighs the insurance costs. However, we point out that although the annuity is tax-deferred, future withdrawals will result in ordinary income tax, while investing outside annuities results in the much lower capital gains tax. Therefore, the tax argument for annuities falls apart, leaving nothing to offset the high internal costs of the insurance product.

I think clients often get overly focused on tax-deferred investments and never consider that qualified dividends and capital gains in most investments are taxed at a maximum of 15%.

For those clients who come to us with annuities already in their portfolio, we often exchange the annuities for others with lower costs. The timing of the exchange is determined by the surrender charge associated with the original annuity. We would like to avoid having our client pay a surrender charge at all, but if the charge is low and the annuity is especially expensive, we may recommend a change during the surrender charge period.

June Schroeder, CFP®, RN: Our bias is to look elsewhere first. Have we recommended annuities? Yes, if the person is over 59 1/2 and it is a no load, no commission product. We primarily recommend 1035 exchanges to no-load programs even if the surrender charge has not expired if it makes sense after we do our calculations.

Mike Busch, CPA, CFP®, CEBS: Unfortunately, annuities are the most oversold product in the financial services industry. They do have their place, but I believe they are generally only suitable for those who have an above average need for creditor protection and/or have maxed out their tax-deferred savings. I also believe fixed annuities are generally more appropriate than

217

variable annuities. Variable annuities tend to have high expenses and also have the nasty tax characteristic of converting what would otherwise be favorably taxed capital gains into unfavorably taxed ordinary income. In contrast, fixed annuities are a bit more straightforward. The guaranteed rate is not reduced by additional expenses. And since they tend to be fixed income or CD equivalents, they are not converting capital gains to ordinary income. Finally, it is relatively easy to compare the rates offered on fixed annuities to CD rates and know if a fixed annuity will produce a better yield.

Tom Wargin, CFP®, CFA: We find many traditional annuities to have high costs and high expense ratios that can sap a person's return. Equity indexed annuities are the biggest culprits today. We are very suspicious of their long surrender periods-- up to fifteen years. I am currently working with a new client who, prior to coming to meet us, put $140,000 into one and $90,000 into another. Surrender fees are $22,000 and $13,000 respectively. That's about 15%! We are in the process of challenging them, including the appropriateness in her circumstances.

Chad Starliper, CFP®, CLU, ChFC, EA: Discussions about annuities—mainly deferred annuities—tend to bring up a lot of heated debate, and for good reason. The abuses that go on in this area are both repulsive and common. But that has more to do with the application than the actual vehicle itself. We have clients that invest in annuities, but it is the exception and not the rule.

My general assessment on the use of annuities—this might include fixed, variable, or equity-indexed versions—is they are principally risk management vehicles. The risks being managed could be income longevity or capital preservation. It goes without saying that there are no free lunches; you don't get something for nothing. And just like any other instrument, they may be well-suited if the investor knowingly and purposefully pays the extra costs associated with the risk management features. If the investor neither understands nor wants these features, then they are paying for something they don't need.

For example, if I need to haul firewood to my parents' house, I might need some kind of truck. But it would foolish to rent a bulldozer to do it. It has nothing whatever to do with the bulldozer, but everything to do with the use of it. It's the same thing with investing.

The other issue is that, even assuming the investor "thinks" he or she wants these features, I believe the advisor (not salesperson) should explain to the client just what these costs are in comparison to other alternatives. Because I think, from experience, most annuities are not purchased with full knowledge of the costs or ramifications of those costs. Regarding variable annuities, when you start talking about expenses in the area of 3%, you're really chopping off some returns. Not to mention that you're restricted to the sub-account selections within the annuity chassis. So we're not huge fans, although the type of annuity in question might elicit a different type of response from us.

Social Security and the Baby Boomers

MARK DIEHL:
Research indicates that 77 million Baby Boomers will begin a retirement tidal wave in the next few years. This will certainly place an even larger strain on the already burdened Social Security system? What challenges do you see ahead for the retiring Baby Boomer generation?

Matthew Tuttle, CFP®, MBA They need to realize that what worked for their parents and grandparents will not work for them. Years ago when someone died at 65 we thought about how he/she lived a long life. Today, if someone dies at age 65, it is a shame that they had to die so young. Longer life expectancies create a number of problems--running out of money, inflation, health care problems, etc. Now more than ever, Baby Boomers need to have a plan in place. There are times when you cannot do your best and still be successful; these are not those times.

Kristi Sweeney, CFP®: I am a part of the Baby Boomer group, so I feel free to criticize. I hope that our demands as the Baby Boomer generation will not impoverish our children and grandchildren. We are a large voting group so we will have an effect for years to come. As we become eligible for Medicare, I am concerned about my group's high demand on a medical delivery system. From long term care to multiple prescription drugs, hip replacements and heart transplantations, my population group has high expectations for long and healthy lives. And high expectations for quality of life as well. For many complex reasons, Boomers have not managed to save for retirement like our parents and grandparents did. My hope is that through education, we will look to solutions that are good for our country, our children and our community.

Wayne Starr, CFP®, ChFC: I think there are three challenges. The first is moving from a regular income provided by salary, business ownership, or a profession to reliance on an investment portfolio. It is a major mental transition.

Next in line are the other two as they are intertwined—meeting monthly needs/wants and not outliving the money. Our focus is on determining the amount needed to meet the client's goals for a retirement standard of living. We spend time analyzing what is required to meet the needs—food, clothes, shelter, medical care, utilities, personal care, and a modest level of gifts. Next we estimate the 'live it up' target or wants—second home, travel, hobbies, gifts to family, etc. These two numbers are the real target income.

We have to know what makes up the standard of living today and what are likely to be expenditures in retirement. For example, assuming the mortgage is paid off by retirement; do the clients want the amount previously spent on principal and interest to be available for travel?

The target income plus an allowance for taxes then translates to a required withdrawal rate. What is the annual target as a percentage of retirement assets? If too high, the danger is running out of money while taking on too much risk in order to get a higher return.

Our job is to identify a sustainable withdrawal rate, often 4 to 5%, so we can account for inflation along with possible life expectancies. Buy-in by the client is vital here as unrealistic goals can destroy the portfolio.

It is important to add here that equities cannot be abandoned in the retiree's portfolio. Monte Carlo analysis indicates a too low or no allocation to equities dramatically reduces the probability of success—not outliving one's income.

Dana Sippel, CPA/PFS, CFP®:   Over the past decade or so the entire definition of retirement has really started to evolve. There was a time when a person would spend most of their career working for a single company or the government, and as a reward for their loyalty they would receive a lifetime pension benefit, frequently with medical benefits, as a part of the pension.

Today, Baby Boomers and younger generations are not staying with a single employer and may reasonably expect to work for numerous employers during their career. The outcome of these job changes means that rather than the employer providing most of the employee's retirement benefits, the employee must save for themselves. Saving for financial independence can be a tough task as their purse strings are tugged by children's expenses and possibly aging parent's financial issues. Since employers are generally not as diligent in setting aside funds for their employees' future financial independence, the end result is that many people will find themselves attaining retirement age without the financial means required to completely stop working.

The definition of retirement is evolving to a period in your life when you slow down from the pace of work that you may have kept up in your 40s and 50s to a more leisurely pace as you move into your 60s and 70s and beyond. You may not fully retire, but merely slow down your work schedule allowing your income stream to continue while also enjoying more time spent pursuing hobbies, recreational travel, leisure and family time.

Cary Carbonaro, CFP®, MBA: The normal age now for Social Security retirement benefits has risen to age 67. I see that continuing to rise. I am a fan of privatization of Social Security. When I counsel my young clients about Social Security most of them indicate that they believe they will never receive any Social Security retirement benefits. I feel generation X and Y will plan better because they realize that Social Security will not be there for them in their older years. I think I would rather invest my 12.5% than let the government do it for me!

Diana Grossman Simpson, MBA, CFP® I see challenges, but I also see opportunities. Being a Boomer myself, I think that the Baby Boom generation will change the entire concept of retirement. So many of my clients are not even counting on Social Security for retirement income, and frankly, neither am I. It's not that I don't have faith in the system, it's just that I don't want to count on it. More often than not, my Boomer clients see themselves working in some capacity during their retirement years. I predict a significant shift in the way our society views work, especially in terms of the traditional "8 to 5" type job. I see our entire culture changing, creating more flexible working hours, job sharing and greater growth in the field of professional consulting. Our economy, already a service economy, will shift even more strongly in that direction, perhaps creating a new economic revolution.

To accommodate Boomers, the real estate market will change as well. I think it is highly possible that we will experience a reduction in demand for "family"-style homes (2- or 3-story, large square footage and yard) and increased demand for garden-style homes. Sectors of the market that serve the elderly, such as retirement homes, pharmaceutical companies, medical supplies, and obviously funeral homes, will experience a boom. We are already experiencing the rapid price appreciation of vacation homes as Boomers plan for their retirements.

These changes will present both opportunities and challenges. The housing market may present a challenge for late Boomers trying to sell their traditional family homes, or purchase resort or vacation property. But I don't buy into the theory that all the Boomers are going to pull their assets out of the market upon retirement--thus creating a huge drop in market values.

John Scherer, CFP®, CLU, ChFC: The biggest challenge I foresee for Baby Boomers in the upcoming retirement years is not really financial. I think the biggest issue will be how to stay connected and continue to put their skills and knowledge to use in a personally meaningful fashion. The old-fashioned notion of spending retirement taking it easy, playing bingo, and catching the early-bird dinner specials will soon be a thing of the past, if it isn't already. With ever-increasing life expectancies, even people working until "normal" retirement age 65 will have another 20-30 years to live. Finding ways to use that time to live a truly fulfilling life will be the real challenge for boomers.

Randy Smith, CFP®, MBA: I can sum up the Social Security dilemma with just two words-- "Means Testing". It is obvious to everyone that there are not enough "haves" to support the "have nots". The next generation (our children) will also not have the assets or the numbers to support Social Security. They will fight and vote, in their "growing a family" years, to not pay the bills of those who did not save before them. So, if you can not raise revenue then you must lower costs, it is that simple.

Thus, you must see who has "means" (money) and those people will not be allowed to access their Social Security benefit. The "common good" of all retirees is and will be the explanation. You can already see signs of this taking place. First, the progressive taxing of the current Social Security benefit. Second, the raising of the Social Security benefit age. Third, the raising of the 415 limits to allow people of means to save more of their *own* money in qualified plans today, so the future loss of their Social Security benefit will be more palatable. Lastly, the lowering of the capital gains rate to stimulate the economy now and to place more wealth in retirees hands for the future. The government does know that individuals, who have and understand money, will save it. They are self-sufficient now and in the future.

June Schroeder, CFP®, RN: Some Boomers have anchored on the traditional age 62 or 65 for retirement, or even earlier. We recently met with a client and explained that retirement at age 55 was probably not in the cards for him and why, but he didn't want to accept it. He wanted to retire in five years because he hated his job. He wanted an aggressive portfolio yet bemoaned the volatility and was not open to discussing a career change that could give him more satisfaction and a longer work life. With increasing life expectancies and the dismal savings history many Boomers have, there are bound to be big changes, like working longer or going back to work years after retirement. By sheer numbers, Boomers (my generation) have always forced change or accommodation upon the rest of the economy.

Tom Wargin, CFP®, CFA: That's for sure and so will it be with Social Security. Many Boomers do not have sufficient assets to last their whole lives, even if they work into their 70s, because life expectancies continue to increase. Social Security will be changed because it has to, perhaps by a rebellion from the younger generations. Remember that age 65 was picked by Von Bismarck in 1840 as the age at which most Prussian soldiers would be eligible for their pensions--an age so high that most would be deceased and not able to collect! It was also arbitrarily selected in 1935 with the advent of Social Security, a core tenant of which was to lure older workers out of the workforce to make room for the large number of unemployed. Now we are in the reverse situation. The age for retirement must be stretched out to 72 or 75 in concert with the expanding life expectancies. I know some who plan to get by on their inheritance, but they don't realize that their parents are going to probably spend it first!

June Schroeder, CFP®, RN: Another challenge that is a great concern is the health care worker shortage: doctors, nurses, support staff. Some of this is in part due to the declining birth rate that has been evident in our society for years and some is due to the many alternative careers women now pursue. When I was in high school girls planned to be teachers, nurses or moms! Perhaps time will show us that this is going to work itself out with working Boomers, foreign workers or better preventative care.

Mike Busch, CPA, CFP®, CEBS: Our clients frequently ask about the viability of the Social Security system and its impact on their retirement. I think reliance on Social Security has to decrease. However, unlike some, I don't believe that Social Security is going to go away completely. I account for the decreasing value of Social Security benefits in my planning by inflating living expenses at a faster rate than Social Security cost-of-living adjustments.

Retiring Baby Boomers have several additional challenges as well. Medical costs continue to consume more and more of retirees' resources. Increased life expectancies have a double impact. Not only are additional medical costs incurred to achieve these increased life expectancies, but Baby Boomers must plan for a longer period of retirement which requires more funds. Many Baby

Boomers are deciding they want to retire or work part-time prior to age 65. Obtaining affordable medical insurance during the period from retirement until reaching eligibility for Medicare is a growing problem with no easy solution. Finally, I think it is important for Baby Boomers to re-evaluate their concept of retirement. Society has trained them to think that they are supposed to quit working and devote their life to leisure from age 65 on. I have seen countless men who deteriorate physically and mentally very rapidly upon retiring. They have never considered that they don't have to stop working just because they reach age 65. And if they do want to quit working, they have not adequately planned how they will keep themselves occupied with charitable work or other endeavors that give them a sense of purpose.

Chad Starliper, CFP®, CLU, ChFC, EA: Maybe Social Security will continue for this group of retirees, but something will give eventually, just like all Ponzi schemes do. That income will have to come from personal assets somewhere.

The biggest challenge is planning for such a long retirement with, typically, less outside income from Social Security or pensions. A higher percentage of income will have to come from investment portfolios, and come for a longer time. That changes the whole game.

When Social Security was first enacted, people were living a couple of years past the retirement age. There weren't these thirty year retirements—which by the way, means about one-fourth to a third of people's lives are spent in retirement now. When they started getting checks, they also had this nice pension coming in. The conditions now are reversed; they live longer with less.

My personal opinion is that people are retiring too early with too little money. It has become normal to assume retirement at 60, for some reason. And most people we see have very little concept of how large an asset base is needed to support that.

Long Term Care

MARK DIEHL:
In the distribution phase of our lives we are certainly older and are at a greater risk of needing long-term care or possibly even a nursing home. Are your older clients concerned about the costs of long-term care? If so, what solutions do you recommend?

Matthew Tuttle, CFP®, MBA: Most of our clients are older, so long term care is a big issue. I believe that long term care insurance is the best solution in many cases. We find that many of our older clients object to long term care insurance because they think it is too expensive. However, I don't think that's the real reason they don't buy it. These same people are paying for homeowners, auto, and Medigap insurance that is also too expensive. I think what most people learn about money, we learn from our parents. If our parents had a house they had homeowners insurance, if they had a car they had auto insurance. For most people over 65 today, their parents never had long term care insurance because it didn't exist and they didn't need it.

This generation of people over 65 is the first generation where medical science can keep them alive longer and longer; they just can't keep them healthy. So this is the first generation that has this risk to their assets. My generation, just about everyone will have long term care insurance because we will see the experiences of our parents and grandparents and it will become just like Medigap insurance, where you know that when you reach a certain age you go out and get a policy.

Kathy Stepp, CPA/PFS, CFP®: Many clients who have seen the effects of the cost of long-term care on their parents are concerned about meeting their own needs for long-term care. Also, with the recent changes in estate taxes, many insurance companies have shifted their focus away from life insurance and are talking to our client base about their need for long-term care insurance.

We analyze our clients' need for long-term care insurance. In many cases, especially of our single clients, the cost of long-term care is actually lower than their current cost of living. This situation occurs because we work with wealthy clients who maintain relatively high living expense levels, whereas the cost of long-term care is fairly fixed.

For married couples, the situation may be different. If one spouse requires long-term care, that cost is added to the other spouse's cost of maintaining the couple's pre-illness lifestyle. In this case, we determine whether insurance is needed to supplement the investment assets to provide enough income to cover the additional cost.

If we feel that long-term care insurance is warranted, we shop around to find the policy we think our client should have. The insurance products offered today are far better than the early products on the market. Of course, since we cannot sell any products, our clients trust that we are only looking out for their best interests when we recommend a long-term care insurance policy.

Kristi Sweeney, CFP®: I think lots of people are confused about whether they will need long term care and they are somewhat resistant to spending money for this kind of coverage. Those who have had a *prolonged* experience with a parent who needs long term care really understand the need to insure. Still, policies can be baffling and policy rate increases concerning to people who will soon live on a limited or somewhat fixed income. They ask if they really need it.

I help my clients insure part of their retirement assets so they can enjoy themselves more during the Phase One Period of their retirement. That's when they are supposed to be able to enjoy their money and the joy of having time and money to pursue their interests. By funding a pot of money especially designated to cover the very good chance (50% or more) that someday they will need care for some period of time, they are less likely to deny themselves the fun they really can have for, hopefully, many years of retirement.

Long term care insurance helps insure that your assets can be there for your spouse or your children. This is particularly important if someone in your family is financially dependent on you, but many people just really *want* to leave an inheritance to the people they care for. This is one of the comments you hear the most from people in the twilight of their lives! As people approach the time of their lives when health changes rapidly, they hate to think it will all be spent on long term care expenses. They resist getting help because it costs so much. If there is an available cache of money in the form of policy benefits, the best care will be acceptable and affordable.

There are several new ways to fund long term care costs. We are seeing annuities and life insurance with long term care features. Sometimes, by combining two types of policies, you spend more and really end up with a modified benefit. I prefer actual long term care insurance policies and really like those that have a cash benefit paid to the insured because of enhanced policy flexibility and freedom to use excess cash benefits to pay for prescriptions or anything else you want. However, I think basic coverage from a very reliable, highly rated insurer is the most important thing. Generally, I recommend a 90 day wait, at least a six year benefit period, enough benefit to cover at least the average cost of a stay in a nursing home, and an inflation factor to keep policy benefits up to date. If a person can afford to self-insure a portion of long term care costs (that has to grow to keep up with inflation) we can decrease the daily benefit. I consult with each of my clients to help them determine the best policy for their situation keeping their budget and health history in mind.

Wayne Starr, CFP®, ChFC: Clients start getting concerned about long term care in their 50s. It is not unusual for us to hear stories about a friend's parents or their own relatives who have needed long term care that has adversely impacted net worth.

As medical costs increase and as the population lives longer, long term care costs become increasingly worrisome. The best antidote to net worth deterioration is to have more than enough so that the cost of care is not an issue. How much is enough?

The second best answer is to purchase long term care insurance from a reputable and stable insurance company. We suggest clients view the policy as portfolio insurance. For example, a husband and wife buy coverage that provides a $150 per day benefit for a lifetime. The cost is $9,276 per year for ten years.

The couple has investable assets of $1,700,000. The premium consumes 0.55% of the annual return. Put another way, to save the portfolio from having to pay out $54,750 for nursing home costs ($150/day times 365), the insurance premium takes 0.55% of the annual return. That $54,750 comes on top of the already existing standard of living being supported by the portfolio and social security.

John Scherer, CFP®, CLU, ChFC: Most of my clients consider long-term care as a part of their retirement costs and are planning to pay it as they go. It has not been a major concern for the majority of my clients, and in the few instances it is, I utilize the services of an attorney who specializes in elder care issues to help sort out the legal options. I will say that I think that long-term care insurance is anti-selective (meaning, unlike life insurance, there's incentive for insureds to want to use it) and will be an issue of great disappointment in the future, so I generally look for ways to fund long-term care without buying insurance

Dana Sippel, CPA/PFS, CFP®: As long term care costs continue to rise, most of my older clients are very concerned with this issue. How we address this issue with each client depends primarily on the client's overall net worth.

The clients that are of most concern to me are retiring or retired couples who, through their diligent planning and savings, have accumulated a level of wealth they feel will comfortably take them through their retirement years. One of the largest dangers to this couple is if one of the spouses becomes ill and requires extended long term care. The remaining spouse would then be forced to spend down the family assets for the care of their spouse. This may leave the healthier spouse in a compromised financial position. The best solution for this situation is purchasing a long term care insurance policy. The purchase of one of these policies shifts the risks of this potentially disastrous financial event to an insurance company. Typically a 60 year-old individual in good health can purchase a very good long term care insurance policy for an annual premium of $2,000 to $3,000 a year.

The wealthiest clients can afford to self-insure against this risk. Clients in this category have accumulated assets far in excess of their needs for retirement. A long term care expense for these clients would not compromise their financial independence and the long term care insurance policy becomes optional.

The final group of clients are those persons who do not have the discretionary income to be able to afford a long term care policy. If these people require long term care they will most likely end up under the Medicaid system. Medicaid is welfare medical care for those who don't have the means to afford it.

Tom Wargin, CFP®, CFA: I'm still on the fence when it comes to long term care insurance. We have one client who has owned a policy for over ten years and now had to drop it since the rates went up 35%. I fear that is just the tip of the iceberg. It is still a new product and relatively untested. Those who can afford it, $1.5 million in assets, might not need it.

June Schroeder, CFP®, RN: We always discuss the insurance issue with our clients. We map out the probabilities, the costs of care and premiums. We have an insurance agent meet with them-- and us-- if they so desire. Then we let them make a decision. Some of our clients, especially the nurses interestingly, have decided against it. My husband and I have one-- he had triple bypass surgery last year and three other hospitalizations, so we might need it sooner than later. Tom and his wife do not own a policy.

Tom Wargin, CFP®, CFA: There are a number of alternatives to reduce the risk of the cost increases. One is the employer sponsored plan perhaps with an individual supplement. Another is a facilities only or a catastrophic plan. Each carries with it short-comings but does offer some protection. We might need to adjust the client's income or spending needs if they decide to purchase a policy and then plan for rate increases.

June Schroeder, CFP®, RN: The best advice is to keep mentally and physically active.

Chad Starliper, CFP®, ChFC, CLU, EA: Not only are our older clients concerned about long term care expenses—and also how the care is delivered— but so are the kids and grandkids. Ultimately, this affects the whole family on a financial, emotional, and spiritual level. I think the publicity and experiences of a lot of people have helped make it a mainstream issue to plan for—kind of a dinner table-level confirmation.

You really have to be forward looking in this area because the time of the care and the cost of the care are so far into the future for most people. The costs of this care are estimated to be rising at about 5% annually—about twice the rate of inflation. The time to start making arrangements is before you need it, and before the options start to disappear due to money, age, or health.

The most straightforward way to manage this risk is through long term care insurance. It would depend on where your clients live, but we'll typically oscillate around $150 per day benefit for our folks. We usually like to see some inflation protection—preferably compounded protection. We've narrowed our list of carriers down to about two or three, only the ones who have been in it long enough to be dependable with claims and coverage.

There are some annuity options for those who might be uninsurable, and there is some cash value life insurance that provides for long term care as well. But these are totally different animals.

Wealthier people may pay for straight insurance, self-insure, or utilize some other strategies with life insurance. One option we're starting to look more toward is the life insurance option for them as a way of recouping some premium costs. To actually get the risk fully insured, though, you need to buy a large amount of death benefit. Otherwise, a couple of years would eat up the benefit—which makes it tough for the middle class to do. There is some pretty good tax precedent for using an Irrevocable Life Insurance Trust (ILIT) to own the policy, but make arrangements for the trustee to pay for the grantor's long term care expenses if need be, if one wanted to try that route.

Randy Smith, CFP®, MBA: Yes, long-term care is a big concern. Most of my clients now have or recently have had a parent in a LTC facility. Without exception, they were not aware of the large cost of this care and the lack of government support. LTC or long term care insurance was not available for their parents, so the children directly funded the care. Many of my clients are high net worth individuals and often can self insure for LTC, but after enduring the costs of their parents care, most purchase a policy. In addition, with actual LTC costs inflating at around 5% per year, compounded, LTC insurance is designed to appreciate with the cost of care. A simple cost/benefit premium analysis illustrates that the need for LTC insurance is a "no-brainer".

Mike Busch, CPA, CFP®, CEBS: Yes, the medical improvements that I alluded to earlier often result in prolonging our lives, but at diminished capacities. This has caused clients to realize that their odds of experiencing a prolonged period of care are increasing drastically and that the cost of that care is also rising rapidly. That being said, long-term care insurance is not necessarily the best solution for everyone. I believe long-term care insurance is most appropriate for the middle-income market. The cost of coverage is generally not affordable for lower income families. And they can generally spend down their assets until they qualify for Medicaid. High-income families may be in a position to self-insure. In fact, for many who have expensive hobbies like travel, a period of long-term care would actually decrease the funds they need for living expenses. Those in the middle have enough assets to protect, but not so much that they can afford an extended period of care. Another issue is the comfort factor. Some individuals may be able to self-insure, but they just feel more comfortable knowing they have the insurance in place--not just to cover costs but also so their family does not have to be burdened with care giving responsibilities.

Diana Grossman Simpson, MBA, CFP®: I work with my clients to make them aware of the level of risk they might face in this area, and appropriate ways to mitigate the risk. Sometimes that involves recommending a client shop for long-term care insurance, a product that can be complex. I generally recommend an experienced insurance agent who can guide the client through the process. The agents I work with know that I will be monitoring their advice, and that I will send them more business if they treat my clients well. As with any type of insurance, I want to make sure my client covers the most risk with the least amount of cost. Occasionally, I am the one who brings up the topic of long-term care. Perhaps the client is unaware of the risk, and I feel it is my job to cover all the bases.

Cary Carbonaro, CFP®, MBA: Yes, my clients are very concerned about long term care costs but the insurance becomes cost prohibitive after a certain age, 70 or so. If you know you want long term care insurance you should purchase it at a young age. I've had clients in their 30s purchase LTC insurance and the policy is paid up in ten years and then they are done! You have to have the cash flow and budget to be able to swing this! I had one client who had an old cash value life insurance policy; he rolled it over into a fixed annuity and used that money to pay the premium on his long term care policy. He had no need for the life insurance anymore. New York State also offers tax incentives if you purchase LTC insurance. I send the tax information to my client's CPA when they purchase it.

Jim Reardon, JD, CFP®: Long-term care may be the biggest costs retirees will face in the next several years. All of us can anticipate having these costs and I don't know anyone who isn't concerned about them. Long-term care policies can offer an attractive way to plan for and meet these expenses. Since these policies came on the market they have improved greatly. Coverage has expanded to facilities such as assisted living which were not envisioned when the first policies were issued. We encourage our clients to visit long term care facilities in order to evaluate them and to become aware of the costs involved. There can be a substantial difference in the cost of services rendered in the nicer facilities.

As a rule of thumb, the premium for your long-term care coverage should not exceed more than 5% of your retirement income. If funding the premiums will reduce your quality of life—if it will prevent you from making a yearly trip to see your children or grandchildren for example or seeing a few plays or ballgames with your friends--you can't afford the coverage.

At one time, I thought that if you have sufficient assets to "self-insure" your long-term care, you would not need or want this coverage. However, many affluent people consider the premiums to be reasonable for this coverage and they enjoy the peace of mind knowing this cost is substantially covered by their policy. Having this coverage means they don't have to reserve part of their retirement assets for long term care. It "frees them up" to spend their resources in the fulfillment of their family goals and in their pursuit of happiness.

By adding the "compound interest" rider to a policy you will double the premium. However, this valuable rider takes on increasing importance as you age. With the cost of care increasing at rates above the inflation rate, it makes sense to cover this inevitable increase now at an affordable premium. When these policies came on market in the 80s and 90s they did not offer this rider. As a result people who purchased this coverage when $50 per day would cover the daily cost of a care facility are finding their coverage to be woefully inadequate today.

Buy what you can afford. The average stay in a long term facility is less than three years. If the premium cost is a major concern, select three year coverage rather than five years or lifetime. You can "self-insure" any additional years. Having this coverage for three years should assure that you will be accepted into a care facility of your choice.

 Many people greatly underestimate the value of in-home care. This coverage is much more likely to be used than nursing home coverage. My mother needed increasing personal care as her physical strength waned. At $15 to $20 per hour (in my region) it is more expensive than being in a facility. For an eight hour day this service can cost $150 to $160. There are people who require twelve hours or more of home care for a period of time.

Remember that you are buying an agreement with an insurance company. Your contract is only as good as your insurer. While most state insurance departments have established minimum requirements for companies doing business in their states, some contracts are more expansive and more inclusive than others. Whether the benefit payment is calculated on a daily, weekly or monthly basis is very important. Be sure your advisor is knowledgeable of these contracts and your insurer is a major player in the health care insurance business and one that has highest ratings by A.M. Best, S&P or Moody's. Cheap is not necessarily better. When these policies first became popular around 1990, a major consumer magazine declared a particular company's policy as the "best buy." The "best buy" company was out of business in less than a year. The company was not a major underwriter of health care programs and did not know how to properly underwrite the insuring risk for these products.

Insurers in the long term care market reserve the right to increase your premium as long as all premium holders experience the same increase. If they have underestimated or understated the amount needed to underwrite the risk, they will inevitably seek an increase in premium cost at your expense. Be aware that several pioneering companies in this field have sold their business to other insurers over the years.

Wealth Distribution
Action Plan

1. Create a retirement budget. Be sure to calculate costs you might not have considered in the past. You might want to allocate more money for travel and leisure in the early stages of your retirement, anticipating increased costs for medical care and prescriptions in the later phase of your retirement.
2. You will want to consider the effects prolonged long term care could have on your investment accounts.
3. Consider how to make sure that assets are available to take care of your surviving spouse.
4. Work with an investment professional to develop a diversified portfolio. You need to have the potential for dependable income but also some exposure to growth. Your accumulated wealth may need to last 20 years, 30 years, or possibly even longer.
5. Find something meaningful to do. Work for a non-profit organization or donate time to something you believe in. Pursue a passion you might have ignored when you were an over-worked stressed-out 40 year-old.
6. Spend time with your family and friends. Play golf, tennis, or go fishing.

Section 4
Wealth Transfer

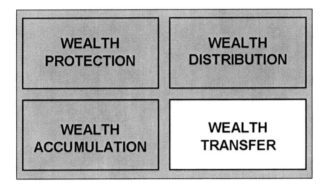

WEALTH PROTECTION	WEALTH DISTRIBUTION
WEALTH ACCUMULATION	WEALTH TRANSFER

Wealth Transfer

Over the course of time we have spent together, we discussed how to protect your assets and how to use your investments to provide greater quality of life. It is my hope that with your accumulated wealth, you can do some good things in the world. Possibly help send your kids or grandchildren to college, or contribute time and resources to those causes that can make a difference in the big picture.

I believe your accumulated wealth can bring you substantial piece of mind. Life will always present concerns that money just can't offer a solution for. There will be illness and death and there is not much we can do about those situations. I don't want you to have to worry about your mortgage payment or how to afford your health insurance premium during those inevitable rough spots.

At the end of your life you will have assets that need to be distributed. How those assets are distributed is up to you. I talked to one couple who expressed no interest in leaving assets to their heirs. If they were successful in their financial planning, they would spend their very last dollar on their very last day on earth. You can just feel the love, can't you?

Estate planning is the process of management, conservation, and transfer of wealth, considering legal, tax, and personal objectives, at death. To be a candidate for estate planning you must meet two criteria:

1. Have assets. (This is you).
2. Limited lifespan.(This is you again).

In other words, everyone needs estate planning. If you do not make plans for the transfer of your assets, the state court will be glad to liquidate your estate after your demise. Dying without a will is called intestate and your state of domicile will liquidate your estate according to their specific formula. Incidentally, their formula may not be exactly compatible with your desires. My recommendation is that you develop your own game plan. Don't leave it up to your state. I know we're treading on sensitive ground here, talking about things that most people would like to put off. Before we move on, let me add that I encourage you to use the services of a capable attorney and possibly the services of your accountant and financial planner.

Exhaustive research on the subject indicates that the average human has a 100% mortality rate. Plan accordingly.

Immediate concerns regarding your estate would include your interest in providing for those closest to you, the ones you love. You're definitely interested in making sure that your spouse is provided for after your death. You want to make sure appropriate funds are available so he/she can have a comfortable and enjoyable life after you're gone. If you have minor children, dependents, or substantial assets, you will want to evaluate all of your transfer options. You may have charitable objectives for some of the wealth you have accumulated over the years. There are certain types of trusts that can provide income to named beneficiaries and leave remaining assets to a charity of your choice.

If you have a child who has special needs, you will want to make sure funds are available for that child's health, education, maintenance, and support. Basically, whatever you want to accomplish, there is probably a solution.

Estate planning can possibly reduce federal estate taxes. Proper planning can also aid in transferring assets in life, as well as in death. If an older married couple would like to start reducing their assets while minimizing gift tax consequences, each spouse could give $12,000 each year to each of their four children. The couple could give a tax free gift of $24,000 each year per child, totaling $96,000 a year. Over a ten year period they can gift $960,000 tax free to their children. This is known as an inter vivos gift or a gift made during lifetime.

Other benefits of estate planning are avoiding probate, meeting liquidity needs, transferring a business, planning for incapacity and completing charitable goals.

Your financial advisor and/or your attorney will need quite a bit of personal information to assist you with your estate plan. Typically, you will need to include information on your mortgages, previous tax returns, current wills, trusts, gifts previously made, annuities, stocks, bonds, retirement plans, and all other assets. This includes all bank accounts, real estate, and small business interests. Also critical to an analysis of your estate is existing life insurance. The benefit amount of the life insurance, named beneficiaries, and the ownership of life insurance is critical to your estate planning analysis.

The Process of Estate Planning

1. Gather your personal information. A statement of your net worth would include the fair market value, basis, date acquired, and the titling of all of your assets. You would also need to provide cash flow statements and family information.
2. Establish your objectives. If you died in six months, how would you want your property to be disposed of? Who would you want specific assets, bank accounts, or real estate to go to? Would you like one of your children to carry on your business or maybe a partner that you have worked with for many years.
3. Determine if there are problem areas. These could include issues that relate to liquidity, disposition of real estate or a business interest, or estate taxes and the costs associated with the execution of your last wishes.
4. Evaluate liquidity needs and reevaluate asset liquidity needs every five years for the rest of your life.
5. Establish a list prioritizing your objectives, from most important to least important.
6. Implement the plan using the services of an attorney experienced in wills, trusts, and estate planning.
7. Periodically review your plan. Your estate planning objectives may change, ownership of assets may change, and possible beneficiaries of your estate plan may change.

To craft a comprehensive estate plan you might need the talents of a team of people. An attorney, accountant, trust officer, financial planner, and life insurance agent may each play a role in plan implementation.

You need to consider how to transfer assets to the people you love or the organizations you care about. You can transfer property while you are still living (inter vivos) or after your death. Let's take a look at some ways that you could transfer assets while alive. This may be important for several reasons. You may have been fortunate enough to have accumulated great wealth over your lifetime, and there may be loved ones or organizations that could use your financial help today. Your children or grandchildren might benefit from your gift today instead of waiting until after your death, and you may derive great personal pleasure from being able to help out the people you love most. There are several options that may be effective for your personal situation.

One issue that seems to be on everyone's mind is reducing or avoiding taxes. Gift taxes, or possibly estate taxes, are usually of concern. Certain lifetime wealth transfers are not subject to gift tax. We should also point out that the person responsible for the gift tax is the person giving the gift.

1. The cost of legal support given to a dependent is not subject to gift tax.
2. If you pay money directly to an educational institution or medical provider for the benefit of someone else, it is referred to as a qualified gift and is free from gift tax. Let me clarify. If you write me a personal check for $15,000 to reimburse my college tuition, $3000.00 of that is a taxable gift. If you write the $15,000 check to be payable directly to the University of Texas, it is a qualified transfer not subject to gift taxes. A qualified gift is an option to consider when grandchildren are the benefactors of the gift.
3. You can give an annual gift each year that is excluded from gift tax calculation up to a limit. For 2006 the annual exclusion limit is $12,000. A husband and wife could elect gift splitting and give $24,000 a year to any one person in a year. There are some special steps required to utilize gift splitting and, as always, I suggest you seek the counsel of a tax professional or your attorney.
4. The ability to disclaim an asset that you have inherited, allowing it to pass to the contingent beneficiary. This enables you to transfer the property as long as you have enjoyed no economic benefit and you have exercised your option to disclaim in the manner and time frame as required by law.
5. Probably one of the greatest ways to transfer wealth is through the unlimited gift to spouses.

Gifts during your life can be given to charities. If an organization enjoys tax free status, the organization can sell donated appreciated stock and not pay capital gains on the appreciation. You might have purchased a stock ten years ago and over the last decade the stock has appreciated 100%.

There are many benefits to making lifetime gifts. One of the concerns to people interested in estate planning is the federal estate tax. There has been much talk about doing away with the estate tax and I am convinced the future of the estate tax largely depends on what political party is controlling Washington at any given time. For 2006 the current estate tax rate is 46%, down from 47% on 2005 and 48% in 2004. For 2006, the estate tax kicks in on an estate valued over $2,000,000.

As an example, let's say you have accumulated $4,000,000 in assets and you are not particularly optimistic about your long-term prospects. You have three children, four grandkids, and a charity that you would like to benefit from some of your good fortune. Over your remaining years, you could gift assets to your children and grandchildren. You might choose to use the 2006 annual gift exclusion of $12,000 and give each of your three children $12,000 a year, totaling $180,000 over the next five years. You could elect to pay your grandchildren's college tuition by paying the tuition directly to the college. Due to your philanthropic orientation, you made five very substantial annual donations to Habitat for Humanity. On the day you pass away, your total estate is now valued at $1,900,000. Your estate is no longer vulnerable to the federal estate tax, according to today's law. More importantly, your financial gifts have touched the lives of those around you.

You will need to visit with your attorney to help you understand what actually defines a completed gift. Generally, you cannot have any incidence of ownership or control over the asset. If I say that I am giving you an automobile, but I reserve the right to ask for the automobile back, it is not a completed gift.

If I create a revocable trust, that is not a completed gift. Revocable means that I can change my mind, I can revoke or terminate the trust for any reason. A revocable trust can be effective for avoiding probate if the terms and beneficiaries of the trust are carefully spelled out and properly funded.

Another type of trust arrangement is the irrevocable trust. If you create an irrevocable trust, it is a completed gift. If the trust is set up correctly, assets owned by the trust will avoid probate and possibly any estate tax. But beware, any assets placed into an irrevocable trust are a completed gift.

A recent survey by AXA Advisors reveals a large share of Baby Boomers -- 66% -- feel it's important to create an inheritance for their heirs or for a charity. Among those who plan to leave behind an estate, 76 percent said they plan to leave at least $100,000 and three-quarters of respondents (76%) believe they will be able to achieve their goal.[25]

Even though you may feel that you do not have money to leave to your children, estate planning is required to make sure your surviving spouse is adequately provided for. Remember different states have different ideas on how assets should be divided between surviving children and spouses. Furthermore, if you have children from a previous marriage or your spouse has children from a previous marriage, issues can become cloudy very quickly.

I can tell you from personal experience that every item that you own has special meaning to one or more of your children. Your mahogany desk was like a throne to your son. When he was a little boy he would come into your study and, as you sat in your desk chair, you looked like a giant to a small six year old boy. Many times when you were working in the yard he would sneak into your study, sit in your chair and imagine he was you. And yes, he would spin around in your chair when no one was looking. Looking back, it seems like just yesterday when your daughter, barely three feet tall, tried to help you set the formal dining table on those special occasions. You were always terrified that she was going to drop one of your pieces of fine china. You knew that she really, really wanted to help, so you reluctantly let her.

Your mahogany desk, your fine china, your dining table with room for ten, means so much to your children. Years after you're gone, your adult son will sit at that desk and maybe pull his own little boy up in his lap. Maybe they'll spin around in that chair together. On Thanksgiving, your daughter and granddaughter will set that same dining room table with the china that always meant so much to you. These pieces of furniture are just things, but after you're gone they will serve as reminders of you, as a way for your children to share stories about you and to reconnect with the vital role you played in their lives.

Wealth transfer means so much more than money or bank accounts. After your gone, your material possessions have a special meaning for those you leave behind. Whether you're concerned about providing for a surviving spouse or which daughter gets your fine china, estate planning is necessary and often unpleasant to think about. I wanted to start our advisor discussion by asking Jim Reardon, attorney and CERTIFIED FINANCIAL PLANNER™, to share his experiences.

Estate Planning Advisor Roundtable

MARK DIEHL:
Jim, as an attorney who also happens to be a CERTIFIED FINANCIAL PLANNER™, I imagine you discuss estate planning in detail with your clients.

Jim Reardon, JD, CFP®: Absolutely. Until recently, it was the practice of the drafting lawyer to draft the documents and then to be removed from the process for months and years at a time. A survey taken several years ago revealed that the typical estate attorney met with an estate planning client once in nineteen years. While that paradigm is changing, the financial planner who meets with a client more frequently is in an excellent position to follow the plan documents and see to the orderly management of the estate. Changes in estate tax laws and other legislative enactments will affect these documents. It is very important that estate planning documents be updated when you move to a new state. One of the best services an advisor can provide is to recognize when a client's documents need to be updated by an attorney.

The prospect of death is not a pleasant topic. For some people it is taboo. Very few people under the age of 45 have executed estate planning documents. Even in this day and age, half of the people in America will never create a will or trust. If they have a will or trust document, it is usually outdated. There are people who think that if they have a will or trust documents drafted, they are covered for life. Many people don't know the difference between a will and a trust. Many people who have had a trust created have never put their assets in their trust--in effect, their trust is an empty document.

Creating an estate plan is one of the most unselfish things you will ever do. You do not create a will or trust to benefit yourself--you do it for the benefit of your spouse, your children and/or to create a legacy that will live on after you are gone. We find that people become most receptive to the idea of estate planning when they have their first child or when they begin to think about retirement.

We begin by discussing the estate planning tools. A will is a document that guarantees that your estate will be probated. In effect, it is a letter to the probate judge explaining your last wishes to the court. In order to understand this, it is important to know that the probate process is designed to assure that your last wishes are carried out. It is a process to conserve and protect your assets from others until they can be distributed to your heirs. Transactions must be carried out by your executor and justified to the court in open session by your lawyer. Therefore, the will is a public document which is available to public view. While probate is an important safekeeping process, it is highly public, it can be expensive and it can be lengthy. In recent years, the trend has been to avoid the probate process unless there is a good reason for it.

As an alternative, a trust document creates a trust for your assets and puts the administration of the trust in the hands of trustees. While the trust concept is new to many people, it is an ancient and time honored practice that has been used by wealthy individuals for the safekeeping of assets for centuries. It is reported that Anglo Saxon trusts were first put in place during the Crusades so that a knight's estate could be protected while he was off fighting a war. In recent years, Middle Americans have adopted revocable "living trusts" as the estate plan of choice.

Living trusts are often used to:
- Avoid probate.
- Reduce or eliminate estate taxes.
- Protect the privacy of the trust maker.
- Provide for the continuing administration of assets for the benefit of spouse and children.

While I tend to favor the use of living trusts for my clients, it is important to point out that wills can be very appropriate, particularly for small estates and young couples. There are not as many safe-guards for trusts so it is important to choose trustees wisely. The creation of trust documents is usually more costly than the drafting of simple wills.

There are a variety of probate avoidance methods available for people with wills and trust provisions can be added or included in a will for administration purposes or estate tax planning. Even if you have trust documents, your attorney will draft a provisional will known as a "pour-over" will to address matters just in case all of your assets don't get into your trust. Think of it as a letter asking the court to "pour over" your assets to your trust.

Estate planning involves more than just the drafting of wills and trusts. These documents don't empower people to act on your behalf if you become disabled or incapacitated. They do not empower people to make heath care decisions for you and they do not give final directions in the event of terminal illness. Prudent estate planning requires that powers of attorney and other documents be prepared for these purposes.

Once the pros and cons have been discussed and the attorney contacted, we prepare a complete inventory of all of the client's assets including personal property and life insurance death benefits for the client to share with the attorney. Once a draft copy of the will is prepared, we will often review it with the client or the attorney before the final documents are created. When the documents are signed and witnessed, we have the attorney prepare a copy for us.

We request that written instructions be prepared for titling each asset to a living trust. This process is very important and we help the client with the entire trust funding process. Since insurance policies, annuities and retirement plans pass according to the terms of a contract or law; they are often not in agreement with the estate planning documents. This means they will pass to the named beneficiaries regardless of what the will or trust documents say.

It is necessary to discuss each asset with the attorney to make sure he or she is aware of any unusual aspects of an investment such as a variable annuity or a variable life policy. It must be clear to the advisor as to how the attorney wants the asset titled to the trust. Costly mistakes can occur during the funding process and I request written instructions from the attorney as to how to proceed.

Estate planning is one of the most important things you can do for your family. Don't entrust it to an amateur. Do not have your documents prepared by attorneys who do not specialize in estate planning. Do not use "boiler plate" contracts or "do-it- yourself" forms. Do not put yourself in the hands of an advisor who recommends that you save taxes by buying a lot of life insurance without reviewing the recommendation with your estate attorney, your accountant and your trustees. While life insurance is a valuable tool for estate planning, it is often not the only tool.

MARK DIEHL:
Do you have discussions with your clients regarding their need for up to date wills and estate planning?

June Schroeder, CFP®, RN: That is standard procedure. It is part of our review sessions. We discuss updating beneficiaries, financial and health care powers of attorney and revising wills or trusts when necessary. We encourage them to rethink their plan, especially when there have been changes in their life, like births, deaths, divorce.

Tom Wargin, CFP®, CFA: Right! We have one client who has been divorced for years and his former wife is still his beneficiary. Perhaps now that he is getting married again, we can get him to make some changes!

June Schroeder, CFP®, RN: Sometimes I think it will take dynamite to get clients to take this issue seriously! My aunt, a woman with two masters degrees, died intestate. I know she would have wanted a different disposition of her assets than what happened. Her partner of 50 years did not inherit a dime, had to move out of the house, while a dozen far flung nieces and nephews split it all.

Kathy Stepp, CPA, CFP®: Because we provide comprehensive financial planning on an ongoing basis, estate planning is always a topic for discussion in any of our regular quarterly meetings. As a rule, clients would like to do their estate planning once and then never have to look at it again. It is not the most pleasant exercise, and their own mortality is not always the clients' favorite topic.

However, we keep estate planning and all the related wealth-transfer issues on our meeting agendas. Changes in family structure or tax laws make it necessary to revisit the estate plan. On the other hand, some clients may wish to make changes to the distributive clauses of their documents when they understand the actual dollar amounts that would pass to their beneficiaries under their current plan or lack of plan.

We consider it our job to help our clients through the estate planning and wealth transfer issues from a layman's point of view. We show them the implications of their distribution choices, so they can alter them as they wish. We emphasize flexibility and control in structuring a plan, and although estate taxes can be daunting, we make sure that our clients understand the cost in terms of loss of flexibility and control when they plan for the sole objective of reducing estate taxes, as many estate planning attorneys are prone to do.

John Scherer, CFP®, CLU, ChFC: Absolutely. We spend an entire meeting during their plan development talking about their wishes regarding estate planning. While I'm not an attorney and don't provide legal services, discussing these issues before clients meet with a lawyer helps them to clarify in their mind what they really want. It's impossible to be financially set without having estate affairs in order.

Chad Starliper, CFP®, ChFC, CLU, EA: Oh, yes! That's really just automatic stuff that starts from the moment we start working with them. We call it the basic estate package, which would be wills, powers of attorney, health care powers of attorney, and living wills. It's relatively inexpensive to have drafted.

But we delve pretty far into the estate planning and transfer tax issues as part of our normal engagement, and that goes beyond the basics of documents. This is not typically something that people come right out and ask for, and it can be a little tough to get them moving on it. They might also not necessarily think of our firm as being able to help them. But it's so important that we have to push it along.

It's almost staggering how little planning is done, even for the wealthy who you might assume have all of the sophisticated advisors already in place. I've learned to assume the opposite—that nothing has been done unless I can see it on paper.

Estate planning can be a fun and rewarding topic once clients see what can be accomplished—or lost, for that matter. A lot of families want to leave legacies and start having some fun with it. One thing is for sure, the initial estate tax savings discussion is sure something to behold: "They're going to take how much in taxes? You've got to be kidding me!"

Wayne Starr, CFP®: Estate planning, including updating wills and related planning documents is a regular discussion topic with my clients. Since the estate tax is in a state of continual change at both the federal and state levels, clients need to revisit their estate plans on a regular basis. Any major life event would be cause to review their estate plans. Life changing events such as the birth of a child or grandchild, death of a family member, divorce, changing residency to another state, or retirement are just a few of the many events that can trigger the need for an estate plan review. Even if none of these trigger events have occurred, there may be other reasons to review estate plans. Some of the ancillary estate planning documents, such as Advanced Medical Directives, may require language changes due to court decisions and/or other legislative changes. Having the proper language in these documents is crucial to allow the designated person to carry out the wishes of the designee with the least possible difficulty.

One of the biggest traps for the unwary is incorrect or incomplete beneficiary designations. Because the distribution of life insurance policy proceeds and retirement plan distributions are controlled at death by beneficiary designations and not the estate documents, the accuracy of these documents is most crucial. Due to the increasing proportion of clients' estates comprised of retirement plan assets, correct beneficiary designations have taken on an increased importance. Estate planning is such a critical piece of an overall financial plan. With proper planning a couple can pass on $4 million in assets to their heirs with no federal estate taxes. Without a well crafted estate plan the results can be costly and disastrous. A good rule of thumb would be to have a qualified individual review your estate plans any time you have a major life event or every 2 years, whichever is sooner.

Kristi Sweeney, CFP®: I always talk to my clients about estate planning when I meet with them. Along with this discussion, I feel that living wills, medical and financial power of attorney are very important.

I urge clients to consider how they want to leave their loved ones. An attorney once said that you do not want to leave your loved ones worse off the day after you die than the day before you die. On all sorts of levels, your will and estate plan is the last word you have and it is how you will be remembered by those you care the most about. It is not just about money but, in my experience, money is still a big measure of love. For instance, what will your child think when you say in your will "I love you just as much as Tommy, but you don't need money as much as Tommy, so I left you my silverware."

Almost everyone should do a will unless they have no dependents and no assets- like your nineteen year old college student. Yet, everyone over age eighteen must consider how they want to live out their lives if they cannot care for themselves. In that respect, living wills, medical and financial power of attorney are very important. In our state and many others, a booklet called *Five Wishes* (www.fivewishes.org) allows even young people to express their wishes for medical care if someday they cannot make decisions for themselves. More people are aware of this thanks to the much publicized recent Terri Schiavo case.

Though everyone should have a will, my special needs clients must do wills and estate planning. They have to set up a viable plan for a child or other loved one who cannot take care of himself for the rest of his life. Families need to protect any inheritance designated to someday benefit that person with a disability or vulnerability. If they leave more than $2,000 directly to a person who would otherwise be eligible for government benefits, that dependent may have to spend the entire inheritance before regaining eligibility and possibly losing some very important medical or housing benefits. But money can be left to benefit that person and supplement their needs without losing control of how these funds can be distributed at the death of the disabled person. I guide these families and help them understand their choices and the critical nature of the special estate planning they will need so they are prepared to see an attorney. I recommend certain attorneys who are knowledgeable in special needs planning to help them designate an appropriate trust (supplemental needs/ discretionary trust) inside their will. Sometimes they need a revocable living trust. At times, planning comes too late and they need to help establish a "pay back" trust. Opening up a Special Needs Trust by the grantor is a way for other family members to leave assets for the benefit of that person with special needs. I urge families to consider how they want to leave their loved ones and whether they have the funds needed to preserve their quality of life as well as leave an inheritance for their normal children.

Matthew Tuttle, CFP®, MBA: We have a lot of discussions with our clients about estate planning. This revolves around updating wills and beneficiary forms, funding trusts that were set up by attorneys, and having conversations about how a client would prefer their children to inherit money---outright or in trust. We also talk a lot about ethical wills. An ethical will is not a legal document, it is a statement of family values and ideas that you want to pass on to the next generation. I am a big believer that everyone should have an ethical will, especially since you do not need a lawyer to set it up. We actually outsource the estate planning to an attorney who is paid out of the annual fee we charge the client.

Mike Busch, CPA, CFP®, CEBS: One of the first questions I ask a client is if they have a will and when it was last updated. It is amazing how many people have no will at all or have not updated their will, even though they were drafted under entirely different circumstances than they now find themselves. I also remind clients that it is critical that they check their beneficiary designations to make sure they are in harmony with their will. Many clients don't realize that the beneficiary designations on brokerage accounts, retirement plans and insurance policies will trump instructions in their will.

Cary Carbonaro, CFP®, MBA: Yes, this is one of the pieces in the financial planning puzzle. It is often overlooked when someone young comes in. I always include it in every plan. The cornerstone of a complete estate plan comprises a will, durable power of attorney, health care surrogate and living will. These documents provide the minimum amount of planning to navigate probate and any incapacity. I attach a *Five Wishes* brochure to address this. This is put out by Aging with Dignity (http://www.agingwithdignity.org/5wishes.html) and the Bar Association.

Five Wishes lets your family and doctors know:

1. Which person you want to make health care decisions for you when you can't make them.

2. The kind of medical treatment you want or don't want.

3. How comfortable you want to be.

4. How you want people to treat you.

5. What you want your loved ones to know.

I gave this to my family members when my grandfather passed away. My wish was that my dad had filled it out. The ways assets are titled is very important for estate planning. I also advise every client about the current estate tax limits and possible estate taxes. The current laws are set to expire in 2010. This is also where we address charitable planning or planned giving. This can really be a win-win. I've had clients set up charitable remainder trusts, charitable gift annuities and private foundations.

Wealth Transfer
Action Plan

Estate planning requires some concentrated thought on your part. The problem is that I am asking you to focus on what happens to your assets and survivors when you die. Definitely not #1 on your list of fun things to do:

1. Make a list of the people you love most and your closest relatives. Make a list of charities or organizations you might like to donate to.
2. If you died today, would you need to provide financial support for a surviving dependent? How long would you need to guarantee that support? Five or ten years, or maybe a lifetime for someone with special needs.
3. If you were in a coma, at what point would you want the hospital to remove life support?
4. Are any of your children emotionally attached to any of your personal items; furniture, jewelry, china, etc.
5. Find an attorney who specializes in estate planning. Communicate your wishes and the attorney will advise you on the best ways to facilitate your last wishes in your particular state of domicile.
6. Discuss titling of property and beneficiary designations on life insurance and retirement plans with your attorney.
7. Review your plan at least every three years or if there is a material change like divorce, death of a beneficiary, or marriage.

Hiring A Financial Advisor

Hiring a Financial Professional

We have covered a lot of material in this book. From this point on, I would like for you to view your financial situation in a holistic manner, with each of the four major components working synergistically together. A book could be written about each of the individual sections of the Wealth Management Quadrant. Instead, I have attempted to give you a broad brush view. Quite a few of you are "do it yourselfers", but many of you will choose to seek the guidance of an advisor. For those interested in working with a professional, I wanted to give you a roadmap or maybe more accurately, a checklist to guide you in your search.

If your financial advisor told you that you could save $48,000 over the next fifteen years by refinancing your home at a lower interest rate, your family would enjoy a quantifiable economic benefit from his advice. If your CERTIFIED FINANCIAL PLANNER™ explained that you could potentially add $12,000 to your retirement account by using low cost exchange traded funds, you would be able to place a definite dollar value on his counsel. In addition to matters of investments and insurance, a qualified financial planner can answer questions regarding budgeting, finance, debt management and income replacement.

If you are considering working with an advisor, you may be wondering what qualities you should look for. What is an advisor, how do they get paid and how much does a good financial planner cost? Are financial advisors really salespeople or is there a difference? Aren't all financial advisors the same? Your neighbor's business card indicates he is a CLU and you are wondering if that is the same thing as a CFP®? So many different designations and so many different letters start to look like alphabet soup. What do they all mean?

Financial Credentials

In many of your business dealings you probably attempt to work with professionals in their respective fields. If you're seeking medical care, you'd find someone with the education and experience to provide the best care for your family. Your general practitioner might refer you to a specialist, someone who has an advanced level of education and expertise in a specific area of medicine. If you wanted to have a trust created for your family, not only would you find a qualified attorney. You might also want to work with an attorney who is board certified as an estate planning specialist. For advanced auditing issues, you might prefer to use the services of a CPA instead of a non-certified accountant.

In the field of financial services, there are over 90 professional designations and many of them do not provide much value to professionals or their clients. It is difficult for financial services consumers to really know what they are getting. We are going to take a look at a few of the flagship financial designations and the education and experience requirements behind each designation.

Our discussion will not include every one of the 90 plus professional designations and our exclusion of a particular designation or certification should not be interpreted as a statement of non-value. I have attempted to include most of the designations or certifications that you may encounter while seeking financial advice.

CFP®--CERTIFIED FINANCIAL PLANNER™ The CERTIFIED FINANCIAL PLANNER™ is the flagship designation for the financial planning profession. To quote an article in The *Wall Street Journal*, "The CERTIFIED FINANCIAL PLANNER™ is the gold standard in the financial planning crowd. CFP®s are required to be knowledgeable about financial planning topics including insurance, employee benefits, investments, taxes, and retirement and estate planning. They must also have at least three years of experience and pass a 10 hour exam."[26] The candidate pass ratio for the 10 hour exam is usually between 50% and 60%. The education requirements to earn the CFP® can take over two years to complete and starting in 2007, newly minted CFP®s will be required to have a bachelor's degree. A CFP® certificant must meet strict education, experience, and examination requirements set by the CFP Board. Certificants must also adhere to a high standard of ethical conduct and commit to biennial continuing education.

The Wall Street Journal, May 31, 2006 ~ To ensure your advisor is knowledgeable, stick with CFPs or, alternatively, folks who have qualified to be Chartered Financial Consultants (ChFC), Chartered Financial Analysts or Certified Public Accountants-Personal Financial Specialists. [27]

CNN/Money, January 31, 2006 ~ The most important thing you want to see is a planner who has CFP after their name. It's the gold standard. This signals the person is a CERTIFIED FINANCIAL PLANNER™ and has undertaken a rigorous 18 to 24 month program in six financial areas including insurance, retirement planning, estate planning, taxes, and investments. A planner must have at least three years of experience before they are certified. A CERTIFIED FINANCIAL PLANNER™ must put in 30 hours of continuing education every two years, according to the CERTIFIED FINANCIAL PLANNER™ Board of Standards.[28]

The Wall Street Journal, October 30, 2002 ~ Some companies are willing to pay for this knowledge. Merrill Lynch believes this training is so important that the company is offering $100,000 to any financial advisor who obtains the CFP designation and also meets certain business requirements within a 5 year period.[29]

CPA--Certified Public Accountant This certification doesn't need much explanation. The CPA designation is easily recognized and is a part of every community from New York to Los Angeles. To qualify to take the CPA exam, a candidate must have a bachelors' degree with a concentration in accounting. Many states require a CPA candidate to have a graduate degree. The CPA exam is one of the most rigorous tests a person can take. Accountants who are non-certified can perform many of the same tasks but CPAs usually command higher fees due to their advanced certification.

ChFC®--Chartered Financial Consultant is a professional designation conferred by the American College. Founded in 1927, the American College is a leading educator of financial services professionals. The ChFC® curriculum includes the study of insurance, income taxation, retirement planning, investments, and estate planning. The coursework for the ChFC® designation is very similar to the CFP®. Both are held in high regard in the financial community and are viewed as broad financial planning designations. The education component of the Chartered Financial Consultant program encompasses eight college level courses and can take over two years to complete. Holders of this designation must abide by a strict code of ethics and complete thirty hours of continuing education every two years.

JD--Doctor of Jurisprudence The Doctorate of Jurisprudence (JD) is the degree earned by a law student. The Doctor of Law or the term JD comes from the Latin phrase Juris Doctor. In order to practice law, an attorney must pass the bar exam in their particular state. The bar exam is an extremely challenging test and is one of the most difficult examinations in the professional community.

CFA--Chartered Financial Analyst This designation is held by investment professionals that specialize in portfolio management. As the name implies, this certification is very analytical in nature and is the education of choice for professionals that manage assets for mutual funds, trusts, pension plans, and separately managed accounts. You will find a large percentage of mutual fund portfolio managers hold the Chartered Financial Analyst credential. Most Chartered Financial Analysts do not work directly with individual clients, choosing instead to focus on the institutional side of investment management.

RFC-- Registered Financial Consultant This designation is conferred by the International Association of Registered Financial Consultants (IARFC) to members who have met certain requirements. To earn this designation, a member must have met education, experience and membership requirements. The member must also agree to abide by its code of ethics and previously have earned one of the following designations: CPA, CFA, CFP, CLU, ChFC, JD, EA, or RHU. One additional requirement that makes this designation unique is that the IARFC requires that the certificant complete 40 hours of continuing education each and every year!

CLU--Chartered Life Underwriter If there is anything you wanted to know about life insurance and estate planning you would want to talk with someone holding this designation. The CLU is a flagship designation offered through the American College. The curriculum includes Fundamentals of Insurance Planning, Individual Life Insurance, Life Insurance Law, Fundamentals of Estate Planning, and Planning for Business Owners and Professionals. To complete the program, the student must also choose three additional financial course electives, totaling eight university level courses to earn the Chartered Life Underwriter designation.

AAMS--Accredited Asset Management Specialist This designation is earned by completing a twelve module education program through the College for Financial Planning, culminating in a comprehensive certification examination. This designation is for the professional specializing in investments and client asset management.

CFS--Certified Fund Specialist The Institute of Business and Finance confers this designation to professionals who complete a 60 hour course and successfully challenge the comprehensive exam. Designees must adhere to a strict code of ethics and complete fifteen hours of continuing education each year.

LUTCF--Life Underwriter Training Council Fellow The American College and the National Association of Insurance and Financial Advisors (NAIFA) jointly confer the LUTC Fellow (LUTCF) designation, which has been earned by more than 65,000 professionals. The LUTCF curriculum covers a broad spectrum including personal insurance, business insurance, retirement planning, estate planning, employee benefits, and disability insurance. The LUTCF program usually requires physical classroom attendance once a week and a student is failed if he/she misses more than 25% of scheduled classes.

COD--Is a fish. I just wanted to see if you were paying attention.

EA--Enrolled Agent To my knowledge, the Enrolled Agent is the only professional designation conferred by the United States Treasury Department. The Enrolled Agent license was first created back in 1884 and now there are approximately 40,000 in the United States. The EA comprehensive exam is only given once a year and is extremely challenging, addressing all aspects of personal and entity taxation. Enrolled Agents are the only tax professionals tested by the IRS on their knowledge of tax law and regulations. Enrolled Agents must adhere to a code of ethics and are required by the IRS to take continuing education.

Advisor or Salesperson?

RIA or Registered Investment Advisor is the term for someone who is registered to provide financial and investment advice, often for a fee. Most practicing financial planners are either registered investment advisors or agents of a registered investment advisor. The RIA is not a professional designation but a registration with the Securities and Exchange Commission (SEC). Advisors who manage assets under $25 million register on the state level with their state's securities department. A registered investment advisor has a fiduciary responsibility to his client. In other words, the advisor must act solely in the best interest of his or her clients. You may be surprised to know that a stockbroker or commissioned insurance agent is not held to that same high legal standard. Let me clarify a point here. The legal standard is higher for registered investment advisors, but there are many stockbrokers and insurance agents who adhere to an equally high self-imposed ethical standard. The smart business person usually learns very early on that the best way to make a great income is with a good reputation.

So how can you be sure what type of financial professional you're working with? It's very simple; just ask. A registered investment advisor or a representative of a registered investment advisor must provide you with Form ADV upon request. Form ADV carefully outlines the firm's fee schedule, type of services offered and brief profiles of the advisors. Also included in Form ADV is an explanation of any insurance, investment or other financial

> I want to be perfectly aligned with my client in an environment of full and open disclosure.
>
> *Nick Nicolette*, President, Financial Planning Association

products that pay a commission to the firm. The SEC feels this commission disclosure is important because financial planning clients should know all factors that could influence the recommendations of their advisor. Since we're on the topic of commissions, this may be a good time to discuss how financial professionals can be compensated.

Commissions or Fees?

Your registered investment advisor's complete fee scale will be detailed in Form ADV. Request his/her form ADV early in your initial meeting, so you can discuss any questions you may have. You should know that advisor fees are usually negotiable within certain parameters. For instance, a firm could waive the planning fee based on a certain amount of assets placed under management. Also, you may be interested in knowing that financial planning fees are currently tax deductible.

Commissions Both salespeople and registered investment advisors can be compensated in the form of commissions from the sale of products, though the trend is for registered investment advisors to earn most or all of their compensation from fees. Most insurance products pay a commission and most investment transactions can be structured to pay a commission as well. One characteristic of the commission-only compensation system is that the representative must sell something in order to generate income. The commission system is more transactional in nature.

Fee-based compensation Remember only registered investment advisors and their representatives can be compensated through fees. The term 'fee-based' means that the advisor is compensated through a combination of fees and commissions. The advisor can charge fees and commissions or use a commission offset method. When using the commission offset method, billed fees are offset by any commission earned by the advisor. If the advisor charges $2000 to craft a financial plan and subsequently earns a $500 insurance commission, the fee offset client would then owe $1500. An advisor could prefer to be a fee-only planner but certain products necessary to a sound financial plan do pay a commission. Long-term-care insurance, disability insurance, and most life insurance products pay a commission. The advisor can either write the insurance or refer it away to another insurance agent.

Fee-only is quite simply the purest way to do business and it takes a bit of courage on the part of the advisor. Imagine you are a fee-only advisor and after meeting with a wealthy client, you determine that the investor needs a $1 million fixed annuity. The average commission on a fixed annuity might be 4% or 5%. By sticking to your fee-only guns, you are going to have to refer away a $40,000 commission. Ouch! Also, many clients need disability insurance, life insurance, or long-term-care insurance, which are all commission paying insurance products.

When working with a fee-only financial planner, you can be sure that his/her advice is not influenced by the possibility of earning a large commission. There are four common fee methods utilized by fee-only registered investment advisors:

1. **Assets Under Management (AUM)**. The client usually pays a flat percentage fee based on the dollar amount of assets managed by the advisor. Since the advisor is compensated based on the value of assets under his/her management, if the account grows from $500,000 to $1,000,000 the advisor gets a pay raise. This fee method places the advisor on the same side of the table as the client. Since this is not a transaction based relationship, if the advisor recommends that the client move from one investment to another, the cash register does not ring and no commission is paid. A common fee is slightly less or slightly more than 1% of assets under management, based on the total dollar amount of invested assets. Some advisors may charge a minimum AUM fee. AUM fees are usually billed quarterly. For instance, a financial planner may charge 1% of assets under management with a minimum of $250.00 billed each quarter. Obviously 1% of $100,000 is $1000. $1000 billed quarterly is $250.00 each quarter. If the client withdraws money from her account and the balance is now $85,000, $250 billed quarterly is equal to 1.175%, still competitive.

2. **Planning Fee** The registered investment advisor will use an industry approved analytical software program. The software will function based on input using client financial information. Most programs create a gap analysis between desired long-term goals and the client's current financial situation. Depending on the complexity of the client's situation, a planning fee can be as low as $500 or as high as $5000.

3. **Hourly Fee** Registered Investment Advisors and financial planners can also bill on an hourly basis similar to accountants or attorneys. I have seen fees as low as $150 per hour and as high as $500 per hour. One point to consider when paying hourly fees are the academic credentials held by your advisor. A financial planner who is a JD, CPA, CFP®, CFA, EA, or a ChFC® is going to be able to justify a higher hourly fee than one who is not.

4. **Annual Fee** Advisors working with high-net-worth clients often charge an annual fee. This is more common with financial planning clients that have large complicated portfolios and estates. If a client

is seeking on-going financial advice regarding investment real estate, several businesses, estate planning and a complicated portfolio, she would welcome consistent advice from someone she can trust.

Growing in popularity is an annual fee based on your total net worth. This type of fee arrangement seems to be most attractive to higher net worth clients, where the advisory firm is serving clients as their personal Chief Financial Officer.

Fee-only financial planners will usually advise their clients on financial planning issues not addressed by their commission-only counterparts. A commission only representative will not help you analyze you asset sheet, annual budget, or debt concerns. Commission representatives will usually provide advice incidental to the sale of their particular products. This is not a bad thing. For instance if a fee-only advisor feels that a client would benefit from a fixed annuity or some life insurance, he must find a trustworthy licensed insurance agent to refer the client to. Any reputable financial planner knows life insurance can play an important role in a financial plan. The fee-only advisor needs ethical insurance agents who can help his clients with disability, long term care insurance, and life insurance.

As you can see, there are three basic forms of compensation: fees, commissions, or a combination of both. A financial services consumer deserves to know how a financial professional is paid, how much, and in what capacity he or she is making recommendations. Have this conversation with your financial professional.

I asked our expert panel what you should consider when selecting a financial advisor.

Hiring A Financial Advisor
Roundtable

MARK DIEHL:
What qualities should people be looking for when they are trying to hire a financial advisor? Obviously, experience, ethics, and a level of professional education are important. What are your thoughts?

Matthew Tuttle, CFP®, MBA: When hiring a financial planner the key thing is "fit". Is there a good fit between what you want and what the planner provides? The first thing you need to determine is what type of person you are---do it yourselfer, collaborator, or delegator. The do it yourselfer does his or her financial planning by themselves. That's fine as long as they have the skill to do it and they enjoy it, life is too short to spend time on things that you do not enjoy. A collaborator is someone who wants someone they can bounce ideas off of from time to time but wants to make most of the decisions on their own. A collaborator is better off with a financial products salesperson. A delegator enjoys the freedom and peace of mind that comes from delegating their finances to a trusted advisor so they have time for the more important things in life that cannot be delegated. A delegator needs to be working with an advisor who they trust has the ability to handle all of their financial matters.

Designations and such are nice, but finding the perfect advisor for you is all about "fit" and after one meeting with him or her you should have a pretty good idea whether there is a "fit" or not. I am not saying that you should understand the aspects of their job, instead you should have a feeling about whether this is someone you can trust or not.

Some key things you should look for are how the advisor handles him or herself. Is your first meeting all about them and their credentials and products or is it all about you and your goals and values? Do you leave their office feeling inspired or do you leave feeling like you have made dumb financial choices and are afraid for your future? Do they have a specific type of client they work with and a specific method or will they work with anyone and does it appear that they are "winging" it? Did you hear about them from a referral or did you get a cold call? Do they meet in their office or will they meet you anywhere, anytime?

You do not need to understand what it is they do but you can learn a lot about what type of advisor they are by how they handle themselves.

Kristi Sweeney, CFP®: Mark, all of those things are really important. Ask the planner some questions. What kind of client do they target in their practice. In other words, do they prefer high net worth clients? Do they have an area of specialty? How do they get paid? Can you work with them on a limited basis or do they do comprehensive financial planning? Are they primarily looking for your assets to manage? Are they fee-based? Are they fee only? Are they willing to refer you for the products or services you need but they do not provide? What will a plan cost? Do they sell products? Ask to see their client agreement before you meet with them. Has the planner been recommended by someone you know and trust? What do they do for their clients on an ongoing basis? What can you expect from their office staff? What you really want to get a feel for is if this is someone who will be responsive to you and whose advice and guidance you will trust.   Look for someone who will care about you and your financial concerns.

Wayne Starr, CFP®, ChFC: A recent article in the *Kansas City Business Journal* (March 31-April 6, 2006) opens as follows: "Choosing the right financial planner can be a lot like selecting a good doctor. There are good ones and bad ones, specialists and generalists, inexperienced beginners and tested veterans. And, after all, you will be entrusting your and your family's financial health to the advisor."

I would not do business with anyone other than a CERTIFIED FINANCIAL PLANNER™. It is the gold standard. You can check with the CERTIFIED FINANCIAL PLANNER Board of Standards to determine whether or not someone is licensed and is of good standing. Call the Board at 888-231-6275 or go online to www.cfp-board.org.

When you meet the planner (you should interview several), inquire about the following:

- Training

- Time in the business

- Willingness to give referrals (be careful, names will be of best clients- but still worthwhile)

- Range of services—One size does not fit all

- Investment philosophy

- Compensation method- "Will I be expected to buy commissionable products from you?"

- Others in the firm—Their experience level and roles. You want to know who will service your needs and how.

- Compliance with state and/or federal regulators such as the Securities and Exchange Commission

Good answers to all the inquiries is no guarantee of a successful relationship. However, candid answers to your satisfaction is a great beginning.

Dana Sippel, CPA/PFS, CFP®: Beside the three "Es" of experience, ethics and education, I feel the most important quality is trust. Trust is the basis of any good working relationship. You need an in-depth meeting with your potential financial advisor to ask him questions, and get a feel of whether you and the advisor philosophically agree on financial issues. I think most of us get a sense of whether or not we meld with someone. This is crucial as this person will be handling your financial well being and you want your advisor to be on the same page as you.

I also believe that the best source of finding the right financial advisor is to ask for a referral from your family and friends who have a similar financial situation. Family and friends will usually be honest about how their financial advisor is doing with their planning, investments, etc. It also gives you the ability to ask pointed questions and hopefully get pointed answers.

As far as credentials are concerned, there is no doubt that the CERTIFIED FINANCIAL PLANNER™ Practitioner (CFP®) is the designation of choice. A CFP® Practitioner has participated in an extensive educational program focusing on issues related to personal financial planning. A person who is in the CFP® program must pass all their exams first, but does not gain the right to use the CFP® designation until they have completed at least two years of experience in the field. A CFP® works predominately in the area of personal financial planning as opposed to someone who's an insurance agent, an attorney, or some other professional where only a small percentage of their time is designated to personal financial planning.

I guess this brings up the question, "Well, what about my CPA? Isn't he qualified to advise me?" My answer would be a tentative yes. A CPA (of which I am one) should be able discuss most aspects of financial planning. The main advantage a CPA would have is a firm grasp of your numbers. I would advise if you're using a CPA that they also have the PFS designation which is a Personal Financial Specialist. This is a designation a CPA can get which means they have additional education in personal financial planning, going beyond the general scope of accounting.

To reiterate, the main thing you want in seeking a financial advisor is someone you can trust, someone who understands your financial picture, where you want to go and has the expertise and experience to implement the plans to achieve your goals.

Cary Carbonaro, CFP®, MBA: Most people agree the following FIVE C's are fundamental factors to consider when choosing a financial advisor:
- Competency: As evidenced by educational background, experience, and credentials.
- Comprehensive Continuing Education: The standard in the industry is set by NAPFA, the National Association of Personal Financial Advisors. NAPFA requires 60 hours for every two-year period with strict distribution requirements across the various topic areas of financial planning.
- Compliance: Is the advisor in compliance with the law, both now and also in the past?
- Conflict-free compensation: Has the advisor minimized potential conflicts of interest to the extent possible, e.g. by operating on a completely Fee-Only ™ basis, by declining business relationships or employment situations that affect objectivity, and by thoroughly disclosing potential conflicts of interest?
- Chemistry: Do you feel comfortable with and trust the advisor? Ethics and values of the advisor are very important.

Jim Reardon, JD, CFP®: This profession abounds with people who have honesty, character and integrity. There are those who are continually striving to learn and to grow in order to reward and justify your faith in them. You will find them actively involved in their professional organizations and frequently enrolled in programs that prepare them to serve your needs better.

Many people are attracted to financial planning from the ministry and from the ranks of teachers and social workers because of the desire to counsel and to serve. I once heard a colleague described as a man who was born with "a servant's heart." That's what you are looking for in your advisor and you will know when you have found him or her.

Diana Grossman Simpson, MBA, CFP®: I encourage prospective clients to "shop around". It is critical that the client is comfortable with, and feels they can trust, the advisor. There has to be a great rapport, because ideally the relationship will last a long, long time. The best way to find some advisors to interview is to ask friends, family and/or coworkers who they use. But even if it is a recommendation from someone you know, it is a good idea to do a background check. The NASD, SEC, and Better Business Bureau all offer such services on financial professionals. If you are meeting someone who was not a referral from someone you know, don't hesitate to ask for names of current clients who would be willing to talk about their experiences. By far, the best clients are the ones who know what they want and communicate their expectations. As hard as we try, we are not mind readers, and unmet expectations can ruin any relationship. I would recommend that they think carefully about what they are looking for prior to meeting with a potential advisor, and then ask specific questions. If you want to make sure that the office hours are convenient for your schedule, ask about that. If you are concerned about how an advisor gets paid, ask him directly. The advisor should be open to discussing all aspects of his business with you. If you communicate your expectations clearly and those expectations are not met, move on.

John Scherer, CFP®, CLU, ChFC: Obviously, having professional education is very important. I wouldn't consider working with a person who did not have the CERTIFIED FINANCIAL PLANNER™ designation. I have multiple designations, and to me the CFP® is the standard when it comes to professional certification. Just because an advisor has the CFP® certification does not make him a good advisor, but why would you want to work with someone who is not a CFP® certificant?

One of the most important things that I would want to know if I was a consumer is how much I'm paying my advisor for advice. Whether it's on a commission only, fee and commission combination, or strictly fee only basis, the only way to assess whether the value of the advice is worth the cost is if you know how much it cost. More often than not when I talk to prospective clients and ask them how much they're paying their current advisor, they don't know. You know how much you pay your attorney and your accountant, you should know how much you pay your financial advisor, too.

Also, I'd want an advisor who has a fiduciary obligation to act in my best interests. Most insurance agents and stockbrokers have contracts which obligate them to their companies, not to their clients. I'd want an advisor who has a contractual obligation to me, not to a brokerage firm or insurance company.

Also, when looking for a financial advisor, people should be sure to ask for references. And not just client references – any advisor, good or bad, can come up with two or three clients who think they're doing ok. The problem is, clients only have experience with that one advisor, or maybe an advisor or two before the current one. It's very important to ask for references to other professionals – attorneys, accountants, and other planners. Those people see the work of many different advisors in the course of their jobs, and they have a better frame of reference as to who provides real value to clients.

Kathy Stepp, CPA/PFS, CFP®:   I think it is important to find a financial planner who not only has the basic education, credentials and experience, but one who has strong listening and communication skills. A planner who is prone to giving textbook answers may not have the skills needed to tailor his or her recommendations to the particular client's needs. Likewise, without the ability to communicate recommendations effectively, the planner may leave the client confused about the recommendations and paralyzed into inaction.

The planner should also be motivated to act in the client's best interest at all times. While this seems like an ethical issue and one that every planner would insist describes his or her business approach, the truth is that if a financial planner is an employee of a company, the planner's first fiduciary duty is to the company, not to the client. In many cases, there is not a conflict between the planner's duty to the company and his or her duty to the client, but sometimes a conflict arises. The prospective client should clearly understand this potential for conflict.

Mike Busch, CPA, CFP®, CEBS: Mark, all of the things you just mentioned are important. In addition, I think people should look for an advisor who will take the time to educate them and will not talk down to them or over their head. They should look for an advisor who talks about risk as much as he talks about return. And most importantly, I think people should trust their gut feeling of who they feel they are most comfortable with and who has their best interests at heart.

Tom Wargin, CFP®, CFA: Personality is important too. We mesh well with some and not with others. In fact June might relate better to one person and I to another. That's why our team approach works well. I find that it helps to find a connection which can help in fostering the compatibility needed for a long term relationship. For example, shared or common life experiences like care-giving for an elderly parent, raising teenagers, or even coming from the same neighborhood or background provide fertile ground for the "bare-all" communication we need to do our jobs well.

June Schroeder, CFP®, RN: "Bare-all" is right. A client needs to be comfortable enough to open up what I call their "financial underwear drawer" so we can really understand what we are dealing with. That means there's trust and compatibility. A person doesn't want to be talked down to, especially women. Also, some clients might want a good teacher; they want to better understand the financial world revolving around them. But they have to be able to "get it" in their own way of learning or their eyes glaze over. I had a client tell me that she was switching attorneys because she said she could not follow the attorney's train of thought or explanations. People learn and hear differently. Some do well with columns of numbers, others need graphs, some just need to hear a verbal explanation, and some just want us to do what's best for them and don't want to know anything more! Now that's trust! And a grave responsibility.

Chad Starliper, CFP®, ChFC, CLU, EA: The most important quality is finding someone that puts the client's interests higher than any other possible objective. And that culminates in trust, essentially. Of course, that gets into how you know you can trust someone, which is a subjective thing.

The best way to get toward the issue of trust is finding someone that is a true advisor with expert knowledge in their field. Educational background, professional status, and those things help. But I would be looking for an advisor to really lay out their process of helping me with the total financial picture. It should be a discussion about addressing issues in a pragmatic way; laying out the planning process; discussing an investment philosophy; and teaching people how they are going to be better off. There should never, ever be anything remotely feeling like a sale of a product or something that specific. How would anyone possibly know what medicine to prescribe to a patient that just walked in the door?

Once the advisor has shown that they are more about process and more about asking questions about goals and current condition, you've gotten closer to the advisor with the right stuff. That gets to the heart of the difference between brokers who represent companies and advisors who represent clients; both legally and ethically. At the end of the day, we're talking about knowledge and care. Both of those things are internal qualities that the advisor will have.

Advisor Compensation

MARK DIEHL:
I think investment and financial planning clients are perplexed by the many different ways that advisors can be compensated. How is your firm compensated?

June Schroeder, CFP®, RN: Fee-only and that is what is most comfortable for us. It seems to fit our philosophy best. Twenty five years ago when we started the company, interest rates were sky high and we put about half of all investable assets into money market funds and the other half into commissionable products. It was hard for me as a nurse to even do that. If I knew about a quality no-load fund, I wanted to share that information with clients. We charged $25 per hour for planning and were lucky to get that. People were not used to "paying" for financial advice. Over time we transitioned to fee only and have been for about ten years. We feel it is a better way.

Tom Wargin, CFP®, CFA: We "morphed" from commissions and fees, to fee-offset, to fee-only. At one time that meant a percentage of assets under management. We are now also using retainers and flat fees. For example, a client owns investment real estate which we don't manage. That client still needs planning advice and guidance in making personal and business decisions. We charge a retainer - negotiated annually. Another client has a large income, college bound children, but the bulk of the assets are in a pension plan. Flat fee up front . . . retainer thereafter.

MARK DIEHL:
Do clients seem to have a preference, one way or another?

Tom Wargin, CFP®, CFA: Why a client comes to us is critical to the kind of service they want. If they view investing as a series of trades, then they are geared to brokers. Most of our clients specifically come to us because they want fee-only. One client asked us to "save him from himself!" He had no plan, no system and was losing money with overactive trading--chasing stocks, etc. We laugh about the fact that he is paying in part NOT to trade! Sometimes it is hard for clients to make the shift to fees, especially if they never paid attention to them or realized how much they were ever paying. We do FULL DISCLOSURE. Our clients know what and when they are paying us and any brokerage fees. Our ADV outlines this fully and every client gets one as well as notices of any updates.

June Schroeder, CFP®, RN: Often when a new client comes to us we find that planning services were not part of their experience and they need to be educated about what planning is and what it can mean for them now and in the future. I often say that it's more important that you figure out how to put the money aside than where you put it.

When we are solving problems or doing retirement planning it is just that - PLANNING. There is no product involved, but there is a spending plan, a net worth analysis, and goal setting. Then we look at the numbers and add back into the equation the individual's personal abilities and personality so we can adjust the planning - and the investments or products needed - to that person. That's the art of planning.

Matthew Tuttle, CFP®, MBA: We are fee-based. We charge a fee to complete a financial plan and then a fee based on the assets under management with minimum assets of $500,000. If the plan calls for life or long term care insurance we will earn a commission on that.

Our clients appreciate the fact that for one annual fee they can delegate all of their finances to us so they can spend their time on the areas of their life that are more important than money and can't be delegated.

Wayne Starr, CFP®, ChFC: Our practice is fee-only. I have been a fee-only planner for about twelve years. The decision to move to this compensation method came after having been commission only in my life insurance planning days. In my opinion objectivity is guaranteed in a fee- only system. We are not being compensated by anyone other than the client. We have no incentives or obligations to meet other than to provide unmatched client service to our client. That said, any guarantee has to be backed by high ethical and moral standards.

We have had success attracting clients and the fee only aspect is important. In marketing our services, we have had to compete against existing commission only and fee/commission arrangements and do not always win. There are quality planners on all sides of this question. We feel strongly that fee only is best for the client.

Dana Sippel, CPA/PFS, CFP®: Our firm is a fee-based practice. We feel it's fairer not only to the client, but to our firm as well. If we have a client who needs a commissioned based product, we will refer them to another professional outside our firm. Being a fee- based firm allows us to serve our clients based on their best interests. We do not feel the pressure to "sell" our clients products that they don't need because of a healthy commission that will boost our bottom line. It allows us to focus on our service to our clients.

Our clients prefer a fee-based practice. In general though, I think the more people are looking for a true financial advisor, rather than only an investment professional, the preference lies more towards a fee based firm. Again, focusing on the client's needs is of the highest importance.

Cary Carbonaro, CFP®, MBA: When founding our firm, we decided that being Fee-Only™ was the most objective method of delivering financial advice to families facing change. Even though this move was somewhat groundbreaking and less profitable, we believed that the marketplace would reward firms who hold the client's best interest at heart. This prediction has turned out to be true, as we are now seeing traditional commission-based brokerage organizations holding themselves out as advisors or financial planners. This distinction is important because commission-based brokerages receive commissions and other forms of compensation that are not disclosed to the client. As a result, it is increasingly more difficult for consumers to find advisors who are truly providing objective advice. I will refer out a client who needs a product such as long term care insurance to someone who specializes in this area.

MARK DIEHL:
Do clients seem to have a preference, one way or another?

Cary Carbonaro, CFP, MBA: I am not sure if it matters to the client, unless they are seeking a fee-only advisor specifically. I don't want a client that doesn't want to pay for my services. If they feel they can get it for "free" down the block, Godspeed! Most clients don't know the difference from a securities salesperson, insurance agent and Registered Investment Advisor or a CERTIFIED FINANCIAL PLANNER™. The general public thinks we are all the same. I use a slide in my financial plans outlining the difference. The biggest issue is being a fiduciary. As a CERTIFIED FINANCIAL PLANNER™ Practitioner and Registered Investment Advisor you have a fiduciary duty to your clients and they come first. The advisor could be sued if he/she does not honor the fiduciary standard. As a registered representative or stockbroker you work for the firm and you can't be held liable plus clients can only seek restitution through arbitration, not the courts as recourse. If you ever heard of the Merrill Lynch rule, this is what I am talking about. It says that even though broker-dealers call themselves financial planners/advisors, the advice they give is "solely incidental" to buying and selling financial products. The Financial Planning Association has a pending lawsuit with the Securities and Exchange Commission over this. We believe as CERTIFIED FINANCIAL PLANNERS™, our advice and planning is the pinnacle of what we do and advice is not solely incidental to our client's lives. I have taught many advisors from broker/dealer firms and once they get their CFP® designation they are fiduciaries. It is interesting to see where our profession is going. I think clients are going to benefit from this lawsuit and where our profession is moving.

Jim Reardon, JD, CFP®: Over 90% of our income derives from advisory fees. The remaining 10% comes from commissions from life insurance, annuities and long term care. My goal is to be fee-only by the end of 2007.

Diana Grossman Simpson, MBA, CFP®: We are a fee-only practice. In fact, my partner insisted that we incorporate the term "fee-only" into the name of the company so that prospective clients would know this up front. For many years I was a fee and commission advisor, mostly compensated for product sales. Frankly, I wasn't very good at it. If the client was already invested in a product that was suitable for their situation, I would tell them so. Although some products pay very high commissions, these are rarely the most appropriate choice for the client, although it is tempting to want to sell them .

Clients are much more comfortable with a fee-only arrangement. Its not that we don't get paid for investing a client's money – we do, but we are always paid only by the client. So if I recommend that a client look into purchasing, for example, long-term care insurance, the client doesn't have to wonder if I really think they need it or if I just want the commission on the product sale. I think my clients have always trusted me, but I also think it's just easier for them to trust me if I am only working for them, and not a third-party mutual fund or insurance company.

John Scherer, CFP®, CLU, ChFC: I am fee-only and my clients clearly appreciate the fact that I have no products to sell and no sales-related agenda. In fact, the reason many clients first contact me is specifically because I operate on a fee-only basis.

Kathy Stepp, CPA, CFP®: Most prospective clients come to us because they are looking for a fee-only financial adviser. True fee-only advisers are few and far between. To be considered "fee only", the adviser can have no source of income other than the fees paid directly to him or her by the clients. In fact, there are many financial advisers who receive fees from clients but who also earn commissions for products sold or derive income through ownership of a related company that sells products or other services to clients. These planners typically refer to themselves as "fee-based", emphasizing the 'fee' aspect of their compensation. To us, the word that should be emphasized is the 'only'. We only accept fees and no other form of compensation.

Financial planners are unique in that we are classified in terms of how we are compensated. We don't refer to doctors or lawyers as "fee only" but rather by their specialties. Fee-only financial planners should perhaps instead be called "objective" financial planners, because that is our specialty in the universe of all financial planners. We are not connected in any way to any particular companies or products, so our advice can be objective. It is our job to act only as a fiduciary for our clients, because we have no incentive or responsibility to act as a fiduciary for any company instead.

Mike Busch, CPA, CFP®, CEBS: For financial services, I really believe a fee-based relationship is best. As a CPA, I was trained to be highly sensitive to conflicts of interest. I want my client to know that my compensation is not tied to my recommendations or to the amount of trading activity in their account. The fee-based model just seems to be best at putting the advisor's chair on the same side of the table as the client's. That being said, I also believe that a client should be able to choose how to compensate their advisor. So, even though I recommend a fee-based approach, I am structured to be able to work with a client on a commission basis, if that is their preference.

The fee-based approach definitely resonates with my clients. Many of them have told me that locating a fee-based advisor was a priority in their search for investment advice. It has taken some time, but fortunately, the public is slowly becoming aware that for financial advice, commission-based salespeople are no longer the only game in town.

Chad Starliper, CFP®, ChFC, CLU, EA: Our compensation consists of both fees and commissions. Predominantly—and preferably—we work on some type of fee basis, whether that is a flat fee, hourly, retainer, or based on the assets we manage. It's certainly, in our opinion, the cleaner way to do business and helps set us up as advisors to our clients.

Commissionable business is typically going to be in the form of various insurance products we help clients implement, i.e. long term care, or if we think it is more efficient for a client with a low asset base to use commissionable mutual funds to get started.

MARK DIEHL:
Do clients seem to have a preference, one way or another?

Chad Starliper, CFP®, ChFC, CLU, EA: Generally speaking, most of our clients prefer a fee arrangement because everything is out in the open. Occasionally, we'll run into some people that see the "hard fee" and think it is a lot. But from a total expense perspective, it's typically less because they have been used to paying hidden fees in terms of commissions or high internal fees on investments. They can see what they are paying—in dollar terms—and what they are getting in terms of service. It's also more congruent to an ongoing professional relationship as opposed to a sales oriented business.

Like any other profession, our clients are paying us for specialized advice and coaching. Much of the time, this advice has little if anything to do with financial products. Some examples of this would income be tax planning, stock options strategies, charitable planning, and any number of other areas. We help them with these things and charge them accordingly—which, by the way, is a very distinguishable characteristic from those peddling financial products and masquerading as advisors. Professional advice is worth professional fees.

Services Offered By Advisors

MARK DIEHL:
Can you tell me about your practice? What kind of services do you offer? What types of clients do you work with?

Matthew Tuttle, CFP®, MBA: Our firm specializes in Values Based Financial Planning™ for retirees and near retirees. Values Based Financial Planning™ is a program that focuses on basing your money decisions on what is truly important to you, your values. As Roy Disney, Walt's brother once said, when your values are clear your decisions are simple.

Mike Busch, CPA, CFP®, CEBS: I offer comprehensive financial planning services, but I do specialize in investment management. My background as a CPA also provides additional expertise in integrating tax planning for my clients.

My clients range from old to young, business owners to employees, and risk tolerant to risk averse. However, I find that I do work with a large number of widows and divorcees. My experience has been that women tend to talk more freely about their finances and are more likely to share stories with each other of how their advisor has been instrumental to their financial success. As a result, I receive a large number of referrals from women who have worked with me and want to help their friends take charge of their finances.

June Schroeder, CFP®, RN: Women!

Tom Wargin, CFP®, CFA: Delegators!

June Schroeder, CFP®, RN: We focused on women early in our business because we felt they were very underserved when we started our company in 1981. To this day, half of our clients are women, single, widowed or divorced, and the other half are couples, which means that 75% of our clients are women! Average age is about 55. Portfolio size is under $1.5 million.

Tom Wargin, CFP®, CFA: On another plane, most of our clients are not Type A's--they are delegators. Also, they are not looking for a quick buck. Sure, some have started a bit late with the planning process, but we emphasize the fact that we believe that slow and steady, mixed with common sense and balance, still wins the race or at least gets to the finish line!

June Schroeder, CFP®, RN: Our clients are smart people who don't take the time, don't have enough knowledge or just plain don't want to manage their own finances. Some would rather golf, fish or spend time with their kids or grandkids in their spare time. Some are embarrassed about the state of their finances, but that passes when we get started and a sense of relief sets in. We have people come to us who don't know what they need. I describe it as being in a dark room, and they are afraid to move because they don't know where the furniture is. We turn on the light!

Wayne Starr, CFP®, ChFC: BKD Wealth Advisors, LLC does specialize in investment management. We have $1,019,500,000 under management as of February 2006. The firm was formed by BKD, LLP, one of the ten largest CPA and advisory firms in the U.S., as part of their firm's overall approach to wealth management, which we call WealthPlan.

While investment management is a primary service, we are heavily involved in financial planning. All clients are exposed to financial planning in some way. A client may need comprehensive planning that encompasses:

o   Tax and Cash Flow Analysis
o   Education Planning for children, themselves,
     grandchildren
o   Retirement Planning
o   Risk Management Planning
o   Estate Planning
o   Investment Planning

Others engage us to focus on one or two issues. Today, we focus quite a bit on retirement and investment planning issues.

In my opinion, financial planners should be able to deliver comprehensive plans and focused plans in order to meet client needs. Further, even though a client may feel that a topic such as estate planning has been addressed via new documents, the planner has an obligation to probe all areas and to make clients aware of things they may have missed. A prime example is the failure to amend beneficiary designations following the creation of a new or revised estate plan.

Our clients are salaried executives, professionals, and small business owners. Some are long-standing clients who have moved into the retirement phase of their lives. Because of our relationship with the accounting professionals at BKD, LLP we are introduced to a number of clients who are selling businesses to which they devoted many years and are now moving into a whole new phase of life.

Dana Sippel, CPA/PFS, CFP®: Typically, our focus has been on the higher net worth individual. Our clientele crosses a broad spectrum, from business executives, doctors, professionals and small business owners to retirees.

Cary Carbonaro, CFP®, MBA: My firm specializes in holistic planning. Financial planning itself comprises risk management, cash flow management, tax planning, investment planning, employee benefits and estate planning. If you tie your goals and dreams in concert with all of the above, that is true financial planning. I am also a Registered Investment Advisor with several years of experience on Wall Street. I would say I also specialize in investment management.

My clients are younger than clients of most other CERTIFIED FINANCIAL PLANNER™ Practitioners. I have a mix of clients in their 30's through 70's. I have high earning young clients with high net worth for their age. I also work with many same sex couples. My average client account has $750,000 in assets. I also enjoy working with self-employed individuals.

Jim Reardon, JD, CFP®: Our core business is managing investment portfolios for individuals, pensions and non-profit organizations and foundations on a fee for service basis. Our minimum account size for individuals and family foundations is $250,000. (We have no minimum account size for non-profit clients.) Our average non-pension client account is $578,000 which would be about the size of a typical life-time 401(k) roll-over from one of our larger corporate employers in Topeka.

We provide a variety of value-added advisory services to our clients, including individual services such as retirement and estate planning. We offer corporate governance services to non-profit associations, pensions, foundations and other organizations with fiduciary responsibilities to their employees and stakeholders. According to a recent report by the Center for Fiduciary Studies, as many as 5,000,000 people may have fiduciary responsibilities. At present, it is estimated that perhaps as few as 10% to 20% are actually aware of this responsibility.

A fiduciary is "one who manages money for others." Fiduciary responsibilities include the management of employee and stakeholder resources according to established legislative mandates such as ERISA and the prudent investor laws that have been passed in the past few years by most state governments. We are also sensitive to the social agendas of our clients. We screen their portfolios to eliminate investments in corporations that are offensive to their sensibilities.

A growing segment of our client base is law firms and their clients who contract my services as an "expert witness" on financial products and transactional analysis. As a CERTIFIED FINANCIAL PLANNER™ certificant with a law degree, I am often called upon to evaluate a case or to analyze the actions of the parties to a law suit or hearing.

Diana Grossman Simpson, MBA, CFP®: Our specialty is hourly consulting. When we started the company, we wanted our advice to be available to a lot of people, not just the ones who have $500,000 or a $1,000,000. We keep our hourly fee low - $150/hr. – and give clients an opportunity to address the issues that concern them the most. Sometimes, that's just an investment review and recommendations; other times it involves comprehensive financial planning or complex issues, such as tax planning for a business owner or estate planning for someone who has remarried and started a second family.

But that's not what keeps us in business. It is our service to our clients – the relationships that we develop – that keeps our clients coming back and sending their friends. Our clients are generally smart people who either have limited knowledge of the financial world or are not interested enough in it to spend the time to gain the knowledge. They want to do the best for themselves and their families but would rather "outsource" the work to a professional. They come in looking for answers, but what they ultimately leave with is so much more – a resource, yes, but also someone who can help them sort through all the complex financial issues in life--now, and down the road.

Because of the way our business is structured, our clients tend to be younger, 40 to 60 year old professionals with families. But we have older clients too, who are already retired, divorcees, widows. I have several clients who are

CPAs or other financial management professionals who recognize their own limitations when it comes to their personal finances.

John Scherer, CFP®, CLU, ChFC: My practice is a holistic financial planning practice with an emphasis on tax planning, investment management, and personal planning for small business owners. I work with small business owners, retirees, pre-retirees, and other 'regular' people.

Kathy Stepp, CPA/PFS, CFP®: Our firm, Stepp & Rothwell, Inc., located in Overland Park, Kansas, performs only one service: comprehensive, fee-only financial planning. We work with all of our clients on an ongoing basis, on all aspects of financial planning at all times. Our clients are either in or near retirement and have accumulated enough wealth to be financially independent, or they are still working and in the accumulating stage. Either way, they seem to have a couple of things in common: they are good stewards of their money but the level of their wealth results in a certain amount of complexity that is beyond their expertise or desire to manage. They are considered wealthy, but not so wealthy that they can afford to make many big mistakes in managing their money.

We meet with every client at least quarterly, usually in person but sometimes by telephone, since many of our clients live in other places. We think it is important to meet face-to-face with our clients at least annually, so we travel to see out-of-town clients or they travel to see us periodically.

When we meet with clients, we discuss their specific financial situations, of course, but we specialize in understanding the 'big picture' aspects to our clients' lives. Our goal is to help them enjoy their wealth now and plan for the distribution of their wealth, now or in the future.

Chad Starliper, CFP®, ChFC, CLU, EA: Our practice is really composed of two pieces that are fairly separate and distinct. One piece deals with qualified retirement plan design and employee benefit planning, which addresses the needs of various size employers, their compensation packages, etc. On that end, we're really dealing with businesses, owners, and human resource managers. The other side of our business is what we call private wealth management, which is comprehensive financial and estate planning for family groups and individuals.

Within the private wealth management arena, the launch-pad that drives everything we do is the idea of integration—that is, dealing with the various areas of the financial pie in such a way that multiple objectives are dealt with concurrently. Integration emphasizes the reality that nothing happens in a vacuum; decisions made in one area affect another.

Investment management is obviously a large piece to the puzzle, because assets—particularly asset growth—are the engine that drives the bus. To accomplish anything financially requires money. Ultimately, the best-laid investment strategy needs to be married to one's financial objectives and resources, which is what we try to help clients formulate.

Our clients are business entities, families, and individuals. We don't have net worth stipulations like some firms do. If people come to us looking for guidance, we try and see that they are helped. The nature of that relationship determines how we proceed, and how in depth we may go with them. Sometimes they just need a quick answer for an isolated event, and we can do that as well.

June Schroeder, CFP®, RN: We're more like a personal CFO. In fact, we often try to get people to look at themselves as if they were a small business: strive for monthly cash flow which is then put towards investment in the future.

We do manage investments, but not in a vacuum. We involve our clients in comprehensive financial planning, step by step, priority by priority and then we feel comfortable managing their investments.

Tom Wargin, CFP®, CFA: Our flyer states "We seek to provide you with whatever it takes to get you 'there'-- wherever your 'there' might be." Like June said, we do it step by step. We identify priorities and work on a time line. We don't write big, long plans anymore like we used to. They just seemed to collect dust on the client's shelf. Action and implementation are key and life happens along the way, so big plans often become obsolete as soon as they are written.

June Schroeder, CFP®, RN: Taking small steps makes the process less overwhelming and reduces the likelihood of making decisions in haste or out of a sense of urgency. Success at each level builds self-confidence and enthusiasm. I tell clients that we will be doing spring cleaning, one financial drawer or closet at a time! It's like peeling an onion.

Tom Wargin, CFP®, CFA: June likes "peeling the onion" and figuring out the alternative recipes, choices, but I like cooking it--allocating the investments, deciphering the probabilities-- the end results of the recipes that are selected. If we feel we need an additional cook, a specialist for a particular issue, we call one in.

Your Wealth Management Team

Is it possible for your CPA, CFP®, or ChFC to be able to handle all of your financial planning issues? Financial planning covers so many aspects that it is hard to imagine that one person can do it all. It actually takes a small team of people to accomplish all that you need to. We'll refer to this team as your personal Wealth Management Team. Often your financial planner can serve as the team leader or quarterback, working with you to coordinate the contributions of the other team members.

Your quarterback often has a specialty of his own. Maybe your fee-only investment advisor is also a CERTIFIED FINANCIAL PLANNER™. He is an expert in the investment field and his CFP® education enables him to recognize some of the gaps in your financial plan. Realizing his own limitations, he recommends you bring in other professionals to help in the implementation of your plan.

Attorney You own a business with a partner and your financial planner feels that a buy-sell agreement would guarantee the transfer of the business to the other partner in the event of premature death. You, your partner, and your financial advisor meet with your attorney to request his input and begin drawing up the needed documents.

CPA – Accountant Your advisor has also suggested that you consider using IRS rule 162, allowing your company to pay you and your partner an accumulation bonus each year. Your CFP® has helped you decide on an appropriate investment plan but you need the accountant to crunch the numbers and determine the tax ramifications of the new bonus plan.

Life insurance agent When you met with your attorney to draw up the buy-sell agreement, he also recommended that you fund the premature death risk with life insurance. Your CERTIFIED FINANCIAL PLANNER™ has the names of three different life insurance agents that he holds in high regard. Your financial planner discloses to you that he receives no compensation from the life insurance sales or from any of the insurance agents. He also informs you that you can use any insurance agent or insurance company that you feel most comfortable with.

This is how the Wealth Management Team works. It would be impossible for one person to adequately perform all the tasks needed.

The Sandwich Generation

Multi-Generational Planning and
Educational Funding

THE SANDWICH GENERATION
ADVISOR ROUNDTABLE

Americans are faced with so many financial challenges these days. People are having children later in life and a 55 year- old person may have kids still in high school. Due to advances in healthcare, it is not uncommon for retirees to live well into their nineties.

A 55 year-old investor who is striving to save for her retirement may also be trying to fund college educations for two children and possibly even be taking care of an aging parent. As you can imagine, this can wreak havoc on a wealth accumulation program. Advisors usually caution financial planning clients to place financial emphasis on retirement and view college funding as a secondary goal. While a prospective college student can work to help fund college, or get a student loan, there will be no scholarships or loans to help you get through your retirement.

Many financial authors have an opinion on the best way to handle the challenges of "the sandwich generation". I thought you would be best served by speaking to advisors who actually work with clients in developing solutions.

MARK DIEHL:
A term that was coined several years ago is the "sandwich generation," describing people sandwiched between trying to raise and educate their children, at the same time dealing with aging parents. Do you counsel clients on multi-generational planning?

Kristi Sweeney, CFP®:   Really, this is a new phenomenon. Since women entered the workforce in greater numbers, there are fewer "people resources" left to care and nurture those in our families who are more dependent, whether this is our children, parents, or family member with special needs. Improved nutrition and advancements in medical care has exacerbated the situation, increasing the numbers of folks who need care and really putting stress on fewer available caregivers. When we have available solutions to cut down on the impact of our own eventual, possible disability and increased dependence on those we love, we really ought to grab them! We ought to really embrace these solutions. I encourage savings for emergencies, promote disability insurance, and encourage clients to have reliable health insurance. Long term care insurance and, in some cases, special needs financial and estate planning helps take some of the burden off of families and caregivers.

It's amazing, isn't it, that the very thing humankind has wished for eons is ours but we have found that it also causes a burden on society, both socially and financially? The fountain of youth is still beguiling to us as we continue our search for prolonged life expectancy. But it is not without a price. At any rate, we help our clients with the things that impact their lives and this is sure one of those things.

Kathy Stepp, CPA/PFS, CFP®: Some clients must help their parents financially. We recommend the best course of action for doing so, given their particular circumstances. However, it is more common for our clients to want to, or feel a need to, assist their own children financially. This is an area that simply requires experience and getting to know the clients, because there are no right or wrong answers. Many clients feel strongly that they should treat all children equally; others feel that they can treat their children equitably without being equal. It is our job to offer solutions and to provide the clients with the information they need to make informed decisions.

Matthew Tuttle, CFP®, MBA: Yes, we complete Financial Roadmaps™ for all of our clients. The Roadmap plots where they are now financially along with where they want to go, the achievement of their financial goals and fulfillment of their values. The Roadmap experience gives our clients clarity on how making smart choices about their money can help them achieve their goals for the reasons that are important to them. It is also the precursor to having a financial plan. One of our client deliverables is that we do Financial Roadmaps™ for all of our clients children and grandchildren (when they get old enough) to help them get financial clarity at as young an age as possible.

We are also very cognizant of issues such as stretch IRAs, planning for incapacitated parents, etc.

Dana Sippel, CPA/PFS, CFP®: Counseling clients in the "sandwich generation" is a task that can be very challenging. These clients can be weary, not only from the time requirements needed to keep up with their children and their activities, but also by the time needed to help their aging parents with any number of tasks from home upkeep, bill paying, and running them to appointments. While trying to split time spent between the kids and their parents can be a challenge, managing the finances can be an even bigger challenge. Those caught in the "sandwich generation" may find their finances being tugged in many different directions including saving for college, saving for their own financial independence, as well as the possibility of having to provide support for parents who may have depleted their own financial resources. The emotional strain, as well as the financial strain, can be quite taxing and a financial advisor can provide support and encouragement for people caught in this dilemma.

Cary Carbonaro, CFP®, MBA: I have many clients in their 30s-50s who are still raising children and concerned for aging parents. I've had many young couples purchase long term care insurance for their parents. I have had clients that added a wing in their home or purchased adjoining apartments and condos for their parents. I find the children who grow up with their grandparents have very rich childhoods.

I have had children in their 40s come with their parents to financial planning sessions with me. I really encourage this. This way the children know what the parents have, where it is and what their goals are. The parents and children partner in the financial planning process. It is much worse when the parents pass away and the children are in the dark.

Chad Starliper, CFP®, ChFC, CLU, EA: We have some extremely wealthy clients where we are heavily involved as part of a team of advisors, sort of a family office. The entire engagement is multi-generational in a sense. We meet with the whole family, manage the LLC, manage family trusts, talk about personal money, and the whole nine yards.

The regular type clients have these issues as well, albeit less complex. Perhaps the grandparent will want to set aside money in a family incentive trust that stipulates some educational goals. You don't have to be rich to do that stuff. Grandparents seem to care an awful lot about values and family-oriented issues where the kids are concerned.

Jim Reardon, JD, CFP®: The expert in our organization on this subject is my wife Linda. My mother lived in our home for the first ten years of our children's lives. While I spent most of my time solving everyone else's problems as a city councilman and as a struggling financial planner, Linda taught school and took care of three small children and two adults (Mom and me) who sometimes behaved like children.

Linda experienced the premature passage of her own mother and father and the long slow decline of Mom's physical and mental health while our children were growing up. Since we are "late in life" parents, all three of our girls are in college at this writing. We lived the "sandwich generation" phenomenon in reverse order. As such, we feel eminently qualified to address this subject with our clients and family. Frankly, this is not something for which you can find all of the answers and there are emotional issues that will affect the participants for years to come.

Most of our clients are retirees or people nearing retirement. They *are* the sandwich generation. Their children are grown and they have experienced the decline and death of their parents. For these people it is not hard to understand the importance of having substantial assets, the likelihood of needing long term care and the value of long term care insurance coverage. They are determined not to be a financial burden to their children or their spouses.

Diana Grossman Simpson, MBA, CFP®: Developing goals and establishing priorities is an integral part of what we do. If a prospective client does not initially elaborate on the topic of family – parents, children, grandchildren – I'll bring it up in the conversation. Ultimately, wealth is not an end in itself, but a means to an end….wealth is the resource that is available to help us reach our goals. But the resources are almost always limited, and so goals must be prioritized. And most people like having the help sorting through them.

I've advised clients concerning how to leave assets in trust to their children, how to deal with their aging parent who is showing signs of senility, strategies for leaving money to charity without "shortchanging" heirs…these are all topics that are important and need to be addressed. Sure, sometimes there is a great deal of emotion involved, especially when a couple can't agree, but the issues need to be addressed.

John Scherer, CFP®, CLU, ChFC: I do help clients deal with issues surrounding both their parents and their children, but I think that the term sandwich generation is overly dramatic. It's just life, something that must be addressed. One aspect of multi-generational planning that I do think is uniquely important is to foster communication between the generations. Money is often difficult to discuss within families and any work I can do to help facilitate interaction and sharing about finances between grandparents, parents, and children is really valuable.

Tom Wargin, CFP®, CFA: Boy, do we! We both have personal experience in that. Although June has no children, this business and her husband have been the other side of her "sandwich." Sometimes we get calls from children who are concerned about their parents. Sometimes the parents are already clients and bring in their kids or refer them to us. That, more often than not, leads to multi-generational planning.

June Schroeder, CFP®, RN: Recently, we met with a man and two of his four children. He recently inherited money from his sister. The daughter had set up the appointment We will be planning and investing for his income needs and estate plan and also doing retirement planning for his two children and their children. The sandwich generation might be facing financial challenges longer than they like since the kids, like Tom's are prone to return home and their parents are living longer lives!

Mike Busch, CPA, CFP®, CEBS: I find that those in the "sandwich generation" have some of the most difficult issues to deal with. They are responsible not only for themselves, but also for their parents and their kids. When you consider that family issues also have the most emotional intensity, the stress levels of the sandwich generation can be incredibly high. With limited resources, should the parents focus on their retirement, their children's education or their parent's care? Spouses may come from different backgrounds and have different priorities. Some parents want to leave a sizeable estate to their children. Others want to contribute the bulk of their estate to charity because they feel it is important that their children make their own way in life. These issues need to be talked about openly and honestly between the generations so everyone is on the same page and relationships are not damaged.

Educational Funding and 529 Plans

MARK DIEHL:
Do you ever work with clients implementing college savings programs, maybe for their children or grandchildren? There has been quite a bit of press lately on 529 plans. Your thoughts?

Diana Grossman Simpson, MBA, CFP®: I have two preschoolers myself, so you can be sure I've done the research on college plans! Many of my clients have young children or grandchildren, and I try to emphasize how expensive the cost of college will be down the road. This is an area where values can vary dramatically, so I don't assume anything. Some parents are adamant their children contribute to the cost of college, by working, taking loans or obtaining scholarships. They want their children to understand the value of the education. Sometimes Mom or Dad will plan to go back to work at some point so they can earn money to save or pay for college expenses. It's always discouraging to see parents who are not prepared. They are blindsided by the expense and it often means postponing retirement by several years because they accrue new debt or dip into their own retirement savings to cover the costs. My experience has shown me that it is far less painful to plan for college in advance.

I love the 529 plans; they are almost too good to be true. The tax benefits can be significant, and the plans are so flexible. But you do have to do the research to determine which plan is right for your circumstances. My favorite website for 529 plan research is www.savingforcollege.com. The site provides information about all of the plans available and allows you to make plan comparisons, calculate the amount you'll need to cover college costs, and even cost information on individual colleges and universities. Clients are more than willing to pay me to sift through all the available information and make specific recommendations for them. It can be a daunting task!

I also bring up 529 plans with grandparents. Sometimes the grandparents want to contribute to the cost of college, but assume that it is best to wait until the child is college age –or at least in high school- to begin making plans. But the 529 plan can also be a useful estate planning tool under certain conditions, and grandparents who are trying to minimize estate tax liability and provide for their grandchildren's' education are missing a huge opportunity if they don't take advantage of the 529.

Dana Sippel, CPA/PFS, CFP®: I do quite a lot of work with clients who are implementing college savings programs using 529 plans, trusts or Uniform Transfer to Minor Accounts.

First people need to understand that there are two types of 529 plans. The first type is the "Prepaid Tuition Plan" in which you can purchase a unit of higher education for your children or grandchildren at today's tuition prices. This can be used for a public university or a private college.

The second type of 529 plan is the "College Savings Plan". This plan works much like a 401(k) plan--you invest your funds into the plan, you make the investment decisions and the final account balance is available to spend on higher education fees.

There are many advantages to the 529 plans including the following:

- Tax-free earnings if used for qualified higher educational expenses.
- State tax deduction if using your resident state plan (most states).
- Numerous asset managers are available through the various plans.
- Ability to fund large amounts in a single year without incurring gift taxes.
- Ability to control assets that have been removed from a wealthier person's estate. For example, if Grandpa has a large estate and wants to reduce his estate value, he can transfer funds into a 529 plan for his grandchild. The money is no longer in his estate but it does remain in his control.
- The accounts can be transferred to another related person with no penalties. For example, your oldest child decides after a year in college, that college is not for him. At that point you can transfer the remainder of the account to a younger sibling.

The main drawback on these plans is that the earnings are subject to a 10% penalty and income taxes on any amounts withdrawn from the accounts if they are not used for qualified higher education expenses.

Cary Carbonaro, CFP®, MBA: I love 529 plans! Of course, not all of them are equal. There are a few that are much better than most due to fees, investment choices and investment management. For financial aid they tell you to put the assets in the parent's name. With a 529 it is in the parents or grandparents name and the child is a beneficiary. The money you put in a

529 grows tax free if you use it for education. If you start when the child is born you have 18 years of tax free growth. The limit is high on these plans and you can front load gift gifting into the plan. That means you can gift 12K per person per year in 2006. If you are a couple that is 24K per year you can gift to your child. You can always gift more but have to file a gift tax return and it goes against your estate when you die. If you five year front load you can put 120K in the plan when the child is born. If you do this and are able to get market performance of 8-10% a year, you should be finished paying for college. I like the age based portfolios that shift as you get closer to college age. They automatically adjust based on years until college and the asset mix changes. 529 plans cover all college expenses.

One problem with college costs is that they have been rising at a rate almost double normal inflation, between 6-8% a year. Based on the current trend, only the wealthy will be able to afford to send their children to college. My sister is a financial aid officer. My nine year-old nephew, Trystian, said when people plan for college they go to Aunt Cary and when they don't plan they go to Aunt Chrissy. Financial aid is shrinking and college debt loans are saddling parents and students. I had a client with their son in a private university paying 40K a year in tuition and the student wants to be a teacher. I love the teaching profession but to come out of school with 150K in debt and know you are only going to make approx 30K. How long will it take you to pay that off? I told them he should switch to a state school or even commute from home. This gets back to managing your career as an asset. A college education does not equal success! You need to have drive, motivation and passion for what you do in your life.

Chad Starliper, CFP®, ChFC, CLU, EA: I'm not all that excited about 529 plans. They certainly can serve some uses, but the expenses can really mount up if you're not careful—even to the point of outweighing tax-free treatment. As I said earlier, one of the few tax give aways remaining is the unlimited gift tax exclusion for direct payments of higher education and health care expenses. If someone has enough to make large gifts to a 529, chances are they might have enough to pay the tuition at some point.

But for large, simple gifts that need to be strictly earmarked, the 529 can be OK. Especially if you need a simple way of having multiple people make gifts to them. It then becomes an issue of selecting a plan, weighing the costs, and seeing which ones have decent investment selections.

Thus far, I'm not real impressed with most of the commissionable products—on any level. What still baffles me is why they don't eliminate these plans from state-level oversight and just allow accounts to be titled according to the tax code like everything else. If I could set up a regular account as a 529 and go about my business, they would become very attractive really fast. Those administrative layers and fees just bother me.

Matthew Tuttle, CFP®, MBA: I am not a huge fan of 529 plans due to a limitation on investment options, lack of control, and financial aid impact. We use them for clients but do not recommend putting large amounts of money into them.

Chad Starliper, CFP®, ChFC, CLU, EA: It is quite common for us to help families with college education planning. Most families have children, and all of them want the kids to go to college. With the way prices are escalating it's best to get started early, if possible.

Wealthier clients, however, might look at education planning from more of a financial and estate planning perspective—and they already have the money. For instance, the grandparents might be looking to minimize estate taxes and gift money each year under the annual exclusion rules to their grandchildren rather than have it cut in half by estate taxes at death. However, instead of funding an education account with these gifts, they could choose to pay the college tuition directly to the institution free of gift tax. That would free up additional money to gift to a trust and have the trust purchase life insurance on their life. The trust would receive the proceeds free of income, gift, estate, and generation-skipping taxes at the death of the grandparent. This would accomplish a couple of objectives at the same time. It's just an example of what someone might do when college is in view and how planning should coordinate things.

A parent might gift money each year to some type of education savings account and hope that pays for all or a portion of the costs down the road. But these gifts are more or less irrevocable, and tend to come with some flexibility issues, such as where will they go to college and if it's in or out of state. In this situation, outright funding gifts aren't always the best course of action. In my opinion—and this is not a hard line at all—just having the parents invest the money in their own names is not a bad course of action.
Some parents look for ways to shift income to the child at an almost 0% bracket; they could gift highly appreciated securities directly to them or through a

custodial account and pay 5% in capital gains taxes; or they might purchase a condo, have roommates pay rent, etc. There are just so many more things that can be done other than setting up an investment account.

Wayne Starr, CFP®, ChFC: Planning for college funding is a significant area of focus in our financial planning work. We use several computer based tools to project costs for public and private schools. We question clients closely about what they envision for their children's education beyond high school and how much they are willing to pay.

We have been recommending the use of 529 Plans since their creation. Our favorite state plan is the Virginia plan because of the fund company managing the assets. We always begin our analysis of what plan to use by reviewing the tax advantages associated with the Kansas and Missouri plans, where the majority of our clients reside.

Another factor of importance is the length of time before college begins. It seems to make more sense to recommend these tax efficient plans for toddlers through young teens rather than for sophomores in high school.

Finally, we are aware of how these plans are viewed in those instances where student aid is being sought. In our firm, student aid funding is not typically an issue because of the parent's income levels.

Jim Reardon, JD, CFP®: Implementing a program for grandparents and parents who want to further a child's education is one of the most satisfying and worthwhile things you can do for a client. It's all part of what we call "legacy planning" and it is an important part of what we do for a client. Most people accumulate money for the accomplishment of their life goals. It's more than just the money--it's about instilling values and caring for those you love.

While I personally like 529 plans and their potential to reward a young child over the years, I also like what the tax treatment does for the donor. In our state and in many states, the contributor gets a tax deduction on state income taxes for contributions into the state approved 529 plans. While these tax perks are added incentive to contribute to a state sponsored 529 plan, there are some plans that are not particularly good or successful.

One real drawback is the distinct possibility that congress or the state legislatures will implement the "sun setting" provisions on these programs in 2010 and the tax benefits will go away. Often an investor is just not willing to put the money into mutual fund alternatives of any kind. We think Series I bonds can be an attractive alternative. There are no state income tax benefits but Series I bonds are government guaranteed, very safe, reasonably high yielding; inflation-protected, tax deferred and when used for educational purposes, tax free. They can also be used for other purposes (without the tax-free benefits) in case the objective changes.

John Scherer, CFP®, CLU, ChFC: I feel that college savings should only be done after retirement savings have been maxed out. If children want to go to college, there will always be money in the form of loans or aid available. If a client gets to retirement age and does not have enough money, there is no formal aid or bank willing to make a loan for retirement.

529 plans are good vehicles in which to save for college, but again only after retirement is fully funded. An even better vehicle to consider is the Roth IRA. The Roth, like a 529 plan, can be distributed tax-free and the 10% early withdrawal penalty can be avoided if the money is used for college. Plus, in financial aid calculations, Roth IRAs are not counted as an asset whereas the 529 plans do get counted, potentially reducing aid eligibility. In addition, the Roth doesn't need to be used for college as it retains its tax-favored status for retirement, where the 529 plan loses its tax advantage if not used for school.

Kathy Stepp, CPA/PFS, CFP®: Many clients wish to help their children financially without creating a disincentive for the children to be fiscally responsible on their own. They also would like to make cash gifts that will be used wisely rather than frittered away on something they may not value. When grandchildren are involved, making gifts to help with their college education is a way to achieve a gift for a specific, valuable purpose while helping their children by relieving them of the future financial burden of college.

We highly recommend using Section 529 Plans for making these gifts to grandchildren. If the current laws remain in effect, the future withdrawals from the 529 Plan account will be tax-free when used for college expenses. If the law reverts to its previous state, then the withdrawals will be taxed to the grandchildren, who will presumably be in a low tax bracket. We believe the likelihood of this happening is slim, but if it does happen, the result is still beneficial.

The size of the gift usually dictates the details of the 529 Plan account. If the gift is substantial, we may recommend that the grandparents own the account. This way, they have the right to make withdrawals if needed. For smaller gifts, we may recommend establishing an account in the name of the child (the parent of the grandchild who will benefit), so that the child can easily make subsequent additions and can make the withdrawal decisions.

Section 529 Plans are administered by the individual states. The states are improving their plans all the time. Therefore, we encourage grandparents to do their homework to determine which plan is right for them.

Mike Busch, CPA, CFP®, CEBS: College planning is a major focus for a number of my clients. And when it comes to saving for college, there really is no better vehicle than a 529 plan. Congress wants to encourage families to save for education and they have created some major incentives to do so. Within a 529 plan, college savings is better than tax-deferred, it's tax free! 529 plans have estate planning benefits as well. They are the only vehicle which allows someone to remove assets from their taxable estate, while still maintaining control over those assets. There was quite a bit of flexibility built into the legislation as well. If a beneficiary does not need the funds for college, a new beneficiary can be named. Even the "worst-case" scenario is not so bad. If the money is distributed and none of it is used for college expenses, you are only subject to tax and the 10% penalty on the deferred gains, not your original principal. It is quite possible that the tax deferral will more than make up for the 10% penalty tax if the funds are not used for education. There has been some concern that the 529 plan provisions will expire if not extended by Congress. While that is true, most commentators agree that Congress so overwhelmingly supports these plans that there is little likelihood that they won't either extend the expiration or make the provisions permanent.

June Schroeder, CFP®, RN: We have clients all over the map on this issue. Some want to finance the entire cost even through graduate school. Some believe in helping but not paying the full freight. Some do not intend to help at all. There might be a disconnect between perception and the reality of what higher education costs and where the money is going to come from.

We talk with our clients about the current costs for a college education. The attitude that "I did it on my own" is relevant but costs for higher education have outstripped inflation and wage increases so we need to once again provide the information the client needs. As with many other issues, things are different than they were before. Sometimes we laugh about needing to make sure the children are able to earn enough to take care of their parents later in life if the markets don't cooperate and things don't turn out like we plan.

Tom Wargin, CFP®, CFA: The 529 plans can be good but they are by no means perfect. They are easy and convenient. There are good ones and some not so good. Like any plan, there are often several ways to solve the problem and fast and easy might not be right.

We look to save outside the 529 accounts, in the parents name or in the child's name, pre-paid or discounted tuition plans. It varies according to the income level, tax bracket, and parent philosophy, public or private school. Then you add in the age, perceived ability and scholarship potential. Our best advice: once again start ASAP!

Small Business Planning

SMALL BUSINESS RETIREMENT PLANNING ADVISOR ROUNDTABLE

Small business owners have unique challenges that must be addressed when evaluating their retirement and wealth transfer options. For the small business owner, wealth transfer and retirement planning is often synonymous. The closely held business is usually the owner's largest asset. It can be difficult to find a qualified buyer in the open market and many times the owner finds a new buyer in his own backyard, in the form of a partner or employee that wants to continue the business. Often business owners want to transfer ownership to a family member, maybe a daughter or son.

As many advisors begin to market exclusively to the wealthy, employees of small businesses can be overlooked by qualified financial professionals. Employer sponsored retirement programs are highly valued by job candidates today but many financial planners are shying away from these smaller accounts. Let's discuss these topics with our Advisor Roundtable.

MARK DIEHL:
On the topic of retirement, do you implement retirement plans for small businesses? If so, what types of plans have you used in the past?

June Schroeder, CFP®, RN: We have used SIMPLEs, SEPs, 401(k)s. It really depends on what makes sense for the business and the owners intentions, including the longevity and retention of employees. Speaking of that, we need to update our plans. You know about the cobbler's children having no shoes? Well, financial planners often need a financial planner to get them to do their own plans!

Matthew Tuttle, CFP®, MBA: We do help business owners implement retirement plans. In that capacity, our main focus is on plan design and tax efficiency. Most small business owners start retirement plans to save on taxes but many plans we see are not tax efficient. For example, if a business owner paid himself a dollar, after taxes he would have about 60 cents. Therefore, for a retirement plan to be tax efficient the business owner must get more than 60 cents of every dollar he contributes to the plan. For business owners who want to put away less than $44,000 we focus on age weighted and new comparability profit sharing plans and possibly 401k's. For business owners who want to put away larger amounts we would use cash balance or defined benefit plans. We would make sure that the plan design favored the business owner as much as possible.

Dana Sippel, CPA/PFS, CFP®: Under the current tax and pension laws there are a wide variety of qualified pension plans available to help business owners and their employees save for their retirement. Small businesses are especially well positioned to implement retirement plans beneficial to their owners as well as their employees. One of my personal favorites is the defined benefit pension plan. This plan works particularly well for the older, higher earning business owner with lots of discretionary income. The defined benefit plan works on the premise of accumulating an amount of assets necessary to provide the retiree with a certain level of income at a defined age. These plans allow the participants to make large annual tax deductible contributions to a qualified retirement plan. For example, a business owner, age 55, earning $500,000 annually, with a target retirement date of age 62 could very reasonably save $200,000 a year into this plan. Defined benefit plans will most certainly favor the older business owner who has a number of younger employees. The younger employees will get a small portion of the total annual plan contribution since under the same targeted retirement age and income the younger employees have a much longer time frame to accumulate assets required to reach the goal.

Cary Carbonaro, CFP®, MBA: I have set up SEPs, SIMPLES, 401(k)s and even defined benefit plans. Today most plans are defined contribution plans like the first three I mentioned. If you can afford to meet the contribution requirements, defined benefit plans are still great plans, especially if you are a one person firm. A defined benefit plan means you get a defined benefit, for example if you put in $25 thousand a year and in 10 years you might get a monthly benefit of $4000 a month for 20 years or life. It depends how the plan is written and how it is funded. This is a traditional pension plan. I use an actuary who will run the numbers for my clients based on income, employees, and goals, to see which plan is best for them. I find most clients are not in the optimal plan for their particular situation.

Mike Busch, CPA, CFP®, CEBS: I implement a wide variety of retirement plans for my business owner clients. One of the most popular plans that I implement for business owners is a 401(k) plan with a safe-harbor employer match and a profit sharing contribution layered on top. We segregate the participants into pools so we can take advantage of cross testing rules. This type of arrangement allows the largest percentage of employer contributions to go to the owner's account and yet still comply with the non-discrimination rules. At the same time, it allows the employees to contribute salary on a tax-deferred basis, while receiving a nice match on their deferral.

Jim Reardon, JD, CFP®: We prefer the benefits of 401(k) plans for most clients who own mature businesses. Recent changes in retirement law have made these plans very attractive for stable business operations and important financial planning tools—particularly for self-employed individuals such as real estate agents.

We specialize in providing 401(k) services to fiduciary clients including plan sponsors and investment committees. In response to the Enron scandal, recent changes in ERISA law have imposed very strict enforcement of fiduciary liability on plan sponsors, executive committees and investment advisors. Most fiduciaries are unaware of these new obligations. A recent study conducted by the Securities Exchange Commission (SEC) found most of the 24 investment service providers studied to be engaged in prohibited transactions in direct violation of ERISA law. Fiduciary behavior is not determined by investment performance or lack thereof. It is determined by the processes implemented and followed in order to act in a fiduciary manner.

Diana Grossman Simpson, MBA, CFP®: We love the opportunity to work with small business owners because there are often so many opportunities available to financially impact both the business and the owner personally. There are many types of retirement plans available, but with some input from the business owner the options usually limit themselves. We have worked with clients to implement SIMPLE and SEP IRAs, one-person 401(k) plans, 401(k) profit-sharing plans and deferred compensation plans, as well as defined benefit pension plans.

John Scherer, CFP®, CLU, ChFC: I do help small businesses implement and manage retirement plans. I have used SIMPLE, SEP, and 401(k) plans, depending on the business' goals.

Kathy Stepp, CPA/PFS, CFP®: We do not administer retirement plans for our clients' companies, but we often recommend them and help our clients to administer their own plans. The most common retirement plans we recommend for clients with small businesses are SIMPLE IRAs, SEP-IRAs, and 401(k) plans.

SIMPLE IRAs and SEP IRAs can be established without a third party administrator, making them attractive, cost-saving choices. For clients with employees who want to contribute by deferring some of their pay, the SIMPLE IRA is the answer. Our client and his or her employees can make contributions in addition to the contributions made by the employer. However, the employee salary deferrals and the company contributions are somewhat limited, compared to other plans.

The SEP IRA does not allow for employee contributions, but the employer can make maximum contributions to the plan on behalf of all employees. For our clients with few or no employees who want to maximize the retirement plan contributions for themselves, the SEP IRA is a good alternative.

The 401(k) plan is a good choice for clients who are looking for some of the best features of the SIMPLE IRA and the SEP-IRA. The 401(k) plan allows for employee deferrals that are currently higher than those allowed for SIMPLE IRAs, yet it allows for employer contributions to the maximum allowed by law. The downside to 401(k) plans is the cost associated with third party administration.

In addition to retirement plans, we help our clients establish appropriate buy-sell agreements and executive bonus plans. Typically, we help the client to identify his or her specific objectives, and then we work with the client's attorney to develop the structure to accomplish those objectives.

Chad Starliper, CFP®, ChFC, CLU, EA: I do not personally handle anything in the retirement plan side, apart from getting into design work for our business owner clients. My cohorts do the actual plan implementation.

However, since this question is an issue of design, we've done about everything you could imagine—maybe apart from a 419 welfare benefit plan or VEBA plans. We've installed SIMPLE IRA plans, 401(k)s with various top-heavy designs, defined benefit plans, SEP-IRAs, 457 plans, etc.

Our favorite way to design the plan—especially a 401(k) plan—is with an open-architecture fee-based plan under a discretionary independent trustee. This helps establish an advice platform for the participants as well as removing most of the liability from the company.

Business Owner Exit Strategies

MARK DIEHL:
Do you work with small business owners regarding owner-retirement planning, buy-sell agreements, and executive bonus plans?

Wayne Starr, CFP®, ChFC: When a part of a financial plan focuses on retirement planning, important issues are:

1. What is the desired date of retirement?
2. What amount in today's dollars will be needed to meet income needs?
3. What assets are available for retirement income generation?

For the majority of business owners. their most significant asset is the business. It is also a great vehicle for providing a formal retirement plan. We have recommended and helped implement SIMPLE, SEP, profit sharing 401(k), and defined benefit plans based on a thorough analysis of the business owner's goals, what the business can afford, and the profile of the employee group.

Also, in order to help the business owner realize the value of the business, we give guidance in the areas of buy-sell agreements, which are effective while living and at death. Estate planning for the business owner is as important as retirement planning. In my opinion one should not be done without the other.

John Scherer, CFP®, CLU, ChFC: I also work with the business owner on personal retirement planning – especially how to maximize the value of their business to help fund retirement – as well as business transaction plans. Many business owners under estimate the true value of their business, and most don't realize that they must start planning for a business sale at least three years, and preferably five years or more, before they actually sell to maximize values.

Mike Busch, CPA, CFP®, CEBS: I find that many small business owners neglect to implement a buy-sell arrangement. They get so busy with the day-to-day operations of their business that they never focus on the bigger issues, or they think they will have time to address those issues later. This can leave a real mess for their family in the event they die or are disabled with no buy-sell arrangement in place.

Chad Starliper, CFP®, ChFC, CLU, EA: I think most people conceptually understand that business owners have a lot of their wealth and success tied up with the business. Because of that, it is crucial to have compensation plans for the top people and succession plans in place to transfer and monetize the business as efficiently as possible.

The place to start with the business owner—and we're assuming some level of financial success here—is what happens if the owner hits one of the big three:

(1) Disability   (2) Death   or   (3) Retirement?

The buy-sell agreement, depending on the type of entity and the overall estate plan, is primarily where this is hammered out legally. While complicated from a technical standpoint, it is quite a logical progression. With answers to the aforementioned three triggering events, you can move into the crux of the matter—namely structuring the sale, where you would: (1) Identify the purchaser; (2) Determine how the buyout will be funded; (3) Structure the terms; (4) Agree on a method of accurately valuing the business; and (5) Adding necessary restrictions, escape clauses, or whatever might be peculiar to the event.

Far too many business owners don't think this is a big enough deal, thinking that the key people will keep running the business or their spouse will handle it. Most businesses look a lot less attractive when any type of uncertainty enters the picture—and everyone suffers for it.

I probably sound like a broken record, but it is important that the business succession plan be integrated with the family estate plan. If it's not, some unforeseen problems could occur with family dynamics, tax problems, business problems, and a host of issues.

Diana Grossman Simpson, MBA, CFP®: It is truly awesome when I can work with business partners on both their personal and business financial goals. I feel that I can add significant value walking them through the "what if?" discussions necessary to develop appropriate retirement plans, buy-sell agreements and executive compensation plans. It's all about meeting the needs of the individual owners--which, sometimes, can also be like marriage counseling!

Special Needs Planning

with

Kristi Sweeney, CFP®

Special Needs Planning

During the interview process for this book, I had an opportunity to visit with Kristi Sweeney, CFP®, and learn more about her area of specialization. When I initially developed the concept of *The Wealth Management Manual*, I had not given any thought to including a section devoted to Special Needs Planning. It just hadn't occurred to me. But after getting to know more about Kristi and her invaluable work, I felt this was an important issue to address.

I was unaware of the large percentage of the population faced with the challenges of caring for a loved one, and ensuring that person will continue to be cared for, long after the primary caregiver is gone. The challenges are great and can literally span generations. From a financial planning standpoint, the obstacles can seem overwhelming.

I had a discussion with Kristi about Special Needs Planning, the challenges, possible solutions, and her own personal experiences. I hope this interview provides some value to you, our readers. This visit was an eye-opener for me. If you have a friend or family member dealing with "primary caregiver" issues, please pass on a copy of this book and bookmark this section.

Let's spend a few moments with Kristi Sweeney.

MARK DIEHL:
Does your firm specialize in a particular area of financial planning, possibly investment management or estate planning?

Kristi Sweeney, CFP®: My company is unusual both for what we don't do as much as what we do. First of all, we do not manage money for clients. As a CERTIFIED FINANCIAL PLANNER™ Practitioner, I focus on Special Needs Planning for families with a loved one who will need lifetime assistance. My firm also services and guides smaller businesses with employee benefits planning and insurance.

Although my company is somewhat unusual, I still consider it a family office. We concentrate on the base of all of our client's financial security needs and have many financial tools we use to solve problems and provide a measure of security. We specialize in asset protection and really compliment other fee only and fee based practices who do not deal with insurance. We provide smaller company benefit packages and individual health, life, disability, long term care and dental insurance plans. Fee-based consultations are available, too. Most of my clients are referred to my practice by my group, individual clients, and other financial professionals.

It may sound like I am going in different directions, but actually, it all fits together. For instance, my knowledge of Cobra and how it affects Medicare, the difference between MediCare and Medicaid, and analysis of employee benefits are integral to special needs consultations.

MARK DIEHL:
What type of clients do you usually work with?

Kristi Sweeney, CFP®: My clients consist of owners of companies who usually have fewer than 50 employees, individuals between jobs, students just graduating from college, people preparing to retire and everyone in between. Everyone understands the need for health insurance so a lot of my time is spent helping people in this area.   It's so hard to find affordable health insurance so people really want to know what their choices are. Sometimes, Cobra is the best bet and we guide our clients this way.

My financial planning clients are primarily families who have a child or adult dependent with special needs.

MARK DIEHL:
Is your practice fee only, or a combination of fees and commissions?

Kristi Sweeney, CFP®: My practice is fee-based, Mark. I find that really meets my clients' needs. What that means is that we can provide consultations or we can broker insurance. However, we do not normally provide both of these services at the same time. If we do, then it is very clear how we are working with our client. We have a comprehensive client agreement that spells out how we work. Our financial consultations tend to be limited. A person may be referred by another planner for an analysis of a life insurance policy or for a consultation about choices of health insurance for a pre-retiree. My Special Needs families are looking for direction, education about this type of planning, and referrals to attorneys or investment advisors so I prefer to meet with them on a fee basis.

I recently worked with a physician on a fee-basis who had problems with her disability claim and needed help sorting out policy definitions and the affect it was having on her ongoing benefits. I could not do this without a lot of knowledge about how a disability policy works and what the insurer requires. That comes from looking at lots of policies.

MARK DIEHL:
Do clients seem to have a preference, one way or another?

Kristi Sweeney, CFP®: The first half hour that I meet with a client in my office is complimentary although I have a minimum charge for a meeting that is fee-based. During that half hour, we discuss how we will work together. When the consultation is fee-based, my clients often comment that it is great to work with someone who is impartial. I understand what they are saying, but I don't think that a good advisor puts herself first even when a product is sold. Generally, it's a perception that people have and they don't trust a planner who makes their livelihood selling products. I think an advisor works very hard to please a client when they work only for commissions. I have to say that I prefer the relationship with my clients when it starts out fee-based. Isn't that something?

MARK DIEHL:
How important is life insurance in a comprehensive financial plan?

Kristi Sweeney, CFP®: Life insurance is key to most financial planning. There is one exception to that rule- a single person without a dependent does not need life insurance. If a person without dependents has a charitable intent or wishes to leave a chunk of money to another person, that's fine. The need arises for couples or families during high debt years and in an asset accumulation phase. When income and growth of assets is important, having enough life insurance for your family if you die before your retirement goals are met, is critical. Since you want to maximize the amount of money, term insurance is a cost effective way to cover this need for twenty or thirty years.

MARK DIEHL:
Do you feel there is a need for life insurance after a person has retired?

Kristi Sweeney, CFP®: Life insurance, in its purest form, is intended to replace income lost due to death. If income and assets are adequate, you won't really need to continue life insurance. But what if it isn't?

About ten years before retirement, assess your need to continue life insurance. How long do you need it? For what purpose? For instance, when the first person dies, the surviving spouse will often be left with less income when social security spousal benefits cease. It can also replace lost pension income. For instance, a covered employee may decide to maximize that income at retirement and elect to have benefits stop when he or she dies. How does that impact the surviving spouse? I know people who choose the maximum pension benefit and the wife signed her permission. They plan on covering that loss of critical pension income for the wife when the husband dies with term insurance. Now ten years into a 15 year level term policy, if the husband dies in five years, his wife's income will consist of only Social Security. Deciding to keep life insurance early allows you to benefit from lower premiums. It can be an effective tool to replace income lost if you predecease your spouse and vice versa.

MARK DIEHL:
Have any of your own personal experiences impacted the type of advice you give clients? Maybe your experiences have influenced the way you deliver advice? Do you have any thoughts on that?

Kristi Sweeney, CFP®: If I could help all of my clients avoid financial distress at the time of a death or disability, I would be so satisfied! My personal experience with my husband's ongoing and chronic debilitating disability from a stroke at the age of 37 influenced my decision to enter the financial field. He has not worked for 21 years and his income consists of Social Security Disability Income and a disability insurance policy. We were so fortunate and relatively well-prepared financially because our advisor at the time made excellent recommendations to my husband, who was the father of two young children and had a non-working dependent spouse (me). The advisor convinced my husband to insure the risk by purchasing disability insurance.. My family is very grateful that my husband listened and bought disability insurance and life insurance with waiver of premium in case of disability. Of course, there was no way we could ever emotionally prepare for this type of life change.

One thing that has also affected me is how some of my clients put off planning and insuring properly until it is too late. That stays with me. I wish I could have been more convincing. One client who is a sole proprietor has the type of cancer that is usually terminal and he has no disability insurance. He has life insurance. The sad part is this will be very difficult financially for his family, even if he survives his cancer.

I have had to reconcile over the years that not everyone will take my advice. Obviously, I believe in what I do. But I have to be careful not to cross the line to "overbearing". I believe that people must make some decisions on their own once they hear my recommendations. What I have learned is that I am a messenger and a financial educator.

MARK DIEHL:
You mentioned that you do Special Needs Planning earlier. Did your personal experiences influence you to enter this specialized area of financial planning?

Kristi Sweeney, CFP®: Absolutely. I am empathetic to those whose experiences are similar to mine. I can relate to people who were caught unaware, unprepared emotionally and financially for death or disability. It throws you when it happens to anyone in your family and it has such a profound affect. We know we won't get out of this world alive and premature death of any loved one is shocking…simply overwhelming. I know because my childhood best friend lost her husband at the age of 36 with three young children to raise. But, you can't imagine the challenges when a loved one doesn't die but instead suffers disability. It's just an amazing challenge and without proper planning, I think it is generally an insurmountable challenge and most families pull apart.

My financial planning practice focuses on Special Needs planning. I work with families who have a loved one with a disability. Sometimes that's a dependent child and sometimes it's an adult dependent like a disabled sibling or spouse. I really have personal experience in both of these areas.

MARK DIEHL:
Are there many families who have a loved one with Special Needs and how would you define Special Needs?

Kristi Sweeney, CFP®: An estimated 10% of families have a dependent family member with a disability severe enough that it is apparent that planning needs to be done to preserve government benefits. However, many more families have someone who will not be totally independent in the future because they are financially, socially, or emotionally vulnerable. These families have to plan as well and the plans are not all that different than they are for a child with a severe disability. You have to protect funds meant for that child, plan around well children, and set up protective trusts. I think it becomes more complicated as far as family relationships are concerned when a young adult can't quite reach independence due to emotional problems, mild learning disabilities, or brain injury. We have had to plan for my daughter who, because of learning disabilities, has needed extra financial and emotional support. She will not be eligible for government benefits so we have always been anxious to maximize her abilities. We certainly cannot ever foresee that she will be totally independent in the future though she works at a retail job and is doing great.

Planning needs to be done around a physical disability, too, since it is difficult when it occurs later in life. Emotional adjustments can set up roadblocks to being able to live independently, especially with increased financial and medical expenses.

MARK DIEHL:
Is the situation different today than in years past?

Kristi Sweeney, CFP®: I think the biggest change has been how long people can live with a severe, progressive or chronic disability. Great medical care and advanced technology are responsible for those cases of what I would call a living death. We can be kept alive for years and years with virtually no quality of life. Even with quality of life, the care of a dependent loved one that goes on for many years has enormous financial costs. In my experience, families will do all they can to keep their loved one alive and provide the best quality of life and care. But parents may not outlive their child with a disability so planning for the future is crucial to ongoing quality of care for their loved one.

It is more critical today that parents start planning. People with Special Needs often live at home so they are more dependent on family for quality care. There's been a positive shift away from institutional care but our social structures have not picked up the slack to assist those families who are really alone in some cases and so overburdened with responsibility. This is when estate and financial planning for special needs can help.

MARK DIEHL:
What is your greatest concern about financial or estate planning for families with a Special Needs child?

Kristi Sweeney, CFP®: It has been my experience that it is hard for parents to start planning. Everyone is busy but parents with a child who has a disability or a person with a disabled spouse really is overburdened. With a myriad of daily care requirements, planning is a low priority until it is too late to make effective arrangements. Many parents wait until it is too late to begin saving and investing to fund a secure future for their child. Interestingly, in my experience, worrying about what will happen to their child with a disability if they are not around is one of the most compelling concerns a loving parent has.

MARK DIEHL:
Are there other reasons why families wait to plan?

Kristi Sweeney, CFP®:   I'm sure there are many reasons. Here are a few I have experienced:

- ❑ They wonder if the rehabilitation and therapies their child receives won't be so helpful that their child will become independent in the future.
- ❑ Parents can't imagine how anyone can take their place as a loving caregiver and advocate. So they don't want to think about it.
- ❑ They must plan for a long lifetime of expensive care. This can be an overwhelming thing to contemplate.
- ❑ They don't know where to go to get help. It's a specialized field of estate and financial planning. It's a little technical and somewhat complex so many people do not even know where to begin.

MARK DIEHL:
What is different about estate or financial planning for families with Special Needs children or adults?

Kristi Sweeney, CFP®:
- ❑ Parents must identify the right people *willing and able* to be future caregivers and money managers in their wills and trusts.
- ❑ Parents should leave written information about their child for a future caregiver and money manager.
- ❑ Using a life planning model, families estimate amounts needed by their dependent in the future to supplement government benefits.
- ❑ When a child is severely disabled, it is likely they will qualify for government benefits. A child or adult cannot inherit more than $2,000 directly or government benefits can be disrupted. That can be disastrous when physical or medical care is costly!
- ❑ A special needs trust can avoid this problem and provide a safe haven for funds.
- ❑ Discretionary trusts protect assets for children or adults who are vulnerable.

- ❏ Assets will have to be titled correctly and beneficiary designations must be changed to fund a trust and avoid loss of government benefits.
- ❏ Assets *have* to last beyond the parent's lifetime. They either have to be saved or created. Then they have to be protected. Of course, that's where insurance comes into play because it is a fine tool for creating wealth where there is none. We try to help our families preserve a secure lifestyle for themselves, as well, or it will be very difficult to leave anything for their loved one.

MARK DIEHL:
Can you tell me something about the families you have helped with Special Needs Planning?

Kristi Sweeney, CFP®:   Here's one example: I worked with one family who has two children with disabilities. One child is profoundly disabled and needs round the clock care. The other child has learning and social disabilities and it's hard to say if she will be independent. It's a second marriage for the husband and he has two other children who he'd like to consider in his estate planning. He has a substantial income, few debts, but savings were minimal. They knew they were spending too much on things that made them feel better but ultimately made them feel terrible because they were so financially vulnerable. Approaching middle age, the couple suspected they could never retire and were concerned about who would care for their profoundly disabled son. We helped them find an attorney to do a revocable living trust with a testamentary special needs trust. We got life insurance for both the husband and wife (caregiver) as well as second to die life insurance intended to fund the special needs trust. We protected earnings with a disability policy and referred the husband to a pension specialist to set up an age weighted pension plan to maximize the amount of money he could save. We helped them with a budget so they could better prioritize expenditures and stay on track. We plan on monitoring the plan, staying in touch with the financial advisor, attorney and the trustee.

I have worked with families who have children with learning disabilities, who want to help supplement living expenses and emergency funding but also want to foster independence.   I also have worked with families with children who have Down Syndrome, Autism Spectrum Disorders, and both child and adult onset brain injury.

Of all that I do to help clients, this is my most gratifying work. I simply receive much more than I give by being able to help out these very special families.

MARK DIEHL:
I really appreciate the time you've shared with me today. What about being a financial planner provides you the greatest personal satisfaction?

Kristi Sweeney, CFP®: There's so much I do to help people live financially secure lives. It's not all about money. It's really all about love. I help people show their loved ones they care. I remember one woman, a stay at home mom, who came to me one day to apply for life insurance one week after her husband died suddenly. She was not going to do to her children what he had done to his family. He had no life insurance when he died. She could not believe he would leave her alone with two young children to bring up this way. She would show her children and those she named guardian that she loved them enough to protect them and their future if she died.

As I mentioned earlier, I get the most satisfaction from helping families with a loved one with special needs. Because I am a caregiver who has lived with a family member with special needs, I like to help other families in the only way that I can, sharing the financial and estate planning solutions I have found that have helped my family. Solutions that helped my family stay together after my husband's disabling stroke.

A Final Word
From Our Contributors

Closing Thoughts

As I mentioned at the very beginning of the book, I am honored to have been joined by the CERTIFIED FINANCIAL PLANNER™ Professionals who have contributed to *The Wealth Management Manual*. They have been candid in their responses and a shining example of their profession. I wanted readers to be exposed to fifteen different opinions, not fifteen versions of the *same* opinion.

I have no doubt that if you read the entire book, cover to cover, you will be able to say it was time well spent. Before we part ways I wanted to ask our contributors if there was anything I overlooked. Was there a topic or question that I failed to address? Their responses are as follows.

MARK DIEHL:
I have discussed some specific financial issues that are on the minds of many Americans; investing, retirement, educational planning for kids or grandkids. Is there a topic that I have overlooked that you feel is important or of interest to readers?

Diana Grossman Simpson, MBA, CFP®: I'm certified as a Divorce Financial Analyst, and I work occasionally with individuals –and sometimes couples-who are going through divorce. For most people, the divorce is a surprise, and they find themselves ill-prepared to deal with it financially. Maybe they don't know much about their own financial situation – this is more common than you'd think –or they have unrealistic expectations about the financial outcome. Or both. It is certainly not unusual for one spouse to have more financial responsibility than another, but it is critical that the spouse who is less involved remain informed. This not only applies to divorce, but also premature death, disability – or simply a spouse being out of town when business needs to be conducted.

Randy Smith, CFP®, MBA: Yes, I think we have missed one of the most important elements of finance. That is the money mindset. Americans, young and old, need to have abundance mentality. Money matters create fear in people because they do not take the time to understand wealth building basics. Day-to-day money management is not that difficult. The difficulty lies with investors developing a plan and then sticking to it. Anything worth having requires a plan: high school degree plan, college degree plan, wedding plan, house plan, vacation plan, retirement plan? The media also has a large hand in this fear. The market goes down and it is on the evening news. But if you are building wealth, market corrections are good. The market is "on sale". Clothes sale, car sale, electronics sale, food sale, stock sale? The contrarian investor is one who buys when everyone else is selling, and sells when it seems everyone is buying. The contrarian investor is rare, but they build true long term wealth.

Lastly, even if investors have the mindset and knowledge, they often lack the discipline to stay on course for many years. Having a plan and adjusting as needed, will heighten feelings of control and reduce fear, but often still has little positive effect on basic discipline. This is where the financial advisor becomes incredibly valuable. We, as advisors, must stay in tune with the economy, trends, investments, education, taxes, but *most importantly*, keep in tune with peoples' needs and emotions. A good advisor has the ability to *see and feel* his clients' personal needs. The advisor must have the ability to match financial skills with people skills. The *healthy* marriage of knowledge, emotions and long term discipline, shepherded by a truly caring advisor are all required.

Mike Busch, CPA, CFP®, CEBS: I think readers could benefit from a discussion of wealth management mistakes and pitfalls that they should avoid. Often, it is not the things that an individual fails to do that cause problems, but the things they actually do that are in direct opposition to their goals. They often don't realize it at the time, but they engage in activities or practices that are counterproductive. If readers were aware of some of these activities before they found themselves practicing them, they might be able to avoid them in the first place.

John Scherer, CFP®, CLU, ChFC: One thing that I really think is important for readers to remember is that money is just a tool for helping them accomplish what's really important to them. It's a means to an end, not the end itself. When you asked me a minute ago about wealth management, what came to mind at first is a definition of wealth that I have on my refrigerator.

WEALTH: an abundance of those things which bring one comfort, security and satisfaction.

Everything else should be a servant to that ideal.

Chad Starliper, CFP®, ChFC, CLU, EA: There are probably tons of little issues that we could write separate books on. But off the top of my head, the most common thing we see and hear is this notion that Everyday Joe is going to pick and choose stocks and dart in and out based on stuff he reads in the newspaper. It is precisely this type of behavior that makes people hugely under perform the market return. We try and try to educate people through this, but some people just won't let go of that feeling that they know something no one else does. Anyone that pursues active stock trading would be far better off putting their money into two index funds—one domestic and the other international—and forgetting about it. I don't advocate that myself, but it is certainly more profitable than playing the online trading game.

There are no free lunches and no magic bullets. There aren't any special financial products out there. The only good products are those that specifically and efficiently create solutions and solve problems. True planning and investment advice is grounded in rigorous research, sound foundational principles, and design.

When people want to know "what are you buying" or "what looks good," it is sort of like asking a doctor what the best drug is right now. It's ludicrous. Everything comes back to risk and reward; they are inextricably connected.

June Schroeder, CFP®, RN: One topic near and dear to my heart is pets. I have always owned and loved animals. I have owned horses, dogs, cats, rabbits, fish, birds, etc. Things have changed a lot since I was a kid. Today Americans spend over $34 billion a year on their pets and sometimes it leads to financial and emotional stress. I have done things for my pets that I would not advise a client to do --it made no sense from a numbers standpoint, but emotionally I could not do otherwise. Several years ago, I spent about $3000 on a cat that a few months later died of lung cancer I didn't know he had! The size and type of pet can put a real strain on a budget so planning is important before someone adopts. Pets are reportedly good for people from a companionship and health standpoint. So they can pay for themselves in a health dividend . . . but a medium sized dog can easily add an average of $100 per month to the spending plan (we shy away from the term budget) according to the ASPCA.

Tom Wargin, CFP®, CFA: It seems that there are fewer children being born so people have more pets. And that brings up the topic of "change." Change has always been with us but it has been more rapid--it is increasing exponentially in some quarters. Life spans are increasing, people have more careers, and information transfer is instantaneous. When we started our business there were around 300 mutual funds, now there are over 15,000. More than the number of U.S. stocks! In addition, Wall Street continues to come up with new types of investments to tantalize the public. And tax laws come and go. That's what makes our job really interesting and emphasizes the need for flexibility in portfolio management and on-going financial planning.

June Schroeder, CFP®, RN: Health is a financial asset. Staying as healthy as possible reduces the probability of having to spend money on health care. A chronic illness or disability can reduce your job possibilities or length of employment and significantly affect your financial well being. For example, obesity, which is often preventable by exercise and/or portion control, is considered by some to be at epidemic proportions. Along with that are the personal and societal costs due to the secondary effects which include heart disease and diabetes, to name a few. Our great strides in computerization have led to a sedentary lifestyle for ourselves and our children. Kids don't ride bikes. We drive them to where they play computer games! We fight over the TV clicker! Perhaps the irony will be that while our life expectancies rise - theirs will decrease - and that will affect Social Security reform and health care costs. Or they might live longer, unhealthier, more expensive lives.

Matthew Tuttle, CFP®, MBA: I think the key issue for most people is to stop reading *Money Magazine* and the *Wall Street Journal*. Stop watching *CNBC*. We call this stuff "financial pornography" because it is designed to get you excited but at the end of the day it is meaningless. Find an advisor you can trust that can handle your finances and spend your time on the things in life more important than money---health, family , spirituality, etc. Do you know the P/E ratio of your favorite stock but not what your cholesterol ratio is? Do you read *Money Magazine* instead of a good book? Do you sign proxy statements instead of cards for your children and grandchildren? You only have 168 hours each week. The quality of your life is directly related to how you spend those 168 hours. If you can delegate your finances you will have more time to spend on things that are more important and that you enjoy.

Cary Carbonaro, CFP®, MBA: I feel you have addressed most of the general questions people have. I would say, don't let greed get the best of you. I've had clients call me when technology was hot and they wanted to put 100% of their money in tech. I would never recommend more than 10% of their assets be invested in technology and that advice served to protect investors that listened. The same mania has happened with real estate over the past few years. I have talked many clients out of speculative real estate. I would put 10% in a diversified REIT. I've had clients call me and tell me they could get 12% guaranteed when bank accounts were paying 2%. I did some research on these accounts and found they were unsecured notes. I have seen many investment scams and ponzi schemes where clients have lost everything they put into it. If it sounds too good to be true, I would not trust it. Be skeptical of anyone promising high returns. I use 6-8% projections in my plans and if we beat projections, expectations are exceeded. Another area clients are interested in today is hedge funds. As of February 1, 2006 hedge funds have to register with the SEC under the Investment Company Act of 1940. I would ask your advisor to do due-diligence on any hedge fund you might be considering.

Personal Experiences

MARK DIEHL:
Have any of your own personal experiences impacted the type of advice you give clients? Maybe your experiences have influenced the way you deliver advice? Do you have any thoughts on that?

Mike Busch, CPA, CFP®, CEBS: I credit my parents for my decision to pursue financial planning as a career. From an early age, they set expectations that I would be responsible for funding most or all of my higher education. I had a paper route from the time I was 11 until I went to college. My parents held me to a simple but rigorous financial management regimen. I had four envelopes into which I placed all of my paper route profits. The first envelope received 10% and was designated for the church. The second envelope received 30% and was for short-term savings, like ski trips. The third envelope received 40% and was for long-term savings, which for me translated to college expenses. The final envelope received the remaining 20% and was available for me to spend as I saw fit. My dad also taught me about what Einstein called the most powerful force in the universe – compound interest. Not only did this early exposure influence my decision to become a financial planner, it also taught me important life lessons and shaped my outlook on financial advice. It is now ingrained in me that discretionary spending comes only after meeting your current obligations and saving for the future. I also understand that it is important to put a plan in place before funds arrive and to be disciplined in following that plan. Finally, I have a real appreciation for the impact that an early start has on your chances for success.

Matthew Tuttle, CFP®, MBA: We give clients advice based on what we believe gives them the greatest probability of achieving their goals and fulfilling their values. We try to keep things as simple as possible. Based on my experiences, this is always difficult. I have an MBA in Finance and I am a CFP® so I have to fight my temptation to show off my knowledge and make sure that I am always keeping things simple for the client.

Chad Starliper, CFP®, ChFC, CLU, EA: That's an interesting question. I'd say that, yes, that's certainly true.

Take for instance a friend of mine that recently had a motorcycle accident. He's a self-employed real estate appraiser who won't be able to work for about six months. Unfortunately for him, he never completed the disability policy we proposed. He has zero income right now. I wish that I'd tied him down and made him submit.

We also have an ex-anesthesiologist who had his legs cut off when a house fell on him during a mud slide. Granted, he's set up pretty well because he had disability and won some lawsuits. But the impetus is still derived from the reality of that situation. People need disability insurance and it isn't cheap, especially for professionals.

Just as a general idea, I have developed my entire skill-set and professional vision around giving real advice to people and helping them manage their money better. That means being an expert; and it means being an advisor and not a salesperson. It means telling people the truth whether they want to hear it or not. There are so many salespeople that are facilitators, just doing what the client asks, even though it may not be in the client's best interest. We see it everyday, at least the carnage from it.

When I go to a doctor, I don't want some collaborative effort on getting my health better. The doctor should know those answers and tell me. If it's collaboration, then we've got the wrong doctor. The story is the same for us. True advisors deliver advice.

June Schroeder, CFP®, RN: My dad died when I was 17. My mom didn't even know how to write out a check. He had handled all the financial aspects of our family. She learned the hard way and became quite good at making ends meet and balancing her checkbook. It made me realize how important it is for a woman to have knowledge about financial issues. Also, he died with very little life insurance. He was unemployed due to his failing health. My mom worked three jobs to raise us kids and I worked three jobs to get through college. The ironic thing is that he had insured me--starting at the age of 0--with hopes that the policies would pay for my college. What he didn't understand was that the endowment policies that he bought were worth less than the premiums he had paid in by the time I was seventeen! Hence, another reason I am *very* careful about explaining and reading contract language. I mentioned earlier that my mom lived in her own apartment for as long as I could provide assistance and then she went into assisted living. She had lupus and passed away in 2001. The experiences of care giving, moving and downsizing her several times, have made it easier for me to discuss the same things with clients and their children.

Tom Wargin, CFP®, CFA: I feel that my personal experiences have made me a better planner. I've lost both parents after prolonged illnesses. My mother-in-law died sitting in her wheelchair in our downstairs duplex. I am part time care giver for my 96 year old father-in-law. My four sons have moved out and then returned! All this has helped me in the psychological aspects of our business since I tend to gravitate to the crunching of numbers more readily than the feelings part like June does.

John Scherer, CFP®, CLU, ChFC: Certainly personal experiences shape what and how I help my clients, but I try to be very neutral in listening to my clients because my responsibility is to help them achieve what's important to them, not what's a priority for me.

One of the biggest benefits I think my clients receive as a result of my personal experiences is the lack of a sales agenda in my advice. Having worked as an insurance agent and in a stockbroker environment early in my career, I was exposed to a culture where "production" was the measure of success instead of helping clients achieve their goals. As a result of that experience, my clients now know that my primary objective is helping them succeed, and that my profits are only as a result of that.

Diana Grossman Simpson, MBA, CFP®: I base my advice on what I have seen work – and not work – with other clients, associates, acquaintances . . . and yes, in my own personal financial life. After all, there is rarely one "right" answer in any given situation. But I think it would be fair to say that I maintain a neutral stance on most issues. I provide clients with their options and help them weigh the pros and cons of each.

339

And I'll tell them if my perspective is subjective. For example, my husband and I are currently getting out of the rental real estate business. We had three investment properties at one time, and are in the process of selling the last one. We made the decision based on our own personal circumstances; with two preschoolers, we haven't been able to put the necessary time into the properties, we've had some pretty bad experiences with renters, and it seemed like more trouble than it was worth, financially. But I don't tell my clients to steer clear of investment real estate. I've certainly had clients who have done quite well with it. But I will make them aware of the pros and the cons, and often bring up issues that they had not considered.

Cary Carbonaro, CFP®, MBA: Certainly, I don't see how you can't be impacted by your life experiences in this role. I feel I was taught by the best! My late father, Paul F. Carbonaro, was a banker for his entire 35 year career. He never made it to retirement. He passed away when he was 58. My personal life experience with my dad enables me to counsel people not to postpone their life waiting for a retirement that may never come!

My mom is a CPA, so both she and my father were strong influences, teaching me the basics of financial planning at a very young age. I managed a budget in college better than anyone. I would always help my friends with money decisions on debt consolidation, student loans, types of mortgages and how much financing they could qualify for. I have been passionate about always learning and taking my own advice. I started at the age of 21 with my first investments, a 401(k) plan and an IRA. I owned my first home at 24. Unfortunately, life happens and even the best planners have experiences that have a negative impact on their finances. I walked away from a very lucrative career in New York City before I started my own firm. I got divorced, which for anyone has emotional and financial consequences.

When I see clients making bad decisions due to emotional stuff, I suggest they speak to a psychologist. I have a client whose husband passed away and she was going through all the money he left her. She lost her job and got involved in a destructive relationship. Every time she called me for money I tried to be an emotional support for her. This was the least I could do. I helped her get her car out of the impound lot. I would even call her just to see how she was doing and she always knew I cared!

The way I deliver advice is much more like an educator. I am an educator at heart. I want to share my knowledge! My clients seem to like my approach of counseling and educating. They never feel intimidated. Women who are going through divorce or the death of a spouse can especially relate to my style. In addition to financial advice, they know I am here to support them emotionally and spiritually.

Wayne Starr, CFP®, ChFC: I tend to be conservative which makes me cautious even for my clients with more aggressive risk tolerances. I do not let my conservative nature get in their way. I do think my cautiousness and desire to really know how an investment works is beneficial to the client.

For as long as I can recall, I have "second guessed" myself. When I am entrusted with other people's money, or when I am helping clients plan for the future, second-guessing is not all that bad. I want the plan or the investment to be as right as it can be. I want to make sure we have looked at all the options.

I came from a broken home of modest means. I feel that spouses need to do planning together and that differences in goals and philosophies need to be reconciled so success can be achieved in meeting common goals.

Jim Reardon, JD, CFP®: We are all products of our environment and our advice is always tempered by our experiences. I paid a large portion of my undergraduate and law school expenses. My mother was a single mom who had to work very hard to make her little dress shop meet all of our financial needs. In the beginning we lived in a little storeroom in back of the building. Mom slept on a fold-out couch and my first bedroom was actually a dressing room with a rollaway cot. She was an awesome woman who achieved a great deal of success. She was a business woman in a time when businesses were dominated by men. My mother was a good manager and a hard worker. I, on the other hand, was no stranger to debt. That's why I hate debt and why I appreciate the simple logic of the *five buckets*.

I enjoy helping people. I learned from twelve years of knocking on constituent's doors and dealing with countless issues as a city councilman that there are often several ways to look at something. Most people want to do the right thing and they want their opinions and their feelings to be respected. They expect honesty and candor. My practice is centered on the premise that most people really desire to be good stewards of their assets.

Among my clients are a couple who are both ninety years old. He takes long daily walks around his independent living facility and he drives his new car to my office or to pick up the great grandkids after school. She keeps meticulous books, pays the bills, and manages the money as she has for decades. She looks forward to the stewardship meetings and she calls me if they are not scheduled in a timely manner. She has a computer and she often goes on-line to check her account or send me an email.

Until recently, both served as volunteer ushers at the Performing Arts Center where they regularly enjoy the shows. They, like so many other people, want to maintain their health, their dignity and their respect to the very end. They want to be responsible for their own outcomes for as long as they are able. They can deal with adversity and they appreciate the work that we do. The major thing they really need from me--in addition to investment management--is a game plan to follow and guideposts to measure their progress. They'll take care of the rest thank you very much.

Wealth Management is a partnership of client and advisor working in tandem. People who want an advisor to make all their investment decisions and who are too busy for the stewardship meetings do not make good clients. They will rarely appreciate our services and they are quick to be displeased. They often hedge their bets with stockbrokers or other advisors and they refuse to take any responsibility for their outcomes either good or bad. We have learned to screen these people out at our first meeting.

Most of my clients have fiduciary responsibilities or they are former corporate leaders or retired working and professional people who had responsible positions and who possess good management skills. These are people who understand that in delegating responsibility they still retain it. My role is similar to that of a personal trainer in stewardship. I am here not just to manage the performance of investments but to enable our clients to realize the achievement of their life goals.

This spring, *Kiplinger's Magazine* invited me to submit one of my client couples to feature as examples of good stewardship. I was pleased to have many choices. My goal is to have all of my clients serve as examples of good stewardship.

Professional Satisfaction

MARK DIEHL:
I really appreciate the time you've shared with me today. What about being a financial planner provides you the greatest personal satisfaction?

Kathy Stepp, CPA/PFS, CFP®: Being a financial planner is interesting because I get to work with clients from all walks of life. My greatest personal satisfaction is in getting to know these diverse clients and forming lasting relationships with them. I truly believe that our comprehensive, detailed approach to financial planning is what enables us to make competent recommendations on an ongoing basis. I am deeply satisfied knowing that our clients, whom we personally care about, are following our advice and doing exactly what we would do in their shoes.

Chad Starliper, CFP®, ChFC, CLU, EA: For me personally, I think it's about helping people make good decisions with a major part of their life. And since most people aren't super good at it, the need is even greater. We're talking about a lifetime worth of working and striving to support a family and put some aside for the future. If they put forth the effort to seek our help, it's rewarding to watch them prosper because of our advice.

In a larger sense, however, I think we all get our greatest fulfillment from operating in our areas of giftedness and giving to other people. It seems to have been that way since the beginning of time, and every great epiphany or saying ends up somewhere along those lines. Financial planning—really, we're talking about teaching and counseling here—is a way for me to combine thinking and strategy with enriching other people.

June Schroeder, CFP®, RN: As an RN, there is joy in my heart when I hear a client say "I feel better already" after only one visit. I bet I could even take their blood pressure and find it to be lower! Research shows that 75% of all illness is caused by stress, much of it financial stress. The best overall satisfaction comes from knowing that for my clients, I am practicing preventative or holistic "wealth care." For years, I have billed myself as a "public wealth nurse." I guess you could say I try to make everyone "healthy, wealthy and wise!"

Cary Carbonaro, CFP®, MBA: I've had a great career even at a young age. I worked on Wall Street and for large Fortune 500 firms. I enjoyed a very large salary and learned a lesson very early in life that "It is not about money." Working one on one with clients and seeing how much you impact their lives is immensely rewarding. I save all the thank you letters and emails I get from my clients. When you work in an ivory tower you can never have this kind of impact.

Tom Wargin, CFP®, CFA: As for me, in the words of Hannibal from the A-Team TV show, "I love it when a plan comes together."

Mike Busch, CPA, CFP®, CEBS: When I used to practice as a public accountant, performing audits and preparing tax returns, I knew I was providing an important service, but the personal satisfaction did not rise to the same level that I now experience as a financial planner. Yes, companies need audits to obtain financing and individuals need to file tax returns, but employees are never happy to see the auditor, and for most people, filing their tax return is just a requirement that can't be avoided. As a financial planner, I see firsthand how my clients benefit from my counsel. I really enjoy seeing "the load come off" of a client when they finally gather the courage to seek assistance in the management of their wealth. Knowing that I have provided a valuable service to my clients and experiencing their thankfulness is highly motivating.

John Scherer, CFP®, CLU, ChFC: I'll share with you the story of a client that illustrates why I do what I do for a living. A 48 year old client came to me with $10,000 in an old 401(k) plan, $30,000 in credit card debt, and had just moved to town from across the country following her second divorce in six years. She had only a part time job earning about $20,000 per year in addition to a business of her own that she wanted to get off of the ground.

I didn't think she could afford to pay for my services, but she insisted, saying "I've made enough financial mistakes in the past and I don't have enough time left to recover from any more. I need your help."

That was two years ago. Six months ago she bought her first condo of her own, her debt is almost paid off, and she's saving enough to be on track to eventually retire. When she had me over to her condo for our tax planning meeting, she said to me "I'm so proud of myself, and so happy to be living here and to be on the path to success that I am. I could never have done it without you."

That's worth more than all the money she'll ever pay for my advice.

Diana Grossman Simpson, MBA, CFP®: I am motivated by being able to help people, and in my field, I can really impact lives. I love that. There is also a high degree of professionalism in this field, and I like the fact that my clients value my advice. But honestly, the thing I like best about what I do is that I get to choose which clients I want to work with. I don't *have* to work with anyone. There are so many truly wonderful people out there, who value my advice and treat me like a professional. I guess life is just too short to work with people who don't!

Wayne Starr, CFP®, ChFC: Satisfaction comes from being told by clients that I am a trusted advisor. Satisfaction comes from seeing a client meet a goal due to following my advice. Satisfaction comes from a quarterly meeting when the client and I really interact and arrive at solutions or plan modifications mutually agreed upon. Satisfaction comes from a phone call by a potential client who was referred by an existing client. It is the greatest compliment. Satisfaction comes from massaging a jigsaw puzzle like set of facts and goals into a comprehensive plan that I believe will cause a positive reaction by the client—the plan will be implemented. Satisfaction comes from successfully fielding a myriad of staff and client questions and phone calls in a day and then going home with that good tired feeling.

Matthew Tuttle, CFP®, MBA: Helping people improve the quality of their lives. By delegating their finances to me, our clients have more time to do what is most important, thus improving the quality of their lives.

Jim Reardon, JD, CFP®: Twenty five years ago, I chose to be a pioneer in the emerging new field of financial planning instead of plying the practice of law. If I had been a better student of American history, I would have realized that it was the pioneers who got scalped or starved to death and it was the settlers who came along later who built the saloons and the general stores and made all of the money.

It was tough going in the early days because I didn't come into the business from a successful career in insurance or securities. I was both naive and foolish. We were fighting to establish the legitimacy of financial planning and the advantages of comprehensive financial advisory services. In spite of the hardships, it has been personally rewarding to be part of the financial planning movement in America. I have met some wonderful people; both colleagues and competitors--mentors all, who have opened up their practices and shared their secrets of success for me to emulate. I have participated on national committees and task forces that were led by the enlightened people who continue to provide direction and guidance to this noble profession.

The practice of law can be adversarial and contentious. It can engender hostility and hard feelings. In financial planning the adversaries are ignorance, poverty, and poor judgment. It is deeply rewarding to instill good stewardship and to see your clients and their families grow and prosper. I am proud to have been chosen for this project and I am grateful for the opportunity to provide direction and guidance to this noble profession.

Dana Sippel, CPA/PFS, CFP: As a financial advisor, my greatest joy comes from sharing my knowledge with others, helping them achieve their life and financial goals. Part of helping people with these goals is an understanding that each person brings to the table their own money and life baggage, and that influences how they think and make decisions. It is a fascinating study of people and what makes them tick. Not only is it related to finances, but encompasses their overall life direction, careers, passions and what drives them. I try to gain the best understanding of my clients' attitudes and beliefs in these areas and then help them integrate these with their financial and life goals so that they can live life to the fullest.

A Parting Thought

Over the past 300 or so pages we have covered quite a bit of ground. I want to personally thank you for purchasing and reading *The Wealth Management Manual.* I am sure we have not answered all of your questions, but I think the most important thing for you to do is start *asking* the right questions. When you start asking the right questions, the right answers will appear.

I hope you will now view all of your financial options as an interlocking puzzle and I do believe you can find a trusted advisor to assist you in your pursuit of financial freedom. Realize that your choices today will definitely impact the quality of your life tomorrow. Protect your assets starting today. Create wealth and, in turn, create a life of contribution to your family, faith, and community. Remember, money is just a tool. It is what you build with your tools that matter.

The advisors who joined me in these pages are among the elite of their profession. If you ever have the opportunity to work with any of them, please do so. You'll be in good hands.

Important Websites

CFP Board of Standards	cfpboard.org
Financial Planning Association (FPA)	fpa.org
National Association of Professional Financial Advisors (NAPFA)	napfa.org
National Association of Insurance and Financial Advisors (NAIFA)	naifa.org
Resource for 529 Information	savingforcollege.com
Financial Information	moneycentral.msn.com
Internal Revenue Service (IRS)	irs.gov
National Association of Securities Dealers (NASD)	nasd.org
Stock Information	bigcharts.com

Index

Endnotes

[1] Peterson, T (n.d.). *The Great Labor Shortage*. Retrieved August-06-06, from http://www.monster.com.

[2] Dohn, A. (2000, July). Gauging the labor force effects of retiring baby-boomers, *Monthly Labor Review*, 17.

[3] Havens, J. J. & Schervish, P. G. (2003). Why the 41 trillion wealth transfer is still valid. *The Journal of Gift Planning, 7*, 11-15.

[4] Federal Reserve Bank of San Francisco. (2003). *Shifting household assets in a bear market* (FRBSF economic letter 2002-16) San Franciso, CA: U.S. Government Printing Office

[5] Opdyke, J. D. (2006, January 28). Wait, let me call my ChFC. *Wall Street Journal*, p. B1.

[6] Savage, T. (2005). Some pros of private accounts. Retrieved Setember 08, 2006 from http://www.suntimes.com/cgi- bin/print.cgi?getReferrer=http://suntimes. com/output/savage/06300sa

[7] Updegrave, W. (2002). An honest financial planner. Retrieved September 08, 2006 from http://money.cnn.com/2002/09/06/pf/expert/ask_expert/index. htm

[8] Lodmell, D. S., & Lodmell, B. R. (2004). *The lawsuit lottery: The hijacking of America*. Phoenix, AZ: World Connection Publishing.

[9] Lodmell, D. S., & Lodmell, B. R. (2004). *The lawsuit lottery: The hijacking of America*. Phoenix, AZ: World Connection Publishing.

[10] National Highway Traffic Safety Administration. (2005). *Traffic Safety Facts* (DOT HS 809 911). Washington, DC: U.S. Government Printing office.

[11] National Highway Traffic Safety Administration. (2005). *Traffic Safety Facts* (DOT HS 809 911). Washington, DC: U.S. Government Printing office.

[12] National Highway Traffic Safety Administration. (2005). *Traffic Safety Facts* (DOT HS 809 911). Washington, DC: U.S. Government Printing office.

[13] National Highway Traffic Safety Administration. (2005). *Traffic Safety Facts* (DOT HS 809 911). Washington, DC: U.S. Government Printing office.

[14] American Academy of Pediatrics. (2003). *Prevention of drowning in infants, Children, and adolescents, 112*, 437-439.

[15] American Academy of Pediatrics. (2003). *Prevention of drowning in infants, Children, and adolescents, 112*, 437-439.

[16] American Academy of Pediatrics. (2003). *Prevention of drowning in infants, Children, and adolescents, 112*, 437-439.

[17] Kraus, L., Stoddard, S., & Gilmartin, D. (1996). *Chartbook on Disability in the United States, 1996*. An InfoUse Report. Washington, DC: U.S. National Institute on Disability and Rehabilitation Research.

[18] Kraus, L., Stoddard, S., & Gilmartin, D. (1996). *Chartbook on Disability in the United States, 1996.* An InfoUse Report. Washington, DC: U.S. National Institute on Disability and Rehabilitation Research.

[19] Kraus, L., Stoddard, S., & Gilmartin, D. (1996). *Chartbook on Disability in the United States, 1996.* An InfoUse Report. Washington, DC: U.S. National Institute on Disability and Rehabilitation Research.

[20] Kraus, L., Stoddard, S., & Gilmartin, D. (1996). *Chartbook on Disability in the United States, 1996.* An InfoUse Report. Washington, DC: U.S. National Institute on Disability and Rehabilitation Research.

[21] Dolan, F., & Harlow, V. (2004). Lifetime income planning. *Fidelity Investments,* 23.

[22] Stocks are represented by Standard and Poor's 500 Composite Index; bonds by the Citigroup High-Grade Corporate Bond Index; Cash equivalents by 30-day U.S. Treasury bills. Indexes are unmanaged.

[23] Dolan, F., & Harlow, V. (2004). Lifetime income planning. *Fidelity Investments,* 23.

[24] Borden, K. (1995). Dismantling the pyramid: The why and how of privatizing social security. *Social SecurityPrivatization.* Retrieved March 03, 2006 from http://www.socialsecurity.org/pubs/ssps/ssp1es.html

[25] Tierney, M. (2004). From spending to savings: *Ten years shows shift in mind-set of nation's baby boomers.* Retrieved August 06, 2006 from http://www.axaonline.com/rs/axa/pressroom/2004/01132004_nest_egg.htm

[26] Opdyke, J. D. (2006, January 28). Wait, let me call my ChFC. *Wall Street Journal,* p. B1.

[27] Clements, J. (2006, May 31). Due dilligence: The five rules to heed before hiring a financial advisor, *Wall Street Journal,* p. D1.

[28] Willis, G.(2006). Get professional financial help: *How to find the best person for your financial needs.* Retrieved September 08, 2006 from http://money.cnn.com/2006/01/30/pf/saving/willis_tips/index.htm

[29] Chu, K. (2002, October 30). Financial-planner certification gains in cachet. Wall Street Journal, p. B5.

Mark Diehl can be contacted at 800-304-1232 with any of your questions, comments, or if you are interested in booking Mark for an interview or speaking engagement.

Subscribe to Mark's financial education updates.

**FAX THIS COMPLETED FORM TO 800-304-1232
OR REGISTER ONLINE AT WWW.ADVISOR90.COM.**

Name:_____

Street:_____

City:_____ State_____

Zip code : _____

Email:_____

Telephone:_____

Mark Diehl, CFP®, ChFC
2323 Clear Lake City Blvd.
Suite 180-144
Houston, TX 77062
Tel. and Fax   800-304-1232
Email: markdiehl@advisor90.com
www.advisor90.com

Mark Diehl can be contacted at 800-304-1232 with any of your questions, comments, or if you are interested in booking Mark for an interview or speaking engagement.

Subscribe to Mark's financial education updates.

**FAX THIS COMPLETED FORM TO 800-304-1232
OR REGISTER ONLINE AT WWW.ADVISOR90.COM.**

Name:_____

Street:_____

City:_____ State_____

Zip code : _____

Email:_____

Telephone:_____

Mark Diehl, CFP®, ChFC
2323 Clear Lake City Blvd.
Suite 180-144
Houston, TX 77062
Tel. and Fax   800-304-1232
Email: markdiehl@advisor90.com
www.advisor90.com

Printed in the United States
68857LVS00004B/79-168